BREAKING DOWN
THE WALL

This book is dedicated to Dan Alpert—

*The force behind this body of work whose strong voice for
social justice and equity has broken down walls and whose conviction has
pushed each one of us to forge exciting new ways of thinking and being.*

With heartfelt thanks,
The EL Collective

Margarita   Maria   Diane

Margo   Andrea   Tonya

Shawn   Ivannia   Debbie

BREAKING DOWN THE WALL

Essential Shifts for English Learners' Success

Margarita Espino Calderón

Maria G. Dove

Diane Staehr Fenner

Margo Gottlieb

Andrea Honigsfeld

Tonya Ward Singer

Shawn Slakk

Ivannia Soto

Debbie Zacarian

FOR INFORMATION:

Corwin
A SAGE Company
2455 Teller Road
Thousand Oaks, California 91320
(800) 233-9936
www.corwin.com

SAGE Publications Ltd.
1 Oliver's Yard
55 City Road
London EC1Y 1SP
United Kingdom

SAGE Publications India Pvt. Ltd.
B 1/I 1 Mohan Cooperative Industrial Area
Mathura Road, New Delhi 110 044
India

SAGE Publications Asia-Pacific Pte. Ltd.
18 Cross Street #10-10/11/12
China Square Central
Singapore 048423

Program Director and Publisher: Dan Alpert
Content Development Editor: Lucas Schleicher
Senior Editorial Assistant: Mia Rodriguez
Project Editor: Amy Schroller
Copy Editor: Lynne Curry
Typesetter: C&M Digitals (P) Ltd.
Proofreader: Tricia Currie-Knight
Indexer: Molly Hall
Cover and Interior Designer: Rose Storey
Marketing Manager: Maura Sullivan

Printed in the United States of America

ISBN 978-1-5443-4261-0

This book is printed on acid-free paper.

21 22 23 10 9 8 7 6 5 4

CONTENTS

FOREWORD

We seem to live in a world of maps, but, in truth, we live in a world made not of paper and ink, but of people. Those lines are our lives. Together, let us turn the map, until we see clearly the border is what joins us, not what separates us.

—Alberto Rios, First Poet Laureate of Arizona

Borders are a uniquely human invention. They signify beginnings and endings, knowns and unknowns, us and them. They mark crossings from past to future lives. For some, they protect the homeland. For others, they are the obstruction to living lives of safety, freedom, and wholeness.

We used to believe that different languages reside in distinct regions of the brain as if separated by strict borders. In fact, neuroscientists have established that when children are exposed to two or more languages in their early years of life, both languages reside in common regions of the brain's left hemisphere. By extension, such findings imply that we are "wired" for multilingualism. Furthermore, when we are exposed to more than a single language at a later stage of childhood, a separate Broca area—one of the two areas of the brain that play a role in language acquisition—will activate in the right hemisphere whenever a speaker switches from one language to the other. Conversely, when we are only exposed to a single language in childhood (a form of impoverishment), no right hemisphere activation occurs. The implication is that such borders are "learned" in monolingual speakers, but eliminated or otherwise "torn down" from a young age in multilingual speakers (Sousa, 2011, pp. 24–25).

Although physical borders had little meaning to me as a child, I cultivated an early awareness of linguistic borders. My mother and father—both second-generation U.S. citizens—had learned a functional version of a nearly moribund language—Yiddish. I was exposed to both English and Yiddish at an early age, but in my boyhood household, it became the language of secrets. My parents reserved its use for aspects of life and human experiences from which they believed I should be protected. In some ways, this gave me a greater incentive to want to master Yiddish—after all, every boy wants to crack a code—but such desires were squelched by the assimilationist fervor among post-war American Jews to strip ourselves of our Jewish identities.

My experience with international borders began later in life, as an undergraduate at McGill University. Motivated by a sense of adventure and a desire to immerse myself in a new language and culture, I took a leap into the unknown. First, there was a physical border crossing—typically through the dingy Swanton, Vermont, Customs station. My interactions with the Canadian Customs officers were usually pleasant enough, albeit perfunctory. I would present my student visa, respond to their questions about the duration of time I was to spend in Quebec, and perhaps get a stray question about my academic interests. In contrast, when I returned to the States, my reception was noticeably different—more akin to a police interrogation. I often was left with the feeling that by having ventured beyond the U.S. border, I had inadvertently transgressed and was marked as a "person of interest."

Quebec in the 1970s was in the midst of a seismic rebalancing act. The spark that ignited this revolution was, in fact, language. In my third year of university, a new premier, Rene Lesvesque of the Parti Quebequois, running on a platform of sovereignty, was elected in a landslide victory. Shortly thereafter, language policies shifted and French became the official language of the province. Ultimately, Quebec voters rejected efforts to secede in several referendums, and despite the shift to a single official language, most residents of Quebec today recognize the value of bilingualism for success in school as well as the workplace. In university, I chipped away at my core language and literature courses but also became fascinated by the process of language acquisition and picked up coursework with several leading psycholinguistic researchers with vast knowledge of language acquisition. But perhaps my biggest takeaway from these years was the realization that multilingualism is utterly achievable, given the right conditions.

Since then, I've learned that one of the benefits of growing older is that we develop a much more nuanced understanding of the nature of social progress. Policies may progress and regress, and new research plays a role in restructuring the landscape of learning, but at the beginning of the school year, most of us still enter our buildings with a sense of unbridled optimism: maybe this year, we'll get it right. And yet, unlike the linguistic revolution in Quebec, it seems that the pace of change—specifically with respect to changing the narrative for our multilingual learners in the United States—is painfully slow. Gary Howard, one of my educational equity heroes, is fond of saying that the arc of justice is a jagged line. And, of course, the downside of growing old is that sobering realization that the changes that we fought for will, most likely, not be realized in our own lifetimes.

At Corwin, I've had the honor of editing the work of some of the most brilliant and influential scholar/practitioners in the field. While each of these individuals has made unique contributions to scholarship and practice, I always wondered what they might accomplish by working collaboratively on a book project with one another. This fantasy grew out of my own realization that our field and, by extension, our children have suffered as a result of a siloed approach to educating English learners. What might it be like to break down the borders that separated my authors' bodies of work and to pool our expertise to cocreate a vision for truly shifting the EL narrative? In envisioning such a change, I also had to grapple with the traditional approach to book publishing—an Industrial Age model that is grounded in cutthroat competition—and to consider a more cooperative alternative in which experts pool their individual strengths and specialized knowledge around the project of creating policies, practices, schools, and classrooms that build on the cultural and linguistic assets of our English-learning students.

What happened next was nothing short of miraculous. We came together on a dark and stormy night in Santa Barbara in January of 2017. It was the night before the Trump inauguration, and talk of the "Wall" screamed across our social media and cable news. Nine Corwin authors convened with the sole desire to envision a world in which our schools can truly support multilingual learners by building on their assets and helping them to realize their full potential. I believe that we were fueled by the idea that our fundamental values were in danger and, while our process wasn't always smooth (collaboration is always beautifully messy!), we worked well into the night to devise a list of shifts from the status quo, shifts that were meant to be enacted at all levels of the educational system, from mainstream classrooms to district- and state-level agencies. One of the first critical shifts we arrived at we deemed *from deficit-based to assets-based.* Until we begin to acknowledge the cultural and linguistic funds of knowledge our children and their families carry with them, we'll fall into the perennial trap of only considering what they lack.

From this essential shift, others began to surface. The authors of this book unabashedly support dual-language education in recognition of the cognitive, cultural, and economic benefits of proficiency in more than one language. We challenge the notion that content and language teachers exist in separate worlds and present them with a mandate for working together. We turn the traditional conceptualization of assessment on its head and replace it with a three-part framework that includes assessment *as, for, and of* learning. We argue that multilingual learners are capable of achieving rigorous levels of learning—especially when challenged by teachers with a rich repertoire of appropriate scaffolds. And we push administrators to refine their focus beyond doing the bare minimum in the interest of compliance and acting from a deep-rooted sense of moral imperative.

And while we acknowledge that there may be other shifts—those that will require adaptive expertise to unpack and implement—we believe that system-wide implementation of those that we identified represents a good starting point for solving our equity challenges, promoting EL excellence in every classroom and school, and breaking down the real and imagined borders that have kept us from becoming our best selves.

We reach out to you to join us in this exciting, border-crossing endeavor!

Dan Alpert

San Francisco, 2019

PUBLISHER'S ACKNOWLEDGMENTS

Corwin gratefully acknowledges the contributions of the following reviewers:

Kelly Alvarez
English Learner Educational Consultant
Michigan Department of Education
Lansing, MI

Michele R. Dean, EdD
Lecturer and Field Placement Director
School of Education, California Lutheran University
Thousand Oaks, CA

Tanya Franca
Director of ESOL, Greenville County Schools
Greenville, SC

Daphne Germain
Director of English Learner Program Planning and Implementation
Boston Public Schools
Boston, MA

Joan R. Lachance
Assistant Professor, Director of TESL Minor Program
University of North Carolina at Charlotte
Charlotte, NC

Olivia Santillan
Coordinator, Multilingual and Humanities Education
Santa Clara County Office of Education
San Jose, CA

ABOUT THE AUTHORS

Margarita Espino Calderón, a native of Juárez, Mexico, is professor emerita and senior research scientist at Johns Hopkins University's Graduate School of Education. She is president/CEO of Margarita Calderón & Associates, Inc.

Margarita has served on several national panels, among others: The National Research Council's Committee on Teacher Preparation; the U.S. Department of Education Institute for Education Sciences' National Literacy Panel for Language Minority Children and Youth; the Carnegie Adolescent English Language Learners Literacy Panel; and the California Pre-School Biliteracy Panel.

She was principal investigator in two five-year empirical studies: *Expediting Reading Comprehension for English Language Learners (ExC-ELL*™*) Programs*, which focuses on professional development of science, social studies, and language arts teachers in middle and high schools, funded by the Carnegie Corporation of New York, and the *Bilingual Cooperative Reading and Composition (BCIRC)*, funded by the U.S. Department of Education.

She was coprincipal investigator with Robert Slavin on the five-year national randomized evaluation of English immersion, transitional, and two-way bilingual programs, funded by the Institute for Education Sciences. Currently, she is coprincipal investigator with George Washington University on a five-year study of the *Whole-School ExC-ELL Implementation*, funded by the U.S. Department of Education's Office of English Language Acquisition.

She has published over 100 articles, chapters, books, reading programs for students with interrupted formal education, and teacher training manuals. She is invited to present at national and international conferences, and comprehensive professional development in schools and statewide.

Maria G. Dove, EdD, is professor in the School of Education and Human Services at Molloy College, Rockville Centre, New York, where she teaches preservice and inservice teachers about the research and best practices for developing effective programs and school policies for English learners. Before entering the field of higher education, she worked for over thirty years as an English-as-a-second-language teacher in public school settings (Grades K–12) and in adult English language programs in Nassau County, New York.

In 2010, she received the Outstanding ESOL Educator Award from New York State Teachers of English to Speakers of Other Languages (NYS TESOL). She frequently provides professional development for educators throughout the United States on the teaching of diverse students. She also serves as a mentor for new ESOL teachers as well as an instructional coach for general-education teachers and literacy specialists. She has published articles and book chapters on collaborative teaching practices, instructional leadership, and collaborative coaching. With Andrea Honigsfeld, she coauthored four best-selling Corwin books: *Common Core for the Not-So-Common Learner, Grades K–5: English Language Arts Strategies* (2013), *Common Core for the Not-So-Common Learner, Grades 6–12: English Language Arts Strategies* (2013), *Co-teaching for English Learners: A Guide to Collaborative Planning, Teaching, Assessment, and Reflection* (2018), and their latest volume, the second edition of their 2010 best seller, *Collaboration for English Learners: A Foundational Guide to Integrated Practices* (2019).

Diane Staehr Fenner, PhD, is the president of SupportEd, LLC, a woman-owned small business based in the Washington, DC, area that provides educators in English learners' education the skills and resources they need to champion ELs' success within and beyond their classrooms. At SupportEd, Diane serves as project lead for all the team's work providing professional development, programmatic support, and research to school districts, states, organizations, and the U.S. Department of Education. Diane is an author or co-author of five books including *Unlocking English Learners' Potential: Strategies for Making Content Accessible* and *Advocating for English Learners: A Guide for Educators,* and a frequent keynote presenter on EL education at conferences across North America. Diane was a research associate at George Washington University's Center for Excellence and Equity in Education, spent a decade as an ESOL teacher, dual language assessment teacher, and ESOL assessment specialist in Fairfax County Public Schools, Virginia, and taught English in Veracruz, Mexico, and Berlin, Germany. Diane earned her PhD in multilingual/multicultural education with an emphasis in literacy at George Mason University. She earned her MAT in TESOL at the School for International Training and her masters in German at Penn State University. She lives in Fairfax, Virginia, with her husband and three children in the public school system. Diane is a first-generation college graduate who speaks fluent Spanish and German and grew up on a dairy farm in New York State's Finger Lakes region. You can connect with her via email at Diane@GetSupportEd.net or on Twitter at @DStaehrFenner.

Margo Gottlieb, PhD, is cofounder and lead developer for WIDA at the Wisconsin Center for Education Research, University of Wisconsin-Madison, having served as director, assessment and evaluation, for the Illinois Resource Center. Her professional experiences span from being an inner-city language teacher to working with thousands of educators across school districts, publishing companies, governments, universities, and educational organizations in 22 countries and across the United States. She has contributed to the crafting of language proficiency/development standards worldwide and enjoys designing assessments, curricular frameworks, and instructional assessment systems for multilingual learners. Being a Fulbright senior specialist in Chile, appointed to the U.S. Department of Education's Inaugural National Technical Advisory Council, and named by TESOL International Association's 50@50 "as an individual who has made a significant contribution to the TESOL profession within the past 50 years" have been career highlights.

Margo's publications include over 90 articles, technical reports, monographs, chapters, and encyclopedia entries. Additionally, she has authored, coauthored, and coedited over a dozen books this past decade, including: *Language Power: Key Uses for Accessing Content* (with M. Castro, 2017*), Assessing Multilingual Learners: A Month-by-Month Guide* (2017), *Assessing English Language Learners: Bridges to Educational Equity* (2016; 2006), *Academic Language in Diverse Classrooms: Definitions and Contexts* (with G. Ernst-Slavit, 2014*), Common Language Assessment for English Learners* (2012), *Paper to Practice: Using the TESOL's English Language Proficiency Standards in PreK–12 Classrooms* (with A. Katz & G. Ernst-Slavit, 2009), and *Assessment and Accountability in Language Education Programs: A Guide for Administrators and Teachers* (with D. Nguyen, 2007).

Andrea Honigsfeld, EdD, is associate dean and professor in the Division of Education at Molloy College, Rockville Centre, New York. She directs a doctoral program in Educational Leadership for Diverse Learning Communities. Before entering the field of higher education, she was an English-as-a-foreign-language teacher in Hungary (Grades 5–8 and adult) and an English-as-a-second-language teacher in New York City (Grades K–3 and adult). She also taught Hungarian at New York University.

She was the recipient of a doctoral fellowship at St. John's University, New York, where she conducted research on individualized instruction and learning styles. She has published extensively on working with English language learners and providing individualized instruction based on learning style preferences. She received a Fulbright Award to lecture in Iceland in the fall of 2002. In the past 12 years, she has been presenting at conferences across the United States, Great Britain, Denmark, Sweden, the Philippines, and the United Arab Emirates. She frequently offers staff development, primarily focusing on effective differentiated strategies and collaborative practices for English-as-a-second-language and general-education teachers. She coauthored *Differentiated Instruction for At-Risk Students* (2009) and coedited the five-volume *Breaking the Mold of Education* series (2010–2013), published by Rowman and Littlefield. She is also the coauthor of *Core Instructional Routines: Go-To Structures for Effective Literacy Teaching, K–5 and 6–12* (2014), and the author of *Growing Language and Literacy: Strategies for English Learners K–8* (2019), published by Heinemann. With Maria Dove, she coedited *Co-teaching and Other Collaborative Practices in the EFL/ESOL Classroom: Rationale, Research, Reflections, and Recommendations* (2012) and coauthored *Collaboration and Co-Teaching: Strategies for English Learners* (2010), *Common Core for the Not-So-Common Learner, Grades K–5: English Language Arts Strategies* (2013), *Common Core for the Not-So-Common Learner, Grades 6–12: English Language Arts Strategies* (2013), *Beyond Core Expectations: A Schoolwide Framework for Serving the Not-So-Common Learner* (2014), *Collaboration and Co-Teaching: A Leader's Guide* (2015), *Co-teaching for English Learners: A Guide to Collaborative Planning, Instruction, Assessment, and Reflection* (2018), and *Collaborating for English Learners: A Foundational Guide to Integrated Practices* (2019), five of which are Corwin best sellers.

Tonya Ward Singer, MFA, is a keynote speaker and professional learning consultant who helps K–12 educators transform teaching for equity and EL achievement. Teachers and administrators describe her work as groundbreaking, dynamic, practical, relevant, and impactful.

Tonya is the author of bestsellers *EL Excellence Every Day* and *Opening Doors to Equity*. An expert in pedagogy for multilingual learners, Tonya has co-authored curriculum for international publishers including Scholastic, Longman, and Oxford University Press.

Tonya has taught at multiple grade levels as a classroom teacher, reading teacher, and EL specialist, and has extensive experience helping school leaders transform learning at scale. She thrives on leveraging research and innovation to solve challenges in education, and in building collective efficacy for educators to do the same.

While raised in only one language, Tonya is now fluent in Spanish and can negotiate the price of a tomato in Mandarin Chinese. Connect with Tonya on Twitter @TonyaWardSinger or via her website, www.tonyasinger.com.

Shawn Slakk is the CEO and Founder of ABCDSS Consulting Consortium and works with teachers, administrators, schools and state agencies to offer strategies and supports for emergent bilinguals and their classmates, both K–12 and adults. As a former Certified WIDA Trainer and Title III SIOP Coach, Shawn brings a wide understanding of a variety of strategies and how they relate to ELs, language acquisition, and lesson delivery.

He is the former Rethinking Equity and Teaching for English Language Learners (RETELL) coordinator for the Massachusetts Department of Elementary and Secondary Education, where he and his team were responsible for training trainers and developing, implementing, and evaluating a Sheltered English Instruction endorsement course for administrators and classroom teachers. The RETELL endorsement is required in Massachusetts to obtain or retain an educator license, with more than 40,000 teachers and administrators earning this endorsement. Throughout his career, Shawn taught ESOL in Grades K through university, Spanish across all grade levels and curriculums, and even once taught Japanese to K–2 students. He has served as an elementary and middle school administrator and served at the central office level as a district coach and as a state-level coordinator. He started his teaching career teaching Adult ESOL at Spokane Community College in Washington State.

Shawn has two bachelor's degrees, one in English education K–12, and another in Spanish education K–12, from Whitworth College, and a master's degree in English: Teaching English as a Second Language from Eastern Washington University. He also has a master's degree in school administration (MSA) from the University of North Carolina at Greensboro; he is completing his EdD at the University of Virginia with a focus on reading and writing for additional language learners.

Ivannia Soto, PhD, is professor of education at Whittier College, where she specializes in second language acquisition, systemic reform for English language learners (ELLs), and urban education. She began her career in the Los Angeles Unified School District (LAUSD), where she taught English and English language development to a population made of up 99.9% Latinos, who either were or had been ELLs. Before becoming a professor, Dr. Soto also served LAUSD as a literacy coach and district office administrator. She has presented on literacy and language topics at various conferences, including the National Association for Bilingual Education (NABE), the California Association for Bilingual Association (CABE), the American Educational Research Association (AERA), and the National Urban Education Conference. As a consultant, Soto has worked with Stanford University's School Redesign Network (SRN), WestEd, and CABE, as well as a variety of districts and county offices in California, providing technical assistance for systemic reform for ELLs and Title III. Soto has authored and co-authored seven books, including *The Literacy Gaps: Building Bridges for ELLs and SELs*; *ELL Shadowing as a Catalyst for Change*, which was recognized by Education Trust-West as a promising practice for ELLs in 2018; *From Spoken to Written Language with ELLs*; and the *Academic English Mastery* four-book series. Together, the books tell a story of how to systemically close achievement gaps with ELLs by increasing their academic language production across content areas. Soto is executive director of the *Institute for Culturally and Linguistically Responsive Teaching* (ICLRT) at Whittier College, whose mission it is to promote relevant research and develop academic resources for

ELLs and Standard English Learners (SELs) via linguistically and culturally responsive teaching practices.

Debbie Zacarian, founder of Zacarian & Associates, provides professional development strategic planning and policy work for educators of culturally and linguistically diverse populations. Known for her expertise in strengths-based leadership, instructional, and family partnership practices, she has served as an expert consultant for agencies, including the MA Parent Information Resource Center and Federation for Children with Special Needs.

Dr. Zacarian served on the faculty of University of Massachusetts–Amherst for over a decade, where she cowrote and was coprincipal investigator of a National Professional Development grant initiative supporting the professional preparation of educators of English learners and taught courses including *managing culturally responsive classrooms* and *developing curriculum for the heterogeneous class*. Additionally, she was a program director at the Collaborative for Educational Services, where she led and provided professional development for thousands of educators. She also directed the Amherst Public Schools bilingual and English Learner programming, where she and the district received many local, state, and national honors.

She has written and cowritten over 100 publications. Her professional books with Corwin include *In It Together: How Student, Family and Community Partnerships Advance Engagement and Achievement in Diverse Classrooms*; *Mastering Academic Language: A Framework for Supporting Student Achievement*; *The Essential Guide for Educating Beginning English Learners*; and *Transforming Schools for English Learners: A Comprehensive Framework for School Leaders*. Debbie can be reached at debbie@zacarianconsulting.com.

TOGETHER . . .

The urgent need for breaking out of isolation and shifting to collaborative planning, teaching, and assessment models is a central premise of *Breaking Down the Wall*. It is the subject matter of one chapter and is reiterated throughout the book.

Collaboration was also a key element in the development of this book from its inception. During our very first meeting, we agreed that the adaptive challenges that we wished to address were beyond the scope of a single author working alone. Rather, they required a *brain trust*. Consequently, every chapter of the book was written by a pair of authors. Moreover, the authors read and commented on one another's chapters throughout our development process. A number of these comments are included in the margins of the chapters.

In this spirit, we want to suggest that our readers consider approaching the chapters in a collaborative setting, e.g., in teams, PLCs, book studies, or with a partner. While this isn't mandatory, we know that it will significantly enhance your learning journey—much as our own collaboration has enriched ours.

Visit the companion website at
https://resources.corwin.com/BreakingDowntheWall
for downloadable resources.

A NOTE ABOUT OUR TERMINOLOGY

The poignant metaphor "Breaking Down the Wall" applies to how we individually and collectively must be proactive in replacing the prevalent xenophobic and assimilationist sentiment that permeates our society with one that places value on its mosaic of languages and cultures. This seismic revolution in mindset and psyche sparks additional paradigm shifts in our thinking and actions, which we articulate throughout the book. As authors and advocates, we are passionate about our commitment to multilingual education and the benefits it reaps, yet we grapple with the language to use to best represent this student population we so honor and support.

As is evident in the pages before you, we have our own style of languaging that is expressed in how we approach our individual shifts. For some, that means adhering to the terms promulgated under federal legislation, in particular, the 2015 reauthorization of the Elementary and Secondary Education Act, the Every Student Succeeds Act. State and district adoption of the terms "English Learners" and "Long-Term English Learners" has sparked acceptance by the general education community. Others prefer "multilingual learners," a broader, more inclusive term that embraces the students' multiple languages and cultures.

Above all, as a professional collective, we are steadfast in establishing and maintaining an assets-based approach to educating language learners; we advocate on their behalf to maximize their opportunity to learn across the curriculum. As authors of this volume, we have contributed to its design and contents, as is evidenced by our pairing in writing and reviewing the chapters. We hope that our collaborative spirit in which we have shaped and articulated these shifts in mindset extends to and is replicated by districts, schools, and classrooms to ultimately provoke action that positively influences K–12 education for our nation's children.

chapter one

From Deficit-Based to Assets-Based

DEBBIE ZACARIAN
AND DIANE STAEHR FENNER

PREMISE

An English-only approach to instruction coupled with standards-based accountability pushes an overfocus and overreliance on what we perceive as missing or deficient in multilingual learners. On the other hand, a much-needed strengths-based approach that draws from and builds on the personal, social, cultural, and linguistic assets and experiences students already possess promotes ELs' engagement and achievement.

VIGNETTE

When Alfredo, a 12-year-old native Spanish speaker, and his family moved from living in a shelter and their car after a couple of years of traveling as migrant workers in various farming communities across the Midwest and the West Coast of the United States, his parents enrolled him in a new school. Imagine his parents, Alfredo, and an interpreter arriving to enroll Alfredo. After being buzzed into the building and finding their way to the office, they met with the school's registrar. She furnished them with a number of forms to complete and asked for documentation of his prior immunizations, health records, and proof of residency. They provided the registrar with the needed documents and, with the support of the interpreter and Alfredo, completed all of the required documentation. These showed that Alfredo had attended a number of schools throughout the United States during the preceding two years, that his family applied for him to participate in the district's free lunch program, and that he speaks Spanish at home. Alfredo is subsequently given a test to determine his proficiency in English, and the results show that he has reached an intermediate level. With all of this information, the registrar meets with his seventh-grade team of teachers and expresses concern that he needs special consideration because of what she perceives as his lack of English proficiency and interrupted prior schooling.

Despite these initial misgivings, Alfredo does well in school. His math teacher reports that Alfredo is a pleasure to have in his class and that she appreciates Alfredo's politeness, curiosity, and willingness to take risks in trying out new ideas, doing his homework, and collaborating with his peers. His science teacher states that Alfredo shows great interest in participating in experiments and writing well-developed lab reports. Even though these contain grammatical errors, he tells us that they demonstrate Alfredo's depth of scientific knowledge. Additionally, Alfredo has adjusted well to his new school. He tried out for the junior varsity soccer team. He has made friends with native Spanish-speaking and English-speaking peers and is engaged in many school and after-school activities including being a member of the soccer team.

While we all want our EL students to be successful in and outside of school, what is it that supported Alfredo's successes in this middle school? Why might we be surprised to read that he's doing so well? In this chapter, we will explore the urgency for moving from a deficit-based to an assets-based approach using three key ideas, including how these ideas are being actively infused in Alfredo's schooling. We will then describe the actions that should be taken to put the three ideas into practice.

The key ideas we will explore are

1. Recognizing the critical importance of students' identities and the strengths of their personal, cultural, socio-emotional, and world experiences.

2. Building upon the assets of students' home languages and literacy experiences.

3. Tapping into ELs' assets—recognizing the assets and all of us seeing ourselves as teachers of ELs.

THE URGENCY

In the United States, every district is required to identify its English learners, notify parents when their child has been identified, and describe the type of program that their child will be provided to support him/her to learn English and acquire academic content (U.S. Department of Education, 2015). Typically, schools and districts engage in this identification process by asking what language(s) a student uses to communicate and assessing the English proficiency of students whose parents/guardians indicate that their child uses a language other than or in addition to English. For example, Alfredo's parents shared that Alfredo speaks Spanish and was born in El Salvador. This information signaled that Alfredo should be given a state-approved assessment to identify if he was an English learner. When the findings showed that he was, Alfredo was placed in a state-approved language assistance program for him to learn English and academic content, and his parents/guardians were given information about the type of program that he was provided. Following this sequence of federal obligations, identified English learners, such as Alfredo, are also required to be assessed annually to determine the progress that his school and district make in supporting ELs to learn English and succeeding academically in school (U.S. Department of Education, 2015).

While all of this data is helpful to collect and is required by federal laws and regulations, two important questions for us all to ask are

- What should we do to build an effective academic and English language development program?

- How does data collection help us in building programming that draws from our students' prior experiences and strengths?

Districts have traditionally responded to this question by performing three activities:

1. Examining English learners' progress in learning English

2. Comparing their performance on standardized tests of reading in English with their peers

3. Comparing their rates of graduation with their peers

However, engaging in these activities has not resulted in closing the opportunity gaps between English learners and their English-fluent peers. For example, data from the National Center for Education Statistics (2017) about eighth graders' performance in reading showed that 79% of English-fluent students scored at the basic or above level in 2015 and 2017 while only 29% of English learners scored at these levels in 2015 and 32% did in 2017. This enormous gap has led far too many to believe that English learners cannot make progress. In addition, the graduation rates of English learners, as exemplified in the following chart, show that English learners have one of the lowest graduation rates among all students on a national level.

While all of this enrollment, assessment, and graduation data is important to know, it describes what many perceive as what English learners *lack* as

Doing only what is required: compliance means that ELs only receive, as the Department of Justice (DOJ) uses the term, "adequate" service. Diane and Debbie give us connections to doing more than just being compliant. When these questions are considered, they help teachers and schools move toward excellence.
—Shawn

FIGURE 1.1 2015-2016 U.S. Graduation Rates of Public School Students

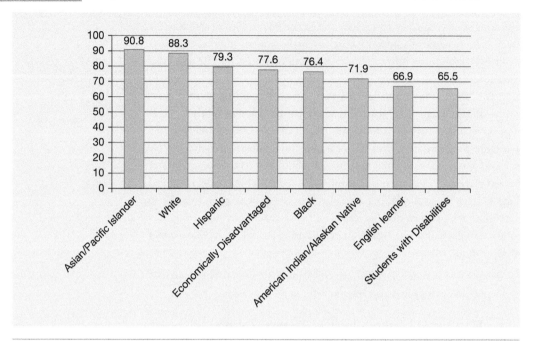

Source: U.S. Department of Education, National Center for Education Statistics. (2017) *The Condition of Education*, Public High School Graduation Rates.

opposed to their many strengths and potential. A deficit-based approach to EL education

- Draws from what students do not possess (or what we perceive that they don't) as opposed to what they do inherently possess or have learned as a result of being reared in a language and culture other than or in addition to North American–English-speaking.

- Has resulted in programming decisions that further distance students' capacity and potential to draw from their strengths and assets.

Indeed, our overemphasis on evidence of deficits, according to many educational scholars, has pushed programming models that are taught entirely in English, a language that all English learners have not yet mastered (Soto & Gottlieb, 2019; Menken, 2009, 2008; Solórzano, 2008). As a result, the majority of EL programming has tended to all but purge students of their precious identities and strengths—their home languages and cultures—and, in many cases, minimized their interactions with native English-speaking peers. In response, the U.S. Department of Justice and U.S. Department of Education (2015) sent a *Dear Colleague* letter to the nation's public schools reminding them of the steps that they are required to take to be in compliance with the federal laws and regulations to recognize the strengths and meet the needs of the nation's English learners. The letter also described two important factors to consider about educating the nation's English learners:

- Over 75% of the nation's classrooms had at least one English learner, and the population is expected to grow.

- Many districts across the nation were found to be significantly out of compliance in meeting the federal obligations of educating English learners.

While our student and family populations are becoming more diverse, we remain a fairly stable homogeneous professional workforce (Musu-Gillette, et al., 2016). The rapid growth that is occurring among the nation's English learners, coupled with concerns about their low performance on standardized measures and rates of graduation, has resulted in many districts having become overdependent on students' performance on state-mandated testing. This overdependence comes at the expense of maintaining and growing students' greatest assets, their home languages and cultures, and socio-emotional growth. The overfocus on state testing results, according to many, has also become the sole driver of programming decisions for English learners *and* purged much of what we know is needed for students' success (Gandára & Baca, 2008; Menken, 2008, 2009).

In 2006, two important meta-reviews of research (August & Shanahan, 2006; Genesee, Lindholm-Leary, Saunders, & Christian, 2006) about successful practices for English learners underscored the critical need to design and implement programming for English learners that includes

1. Instruction that is explicitly and meaningfully connected to students' personal, social, and cultural world and backgrounds and experiences.

2. Instructional programming that systematically provides explicit development of language and literacy that is needed for school success.

Additionally, in 2015, the U.S. Department of Justice and U.S. Department of Education provided information about the importance of supplying English learners with access and opportunity to the same types of school-related curriculum and activities that their peers receive: "Ensure EL students have equal opportunities to meaningfully participate in all curricular and extracurricular activities, including the core curriculum, graduation requirements, specialized and advanced courses and programs, sports, and clubs" (p. 8).

> When ELs are provided excellent service that helps them with content and language and it is done whole-class and whole-school with their classmates, as Margarita and I suggest in Chapter 6, "From Language to Language, Literacy, and Content," of this book, every child in every classroom and school benefits.
> —**Shawn**

THE VISION

Given all of the data that we have presented about ELs' performance in reading and their graduation rates, it is certainly not that all English learners are doing poorly. Many English learners do well in school

(Umansky & Reardon, 2014; Valentino & Reardon, 2015), including our focal student, Alfredo. What's key for us, and what we'd like to share with you, is to understand this positive outcome more deeply so that we can enact practices that are the most likely to yield the same outcome repeatedly. What we propose is a shift in practice toward the strengths and assets that all ELs bring and to build programming based on these inherent strengths.

AN ASSETS-BASED PERSPECTIVE

Let's begin this vision by first ensuring we are operating from a working definition of what an assets-based approach is. Research in psychology, child development, and education show the critical importance of looking beyond what we might perceive as missing or lacking or a deficit in our students so that we can operate from the strengths and assets that all students possess or what is already there. For example, a large body of growing research in psychology suggests that focusing on people's strengths, that is, what they already possess inherently or have already learned and experienced, can lead to far greater academic and social emotional success than does focusing on what we perceive are their weaknesses (e.g., Seligman, Rashid, & Parks, 2006). In addition, educational research points to how we can support students to be more successful in school and beyond when we build from their internal strengths and assets (Biswas-Diener, Kashdan, & Gurpal, 2011).

Further, a student's home language and cultural ways of being and acting play an essential role in their academic, social, and emotional development (Zacarian, Alvarez-Ortiz, & Haynes, 2017; Staehr Fenner & Snyder, 2017; Staehr Fenner, 2014; Zacarian, 2013, 2012). Further, an assets-based perspective recognizes that parents of ELs engage in their children's education and support their children in a multitude of rich, varied, and perhaps unrecognized ways (Zacarian & Silverstone, 2015; Staehr Fenner, 2014; Zacarian, Alvarez-Ortiz, & Haynes, 2017; and Gonzalez, Moll, & Amanti, 2005).

For example, EL parents may encourage their children to complete their homework and listen to their teacher, which is an example of supporting their education that most educators may not be aware of (Staehr Fenner, 2014). Another example is the parent of an EL who attends school-related events to show support for his or her child's education. A further instance is the family who goes to the local laundry on a weekly basis and has their child support the cleaning process by measuring the soap, folding the laundry in thirds, and so forth, supporting mathematical thinking. In addition, Alfredo's parents also provide us with a rich example of the ways in which they show him their deep knowledge and passion for science and mathematics. As migrant farmers, they are keenly aware of the effects that weather patterns, soil conditions, watering, and fertilization have on the health and well-being of fruits and vegetables. They have passed this crucial information on to Alfredo. These real-world experiences and understandings greatly help children to understand the world around them in ways that many educators might not be aware of or imagine.

Engaging in a strengths-based approach requires a shift in our thinking from what we believe is lacking in our students to the many strengths and assets that they and their families already possess. To do this, we must take time to learn about the invaluable personal, cultural, social, and world experiences of our students and their families and draw from these strengths-based understandings to create programming that is meaningful, purposeful, *and* appealing to our students.

BUILDING UPON THE ASSETS OF STUDENTS' PRIOR PERSONAL, SOCIAL, CULTURAL, LANGUAGE, AND ACADEMIC EXPERIENCES

When we look at EL assets, we should expand our resources beyond what it is that we are required to do according to federal regulations. This means looking at more than a language children use to communicate and their performance on state-approved assessments. Broadening our perspectives and cultivating a deeper understanding of our students can greatly help us to build more successful programming. For example, it's very helpful to understand the rich and varied interactional experiences that all children have experienced during development. Seminal developmental psychologist Mary Gauvain (2001, 2013) describes the importance of understanding the practices that all children experience by repeatedly observing, interacting, and participating with others and the ways that they gain meaning about the world around them through these ever-growing developmental interactional experiences. Figure 1.2 illustrates this growth process (see page 8).

In the figure we see that when a child is born, the first people that they interact with are their parents/guardians and siblings. Following this train of thought, as a child develops, they then interact, observe, and participate routinely in a range of routines and practices with their family community. These form the fabric of their development including their personal, social, cultural, and linguistic ways of being and acting in their home environment and family community.

For example, let's say that Alfredo's parents have routinely brought him to the farms where they have worked throughout his childhood. He has regularly observed them engaging in a variety of invaluable tasks and activities that have formed his way of thinking about the world around him. Another example of the type of observation in which children frequently engage is observing the steps a parent/guardian normally follows in preparing family meals. During these routinized re-occurring events, children closely watch their parent/guardian grocery shopping, measuring, timing, and more. A third example is a child who is being cared for by an extra-familial support

FIGURE 1.2 **Developmental Circle of Interactions**

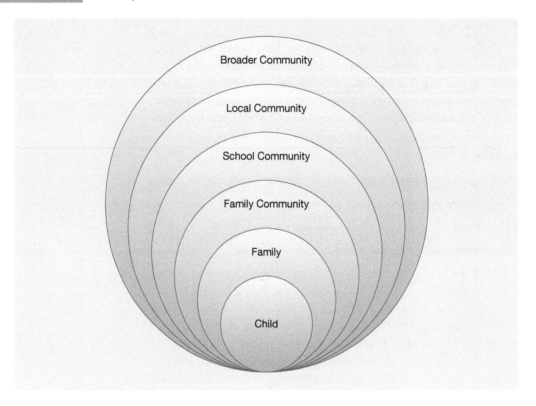

Broader Community

Local Community

School Community

Family Community

Family

Child

Source: Adapted from Zacarian & Silverstone (2015); Zacarian, Alvarez-Ortiz, & Haynes (2017).

such as a child care provider. In this environment, on a routine basis, the child is given a sequence of events to follow. It might be a morning snack followed by nap time followed by playing outside. Thus, children learn about the world around them through these continuously reoccurring routines and practices.

All of these examples we mention help to form children's identities as members of their family, family's community, and more. What is important to note about all of these routines and activities is that children are generally cared for and about by the loving and caring adults in their lives. In addition, as a child matures and reaches school age, their family and family's community (e.g., extended family and extrafamilial members with whom children socialize frequently) hope and even expect that their child will be cared for and cared about by their school community including the teachers, administrators, support staff, peers, and everyone in this environment. The same holds true as a child matures and engages in a range of what we might call typical childhood activities such as town sports activities, dance communities, clubs, and more. That is, as these ever-growing circles of developmental experiences occur, we generally hope that children are cared for and about and that they flourish (Zacarian & Silverstone, 2015).

Additionally, all of these personal, cultural, social, language, and world experiences and practices become part of what we know as our students' developmental experiences and form their diverse identities (Zacarian, 2013). Our essential task is to draw from the many and numerous strengths and assets that all English learners have experienced throughout their life experiences so that we may create programming in which they feel safe, a sense of belonging, acknowledgment, and competence, and we see the many strengths that we bring to the work of being an educator of all learners, including English learners (Zacarian, Alvarez-Ortiz, & Haynes, 2018).

THE CALL FOR ACTION

In this section, we provide specific, tangible recommendations on how to enact the change from a deficit- to an assets-based perspective to fulfill our vision. Our call to action is centered around five practical ways to help educators shift from a deficit- to an assets-based perspective when it comes to educating ELs. While some of these actions can be enacted at the individual educator level, we suggest collaboration as a way to strengthen the impact of these actions. The final action entails wider, system-level supports that are needed to implement our proposed changes at a larger scale so that our vision of a focus on ELs' strengths comes to fruition.

The actions are outlined in Figure 1.3, Actions and Level.

Diane and Debbie show again how functional it is to move beyond compliance with these five shifts towards the assets-based perspective. They fit hand in hand with DOJ suggestions and guidelines. Additionally, in Figure 1.3, they provide great starting places to make those all-important connections to ELs' families, bringing them in as a part of the educational team.
—**Shawn**

FIGURE 1.3 Actions and Level

Action	Level
1. Building relationships with students and families	Individual School District
2. Engaging the school community in building understandings of and relationships with ELs	School Community
3. Challenging colleagues' thinking to help them recognize ELs' assets	Individual
4. Using storytelling as a way to highlight ELs' strengths	Individual School District Community
5. Building upon the assets of ELs' home languages and literacy experiences	School District

BUILDING RELATIONSHIPS WITH STUDENTS AND FAMILIES

In the opening of our chapter, we listed the typical steps that schools use to follow the federal obligations for identifying and annually assessing English learners. While this information is important to know, it's also critical to convey the following messages to families:

- We believe it's important to get to know each other.

- We value your participation.

- We want to work together.

- We are comfortable and embrace your involvement. (Zacarian & Silverstone, 2015)

To do this, it's critical to learn as much as we can about students' and families' personal, social, cultural, and life experiences. This information is invaluable for building instructional programming that capitalizes on students' and families' experiences and welcomes and values students' and families' participation. Whether we do this in a school registration office, in a welcome center, while families are taking a tour of the school, in a classroom, or as a home visit, it's critical to demonstrate a genuine interest in partnering with families and honoring, valuing, and acknowledging the many strengths that they share with us. Figure 1.4 provides suggested topics for discussion with accompanying discussion questions.

For example, when Alfredo's parents met with the school registrar, they shared that Alfredo loves to play soccer and that his favorite subjects are mathematics and science. They explained in detail the types of activities that he likes to do in these subjects. They also proudly shared that in one of Alfredo's prior schools, they helped to build a community garden.

Drawing from this information, the school registrar encouraged Alfredo to try out for the school's soccer team. During the meeting with him and his parents, she asked the coach to come to her office and made introductions; she arranged for Alfredo to meet with the coach and the soccer team during the first week of school so that he could try out for and be part of the team. She relayed the information that she'd learned about his science and mathematics interests to his teachers. They, in turn, took time to learn more about Alfredo's interests and were sure to connect these to his academic studies. She also shared the family's experience building a community garden with the school principal, who had been seeking ways to partner with families. The principal plans to meet with Alfredo's parents to learn more about how his new school might do the same type of community service. Each of these partnership activities greatly supports Alfredo and his family to be active participants in his new school. And they activate the circles of interactions that support a child's well-being and development.

FIGURE 1.4 Suggested Topics and Questions for Meetings With Parents/Guardians and Students to Build Strong Partnerships

Topics	Suggested Questions
1. Find out about qualities and values that make the student unique to his or her family.	What makes [name of child] special (things that set him or her apart from others, qualities he or she has, things he or she values)?
2. Find out about what makes the relationship special between the parent and the student.	What are some things you enjoy about [name of child]?
3. Find out what qualities and values the parent appreciates from the student.	What particular talents and skills would you like me to know about [name of child]?
4. Find out about the subject matters that the child particularly likes and why the child likes these.	What subjects does [name of child] like studying at home and in school, and what does she/he like about them?
5. Find out about the family's values and how they share their life together.	What are things you enjoy doing as a family?
6. Find out about the family's likes and strengths to show that they are valued and they belong to the school community.	We want to be a welcoming place for you and your children. What would make the experience of coming to our school more enjoyable?
7. Set the stage for partnership and collaboration while valuing the family's input.	We see parents as our partners. Is there any particular way you would like to help me make your child's school experience a great one?
8. Find out about ways that the family was involved in their child's prior schooling.	In what ways were parents encouraged to be involved at [name of child]'s prior school?
9. Set the stage for partnership and collaboration while leveraging the family's assets.	What special talents or interests would you consider sharing with the students in [name of child]'s class or with students' families (e.g., work, interests, hobbies)?
10. Find out about family's values and dreams for the student and acknowledge them as family's assets.	What are your hopes and dreams for [name of child]'s education?
11. Set the stage for honesty, trust, partnership, and collaboration, along with a clear message of inclusiveness and belonging.	What questions do you wish I had asked and would like to be sure are included?

Source: Adapted from Zacarian, Alvarez-Ortiz, & Haynes (2017).

ENGAGING THE SCHOOL COMMUNITY IN BUILDING UNDERSTANDINGS OF AND RELATIONSHIPS WITH ELS

Our school communities can and should support ELs in building relationships with their teachers and other adults in their schools. There are a number of easy-to-implement activities that offer ELs an opportunity to become known in their schools and for school staff to take a more active role in welcoming, supporting, deepening their understanding of, and caring about their students.

An example is the work that ESOL teacher Angela Ghent and Principal David Shamble do at Indian Land High School in Lancaster County, South Carolina. Angela engages newcomer students in writing a personal narrative and sharing it with their subject matter teachers, school principal, and/or others (Zacarian & Silverstone, 2015). Angela begins the personal narrative writing and sharing project by interviewing students and asking them to write about themselves in their home languages.[1] Students write about a range of topics from their prior experiences in school, with friends, and their home communities to their move to South Carolina and acclimation in their new Lancaster, South Carolina, home and making new friends. They then spend time writing their personal narrative in English with support from Angela (who possesses intermediate fluency in Spanish) and their EL peers, and alumni. Angela's goal is to engage her students in writing *and then telling* their personal story to at least one of their teachers and/or Principal Shamble. Further, during the writing process, it's commonplace for teachers and the principal to come to Angela's class to learn about their writing project, ask questions, get to know the students, and help them to be comfortable sharing their personal narratives. Angela shares her reflections about the strengths of this project:

> To borrow terms from literature class, newcomers who don't speak English have no voice. They are "flat characters" to their teachers. Newcomers who can present personal narratives to their teachers and talk about themselves through writing become "round characters." Essentially, the more we know about the lives of our students, the more we care. (Ghent in Zacarian & Silverstone, 2015, pp. 87–88)

Educators of younger students can easily adapt this project by engaging students in drawing a personal narrative storyboard, writing a response to the sentence prompt "What I wish my teacher knew about me." Each of these activities supports the process of learning more about students' lives and experiences so that we, as educators, develop a better understanding of the linguistic and cultural assets that ELs bring to our classrooms.

STORYTELLING

In addition to engaging students in writing a personal narrative to promote EL assets, another strategy that can be implemented at the individual, grade, or school level is to use storytelling to help others recognize the critical importance of ELs' identities and the strengths of their personal, cultural, socio-emotional, and world experiences as well as to develop empathy. Like the personal narrative, project-based writing experience, this tool is one way to move the needle, even if slightly, to help others to recognize the rich identities of ELs and their assets. When we have had to make challenging presentations to administrators or school boards who may not share the same level of expertise on EL assets and education, we have found telling a personal story about ourselves or an EL student is a way to put a human face on a complex situation and increase others' understanding. Often times, colleagues who employ a deficit perspective do not have a strong grasp of EL pedagogy, including knowledge of second language acquisition and the crucial role of the home language and culture (Staehr Fenner, 2014). These same colleagues may not have learned a language in addition to English or spent time experiencing life in another culture, but, like ELs, these colleagues have many strengths to offer. Storytelling is a way to help develop empathy in others who may not be prone to empathizing with ELs or their families and recognizing their assets for a multitude of reasons.

One powerful way to help convince others of ELs' assets is through telling stories about individual ELs. We often find that a lot of people we encounter just don't "get it" when it comes to ELs. However, when you focus your story on a single EL, it helps others to appreciate that student on a more humanistic level and find some common ground. Laura Grisso, executive director of language and cultural services in Tulsa Public Schools, Oklahoma (2017), notes that it's crucial for educators to share their ELs' and families' stories to help others put a human face to such hot-button issues as immigration and language learning.

Similarly, she notes it's also important for ELs to share their stories, to the degree they feel comfortable, with other students and educators in their school community who may be unaware of the strengths they bring and obstacles they have already surmounted. She writes, "Storytelling provides a way into those difficult conversations and an opportunity to remind us of the common ground that we do share." We must exercise caution, however, when we ask students to write about or share their stories. As educators, we need to give our ELs the choice to share as much as they feel comfortable or to have the option to not share them at all. Students and their families who are open to the idea could also share their stories in school newspapers or in books to reach a wider audience. Green Card Voices (http://www.greencardvoices.com) is one powerful example of how ELs can share their stories through a multimedia approach on a large scale.

Another opportunity for ELs to tell their own stories is through artwork. A project called "Finding Home" with the Toronto School District and the Aga Khan Museum in Toronto invited refugee high school students to work with local artists to share their experiences of home through art. This moving student artwork was on display at the museum and then at the Toronto School Board office.

A different form of storytelling comes through using teacher-created vignettes or case studies to help others get a deeper sense of ELs' assets, such as Alfredo's vignette, which we shared earlier in this chapter. Sharing carefully worded vignettes or case studies with colleagues can help them form a connection with an EL they read about, see a complex situation through the eyes of a fellow human being, and allow them to brainstorm solutions collaboratively. We recommend these case studies and stories be told when interacting with administrators and other decision makers to provide them a more nuanced understanding of ELs' strengths.

One final way to help educators see the assets ELs bring is to do a deep dive on EL data, having participants use the data to tell a story about what they see happening in terms of ELs' progress and assets. In looking at such data as EL performance and progress over time, it's crucial to follow ELs' achievement in the long term. For example, in Fairfax County Public Schools, when the district followed their former ELs' (those who had exited ESOL services) achievement, they found many of these former ELs actually outperformed native English speakers on state content assessments given in English. Looking more deeply at an explanation for this incredible achievement, we know that bilingual students tend to develop a deep sense of metalinguistic awareness (Bialystok, Peets, & Moreno, 2014; Rauch, Naumann, & Jude, 2012) when they grapple with learning content and developing academic language at the same time while developing their home language skills. They are able to make comparisons between their home language(s) and English and also learn to internalize strategies for learning new vocabulary in English. Also, ELs must learn to acquire specialized study skills as well as exhibit determination and resilience to adjust to learning academic language and content in English. How often are stories like this one shared? We have to realize that ELs don't acquire English and achieve this type of success overnight. It takes years of determination and buy-in from all stakeholders who work with students.

CHALLENGE COLLEAGUES' THINKING

As educators and advocates for ELs, we hear deficit-based statements such as the following all the time: "Maria doesn't speak any English and can't even read in Spanish." "Phuoc's parents don't care about his education and don't bother to come to parent-teacher conferences." "Naila doesn't have the basics in math—she didn't even learn simple addition and subtraction in her country." "All the Spanish speakers in my classroom aren't even trying to learn English." When advocates for ELs hear statements such as these, we must think of ways to support a shift from a deficit- to an assets-based disposition.

We have to take the opportunity to challenge others' thinking in order to shift the narrative when colleagues approach ELs from a deficit perspective. All educators—no matter what their title or how many years of experience they have—are positioned to serve as agents of change in helping others move ever so slightly to an assets-based approach when it comes to ELs and their families (Staehr Fenner, 2014). But how best can we challenge others' deficit thinking when we find ourselves in the uncomfortable space in which we hear someone apply a deficit perspective in describing an EL or an EL's family? We all have the agency to "shake up" someone's deficit thinking around ELs to promote an assets-based perspective, but this change has to occur

While working on changing the deficit-based narrative when colleagues approach ELs, we encourage teachers to take a similar tact with the narrative of the ESOL teacher being the language provider for ELs. Shifting to a mindset that ELs need content-based academic language instruction from the core-content teacher is a key factor in moving from compliance to excellence and shows ELs that they are valued. Yes, content teachers are the language and literacy teachers of their content. Yes, ELs are fully capable of participating in content-based discussions; they just at times need the academic language to do so—who better to provide that support than the core-content teacher?

—Shawn

more toward the end of such an encounter, not at the very beginning (Staehr Fenner, 2017). When we encounter someone espousing a deficit-based belief about an EL, we suggest following the steps outlined in Figure 1.5, Steps for Moving Colleagues From EL Deficits to Assets and Considerations.

FIGURE 1.5 Steps for Moving Colleagues From EL Deficit to Assets and Considerations

Step for Moving From EL Deficits to Assets	Consideration
1. Approach a deficit-focused situation thoughtfully.	Take a minute to think about the situation, who the players are, and the possible ramifications of your actions on ELs and their families. Many teachers and administrators haven't received coursework or training on educating ELs. Keep in mind that their deficit perspective may come from a lack of confidence or strategies in working with ELs.
2. Recognize and acknowledge other colleagues' expertise aloud.	When you point out something positive a colleague is doing (e.g., how well they know their content area), you'll start to build their trust or continue to build the trust you've already established.
3. Model unwavering empathy for ELs.	Demonstrate your character and leadership by remaining an empathetic ally for ELs and their families. In this way, others will look to you as an expert on EL assets and education.
4. Try to first listen and understand others' perspectives, even if you may not agree with them on their approach.	Try to put yourself in someone else's shoes to understand where they may be coming from in focusing on ELs' deficits. This openness to understanding others' frustrations will provide you a greater depth of understanding of their perspective. Your listening to them will also help strengthen their trust in you.
5. Consider what might be happening on a systematic level to promote deficit thinking around this issue.	Reflect on what is happening to cause your colleague to focus on ELs' deficits. Think of some potential ways to address systematic inequalities that promote EL deficit thinking. See Figure 1.6 for barriers and solutions to EL family engagement as an example.
6. Suggest some potential solutions and/or strategies to them.	After you've listened to their frustration, know when to gently shift the narrative to what can be done to support ELs and/or their families in this situation. By offering support, you can help them see the potential for a focus on EL assets instead of deficits.
7. Follow up on your support and solutions for ELs.	To demonstrate your commitment to ELs and their families' assets, check in with a colleague who you've helped by offering solutions and support to see how your suggestions are working. Revisit regularly and revise your approach as needed.
8. Find outlets to share EL achievement.	Share positive stories of EL and family assets with your school or district, such as instances in which former ELs become school valedictorians, honor roll students, and/or graduates. Invite successful former ELs to the school in person or by video to share reasons for their success. Investigate multiple ways to share your message, such as in assemblies, in newspapers, and on social media (with students' and families' permission).

Source: Adapted from Staehr Fenner (2014, 2017).

For an example of some ways to shift the narrative from a deficit- to an assets-based perspective, consider common deficit statements about why EL families may not come to school events as often as non-EL families. Instead of focusing on a perceived personal deficit of the EL or family (e.g., they don't care about their child's education), instead devote resources to examining what policies and practices in your building or school may be preventing ELs' assets to shine. Then brainstorm actionable solutions that you can put in place with colleagues to support your ELs and promote their assets. Figure 1.6 outlines six possible barriers or deficits related to EL family engagement and potential solutions to encourage and promote ELs' assets through family engagement.

FIGURE 1.6 **Possible Barriers to EL Family Engagement and Solutions**

Possible Barriers	Possible Solutions
Language	• **Parent** liasions • **Bilingual** staff • **Translated** materials • **Home language** phone tree/volunteers
Transportation	• **Rides** to school events • **Ride sharing** resource • **Information** about public transportation • **Meeting with families** in their community
Time	• **Flexibility** in scheduling conferences and events • **Parent** survey
Childcare	• **Provide childcare** for conferences and school events
Understanding of school system and role of parent	• **EL meetings** to provide information about school and education • **School tours** • **Community volunteers** to share information in home language
Fear	• **Demonstrated support** for EL families (regardless of status) • **Adult education** programs • Family **support groups**

Source: SupportEd, https://getsupported.net/free-tools.

BUILDING UPON THE ASSETS OF STUDENTS' HOME LANGUAGES AND LITERACY EXPERIENCES AT THE PROGRAM LEVEL

Finally, we would like to offer two ideas for how to tap into ELs' assets at a more programmatic, systematic level to have an even bigger impact. We underscore the notion that all school staff recognize the assets of ELs and see themselves as teachers of ELs, no matter what their job title may be. To do so, we first encourage those who make hiring decisions to position themselves for a focus on EL assets by prioritizing the hiring of those who are more likely to be ambassadors and allies for ELs and their families. While it's important to learn about potential teachers' and administrators' experience with ELs, it's also crucial to get a deeper sense of their disposition toward serving as ambassadors and allies for ELs (Staehr Fenner, 2014). We encourage ESOL and/or bilingual teachers, social workers, and parent liaisons to participate in the hiring process. These stakeholders can review job descriptions and suggest questions that would help administrators determine job applicants' dispositions toward working with ELs as well as the skills they possess in working with these students. We also highly encourage administrators to include these stakeholders during candidate interviews and decision making to the extent possible.

In addition to hiring and maintaining staff who will serve as EL ambassadors and allies, we encourage schools and districts to explore and adopt the seal of biliteracy as a way to highlight ELs' great assets. In 2012, California and New York adopted a Seal of Biliteracy to recognize high school graduates who demonstrate academic excellence in attaining proficiency in all domains (e.g., speaking, listening, reading, and writing) in one or more languages other than English. The state seal of biliteracy is included on graduates' diplomas and transcripts. Since that time, 36 states have fully adopted the Seal of Biliteracy with three considering the Seal and eight in the early stages of adoption, underscoring the growing momentum around highlighting ELs' assets. While the Seal of Biliteracy was designed to be awarded by school districts or states, individual schools or programs may also implement the award, even in states that have not adopted the Seal and in districts in which dual language or bilingual programs are not in place. In districts where high school graduates can earn the Seal, we suggest exploring whether districts can create an elementary-school-level Seal to encourage EL students to maintain and develop their home language.

> Margarita and I totally concur! Having and developing a staff that recognizes the importance of an EL's primary language is critical to moving toward excellence in serving ELs and their classmates. Further, language, literacy, and content competency, as we show later in the book, can be taught with whatever curriculum and language the EL needs for success.
> —Shawn

Summary and Conclusions

In this chapter, we discussed the urgency of recognizing the critical importance of students' identities and the strengths of their personal, cultural, socio-emotional, and world experiences. We showed how we can build upon the assets of students' prior personal and social, as well as home-languages and literacy experiences. We discussed how tapping into ELs' assets can occur when we recognize their assets and when all of us who work with ELs see ourselves as teachers of ELs.

We recognize the many challenges in helping to move colleagues from a deficit to an assets perspective when it comes to ELs and their families. It will take small steps to get there and will not be an immediate change, happening overnight. While it may prove overwhelming to think about changing the system as a whole, we advise you to instead reflect upon your successes in helping just one colleague start to shift from a deficit to an asset view of one EL or EL family at a time instead of ELs as a whole. By making connections with individual ELs' stories and starting to value the often-hidden strengths that our amazing community of ELs brings, multilingualism and multiliteracy have a fighting chance at being seen as the assets they truly are.

References

August, D., & Shanahan, T. (2006). *Developing literacy in second-language learners: Report of the National Literacy Panel on Language-Minority Children and Youth.* Mahwah, NJ: Lawrence Erlbaum Associates.

Bialystok, E., Peets, K., & Moreno, S. (2014). Producing bilinguals through immersion education: Development of metalinguistic awareness. *Applied Psycholinguistics, 35*(1), 177–191. doi:10.1017/S0142716412000288

Biswas-Diener, R., Kashdan, T. B., & Gurpal, M. (2011). A dynamic approach to psychological strength development and intervention. *Journal of Positive Psychology, 6*(2), 106–118. doi: 10.1080/17439760.2010.545429

Cummins, J. (2004). Multiliteracies pedagogy and the role of identity texts. In K. Leithwood, P. McAdie, N. Bascia, & A. Rodigue (Eds.), *Teaching for deep understanding: Towards the Ontario curriculum that we need* (pp. 68–74). Toronto, Canada: Ontario Institute for Studies in Education of the University of Toronto and the Elementary Federation of Teachers of Ontario.

Gandára, P., & Baca, G. (2008). NCLB and California's English language learners: The perfect storm. *Language Policy, 7*, 201–216. https://doi.org/10.1007/s10993-008-9097-4

Garcia, E. E., Jensen, B. T., & Scribner, K. P. (2009) Supporting English learners. *Educational Leadership, 66*(7), 8–13. Washington, D.C., Association for Supervision and Curriculum and Development.

Gauvain, M. (2001). *The social context of cognitive development.* New York: Guilford Press.

Gauvain, M. (2013). Sociocultural contexts of development. In P. D. Zelazo (Ed.), Oxford handbook of developmental psychology: Vol. 2., Self and other (pp. 425–451). New York: Oxford University Press.

Genesee, F., Lindholm-Leary, K., Saunders, W., & Christian, D. (2005). English language learners in U.S. schools: An overview of research findings. *Journal of Education for Students Placed at Risk, 10*(4), 363–385. Retrieved from http://citeseerx.ist.psu.edu/viewdoc/download?doi=10.1.1.465.9404&rep=rep1&type=pdf

Gonzalez, N., Moll, L. C., & Amanti, C. (Eds.). (2005). *Funds of knowledge: Theorizing practices in households, communities, and classrooms.* Mahwah, NJ: Lawrence Erlbaum.

Grantmakers for Education. (2013). Educating English language learners: Grant-making strategies for closing America's other achievement gap. Retrieved from https://edfunders.org/sites/default/files/Educating%20English%20Language%20Learners_April%202013.pdf

Grisso, L. (2017). Building bridges through storytelling: What are your students' stories? Retrieved from http://www.colorincolorado.org/article/building-bridges-through-storytelling-what-are-your-students-stories

Menken, K. (2008). *English learners left behind: Standardized testing as language policy.* Clevedon, England: Multilingual Matters.

Menken, K. (2009). No Child Left Behind and its effect on language policies. *Annual Review of Applied Linguistics* (29), 103–117. Cambridge, UK: Cambridge University Press.

Musu-Gillette, L., Robinson, J., McFarland, J., KewalRamani, A., Zhang, A., & Wilkinson-Flicker, S. (2016). *Status and trends in the education of racial and ethnic groups 2016* (NCES 2016-007). Washington, DC: U.S. Department of Education, National Center for Education Statistics. Retrieved from https://nces.ed.gov/pubs2016/2016007.pdf

The Nation's Report Card. (2017). *NAEP reading report card.* Retrieved October 17, 2018, from https://www.nationsreportcard.gov/reading_2017/#/nation/achievement?grade=8

National Center for Education Statistics. (2017, October 5). *Common Core of data US public schools.* Retrieved from https://nces.ed.gov/ccd/tables/ACGR_RE_and_characteristics_2015-16.asp

Rauch, D. P., Naumann, J., & Jude, N. (2012). Metalinguistic awareness mediates effects of full biliteracy on third-language reading proficiency in Turkish–German bilinguals. *International Journal of Bilingualism, 16*(4), 402–418. https://doi.org/10.1177/1367006911425819

Seligman, M. E. P., Rashid, T., & Parks, A. C. (2006). Positive psychotherapy. *American Psychologist, 61*(8), 774–788. Retrieved from http://dx.doi.org/10.1037/0003-066X.61.8.774

Solórzano, R. W. (2008). High stakes testing issues, implications and remedies for English learners. *Review of Educational Research, 78*(2), 260–329.

Soto, I., and Gottlieb, M. (2019). From monolingualism to multilingualism. In *Breaking down the wall.* Thousand Oaks, CA: Corwin.

Staehr Fenner, D. (2014). *Advocating for English learners: A guide for educators.* Thousand Oaks, CA: Corwin.

Staehr Fenner, D. (2017). SupportEd's top 10 ways to support English learners in 2017. Retrieved from https://getsupported.net/supporteds-top-10-ways-support-english-learners-2017/

Staehr Fenner, D., & Snyder, S. (2017) *Unlocking English learners' potential: Strategies for making content accessible.* Thousand Oaks, CA: Corwin.

Umansky, I. M., & Reardon, S. F. (2014). Reclassification patterns among Latino English Learner students in bilingual, dual immersion, and English immersion classrooms, *American Educational Research Journal 51*(2014), 879–912.

U.S. Department of Justice and U.S. Department of Education. (2015, January, 7). *Dear colleague letter.* Retrieved from https://www2.ed.gov/about/offices/list/ocr/letters/colleague-el-201501.pdf

Valentino, R. A., & Reardon, S. F. (2015). Effectiveness of four instructional programs designed to serve English learners: Variation by ethnicity and initial English proficiency. *Educational Evaluation and Policy Analysis 37*(2015), 612–637.

Zacarian, D. (2012). *Transforming schools for English learners: A comprehensive guide for school leaders*. Thousand Oaks, CA: Corwin.

Zacarian, D. (2013). *Mastering academic language: A framework for supporting student achievement*. Thousand Oaks: Corwin.

Zacarian, D., Alvarez-Ortiz, L., Haynes, J. (2017). *Teaching to strengths: Supporting students living with trauma, violence and chronic stress*. Alexandria, VA: ASCD.

Zacarian, D., & Haynes, J. (2012). *The essential guide for educating beginning English learners*. Thousand Oaks, CA: Corwin.

Zacarian, D., & Silverstone, M. (2015). *In it together: How student, family, and community partnerships advance engagement and achievement in diverse classrooms*. Thousand Oaks, CA: Corwin.

Note

1. See Cummins (2004) for more information on identity texts.

chapter two

From Compliance to Excellence

SHAWN SLAKK AND
MARGARITA ESPINO CALDERÓN

PREMISE

Federal guidelines and district and school policies can be useful for stating minimum expectations for effectively educating ELs. However, when education professionals are driven by a profound sense of justice and a moral imperative that takes them *beyond compliance*, the likelihood of achieving equitable outcomes is dramatically enhanced.

VIGNETTE

Like many districts and schools in August, Winterhaven Schools is gearing up for the new school year. Samuel White, the superintendent, has just been informed that Winterhaven will be a refugee site this coming year and that the district should prepare for a large influx of refugees, mostly from Puerto Rico and the Caribbean. Mr. White has already started the process by convening a committee to review the processes, programs, and services the district has in place. Since Winterhaven is a small suburban Florida district and currently only has a few ELs, he is concerned about how they will properly serve the new students. The EL committee has reached out to several other districts in the area, including a nearby district that is working with the U.S. Department of Justice to remedy the DOJ's concerns about their inadequate service and programs for ELs. Winterhaven is known for its excellence in education, low dropout rates, and higher-than-average college acceptance rates. They hope to learn from their neighbors' experiences. With that in mind, the committee has committed to developing an action plan that will continue that excellence while balancing between service that is above the bare minimum of compliance and available funding, moving forward into a plan that involves the community and business members in welcoming the newly arrived students and their families. Eventually, they hope to help the community's policy makers see the benefits of welcoming, supporting, and encouraging these new families to stay in Winterhaven. Winterhaven's continuing goal is to be the number-one school district in the nation—inclusive of all its students.

THE URGENCY

The United States is a nation of immigrants. This wonderful fusion of culture and global richness is a historical constant. As part of this annual growth in diversity of our nation, our schools also continue to see an influx of English learners. Some states see more students and have figured out how to properly serve them; other states have traditionally had less, so those states are still working on how to best reach ELs. The Migration Policy Institute's findings in its 2018 publication on superdiversity report that ELs account for at least one-fourth of enrolled students in 19 states plus Washington, DC. Not surprising since Goldenberg in 2010 projected that the EL population will rise to 1 in 4 over the next 20 years and that states such as South Carolina, Tennessee, and Indiana will have an EL population growth of up to 400% by 2020. According to the National Center for Education Statistics, in 2014–2015, West Virginia's EL student population was 1% while California's was 22.4%. Also, from the NCES, in 2015 the nation's EL population was 9.5%—a significant increase from the 8.1% figure recorded in 2000. Sixty percent of our nation's EL students are enrolled in schools in California, Texas, and New York. Kansas, of all places, saw the highest increase (7.5 percentage points) and Arizona saw the largest decrease (9.0 percentage points). While immigrants account for much of the EL population growth in a number of states, immigrant children are not the only EL students. Nearly 85% of pre-kindergarten to fifth grade ELs and 62% of secondary level ELs in 2013 we are native-born, and 11.5 million children between 0 and 8 we are dual language learners and accounted for one-third of the 36.6 million children in that age range (Migration Policy Institute, 2015, 2018). Perhaps even more surprising to some readers is the rate of Long-Term ELs (LTELs) in our schools. Long-Term English learners are students who have been in our schools for six or more years and are still classified as ELs. Olsen (2010) reminds us that the majority of ELs in our schools—59%—are LTELs. Maxwell (2012) echoes that finding while adding that the literacy gap between non-ELs and their EL peers is widening with an average of only 62% of ELs graduating in 2014, and even fewer enrolling, being successful in, or graduating from college (Kanno & Cromley, 2015; Núñez, Rios-Aguilar, Kanno, & Flores, 2016). The main conclusion that can be drawn from these findings is that a large percentage of ELs have not been well-served by their schools. Moreover, even schools that are in compliance with federal, state, and local policies have a moral imperative to do more to ensure the success of their ELs.

In September 2017, hurricane Maria ravaged the Caribbean and many parts of Florida. As a result, the continental U.S. school districts in Florida, Massachusetts, New York, and Pennsylvania have absorbed an influx of the students who left Puerto Rico, most of whom are Spanish speakers and English learners. While the devastation of Puerto Rico's education system may be a once-in-a-lifetime happening, it underscored the responsibility of the receiving school districts, many of which already struggled with over-burdened, understaffed, and underfunded support structures. Such over-taxed systems striving to meet the needs of immigrant ELs face an especially urgent need to find a solution with effective outcomes for the success of their multilingual learners.

Puerto Rico is only one of the sources of the influx of new ELs into our public schools. All school systems, even those that were historically too small or exempt from serving ELs, are now responsible. Every school system, private or public, needs to have a plan in place to serve ELs, whether refugees from war-torn countries, immigrant unaccompanied minors, or native-born non-English speakers.

> The fact that the majority of ELs are actually born in the United States is often surprising to many educators and policy makers!
>
> —Diane

FEDERAL GUIDELINES AND REQUIREMENTS

Schools and districts have spent the last 15 years working on the account-ability system and guidelines set out first in No Child Left Behind (NCLB)—the 2001 reauthorization of the Elementary and Secondary Education Act—and then in its latest (2015) reauthorization, the Every Student Succeeds Act (ESSA). All districts and states are required to address iden-tification, reclassification, and performance accountability of ELs set out in the NCLB mandate. With the changes made in ESSA, accountability moved from Title III to Title I, and individual states now have more flexibility in reporting accountability calculations, have longer monitoring periods for students who have exited services (increased from two to four years), have more defined reporting (greater disaggregation of subgroups to include dually identified ELs and Long-Term ELs), and are now required to develop a stan-dardized procedure for screening and exiting EL students (U.S. Department of Education, 2018a).

However, the above policy work is always subject to change. Regulations fluctuate according to the whim of the current policy makers. What will it look like in years to come? What will be the differences in implementa-tion between various states and local education agencies (LEAs)? When will compliance be more than just the current required minimum? The shift described in this chapter suggests that all stakeholders must think beyond the minimum expectation with respect to serving our English learners. States, districts, communities, policy makers, community members, and schools must act now to move these expectations from compliance to excellence. Few can dispute that a well-educated population, thriving schools, and vibrant community are imperatives for a healthy economy and society. And, as noted in Chapter 6 of this book, when instruction to multilingual learners and all students is embraced as a schoolwide initiative, schools show positive gains for years and low-performing ones achieve exemplary results. The good news is that we know it *can be done*, as evidenced by this chapter's examples of what it means to move beyond compliance in the pursuit of equity and excellence for all students.

EVERY STUDENT SUCCEEDS ACT

While the Every Student Succeeds Act (ESSA, 2015) was enacted for all students, it specifically highlights expanding requisite services and programs to ensure equitable access for ELs. The ESSA's goals include holding all students to high academic standards that prepare them for success in college and careers. With this goal comes accountability to guarantee that states redirect resources into what works to help ELs and their schools improve. It empowers state and local decision makers to develop research and evidence-based plans of service to create strong systems of sustained school improvement, avoiding cookie-cutter federal solutions like the No Child Left Behind Act (2008).

OCR/DOJ EXPECTATIONS OF MINIMUM ADHERENCE TO ESSA

To assist states and districts with meeting their obligations to ELs under the newly reauthorized ESSA, the U.S. Department of Justice Civil Rights Division and U.S. Department of Education Office for Civil Rights (OCR) distributed a set of guidelines laid out in a "Dear Colleague" letter on January 7, 2015. These guidelines, discussed and used as the basis for this chapter, also included discussions of how states could meet these obligations and implement Title III grants consistent with ELs' civil rights. These rights range from proper identification, educationally sound research-based instructional programs with adequate instructional staff, to meaningful participation in any school activity or curricula with other non-EL classmates regardless of acceptance of EL services, plus appropriate assistance for dually identified ELs and reclassified ELs. In addition, the guidelines discussed meaningful parent and family outreach. The complete list of guidelines and suggestions can be found on ed.gov or by Googling "Dear Colleague Letter on English Language Learners" (U.S. Department of Justice & U.S. Department of Education, 2015).

As part of this accountability and guarantees, required testing has been reduced, leaving more time for teaching and learning, yet continuing the accountability of clear, annual information parents and educators need to make sure children are learning. In the end, ESSA expects that ELs and their peers will receive a well-rounded education based on college and career ready standards (ESSA, 2016), expanding STEM (science, technology, engineering, and mathematics) to include the arts or the revised STEAM. ELs and the nation benefit tremendously because ELs can begin participating with their artistic talents not limited by their language skills.

All schools need to plan for and provide services as outlined by the OCR/DOJ's "Dear Colleague" letter regarding English learners. In these guidelines, the DOJ provides 10 key necessities for the adequate teaching of ELs. Before embarking on a review of these 10 items, it is important to remember that the overarching goal of ESSA is for all students to have equity of access to education. That equity encompasses not only academic success but also opportunity for all activities, curricular or extracurricular, offered to any of their peers regardless of their language ability. They are to be considered a fully participating member of the educational community of learners. The following items are the guidelines assessed by the OCR for compliance and adequate services for ELs in any school, district, or state. As you review the list in Figure 2.1, consider what it might take to move beyond the minimum expectations to a place where the aforementioned goal of equity can be fully realized.

Starting from the day a student arrives at the school, each education agency must have a process in place to properly identify ELs' English language

> I'd also suggest assembling a team of EL advocates at your school, district, or state to examine these 10 items together in order to prioritize which ones you'd like to focus on first as you advocate for your students. You can create an action plan that maps out your priorities, your goals and objectives, a timeline for taking action, and how you can measure your success.
> —Diane

FIGURE 2.1

- Identifying all English learner students
- Providing English learners with a language assistance program
- Staffing and supporting an EL program
- Offering meaningful access to all curricular and extracurricular programs
- Creating an inclusive environment and avoiding unnecessary segregation
- Addressing English learners with disabilities
- Serving English learners who opt out of EL programs
- Monitoring and exiting English learners
- Evaluating the effectiveness of a district's EL program
- Ensuring meaningful communication with limited English proficient parents

development level and the type and amount of service required to properly support their academic success and growth. The program and amount of service must include adequate staffing and support to provide meaningful and equitable access to all educational activities, fostering an encompassing environment integrating all students together into one body. Dually identified ELs with special physical or educational needs are specifically noted as needing proper integration and service.

All ELs regardless of acceptance of specialized additional support by the parents must be monitored and assessed annually while receiving EL services and identified as having EL status. Monitoring and remediation is also an expectation up to four years beyond exiting EL status.

Annual assessment of the school or district's program and effectiveness and meaningful communication with EL parents and families is also part of the equity of service and one of the DOJ's main guidelines for compliance.

THE VISION

After reviewing processes, staffing, and programs, the next step is to assure that every teacher who serves an EL has the proper training to help them succeed with not just their content, but the language and literacy of the content. Many education agencies are working toward that goal.

Massachusetts is one of those agencies that has implemented a process to ensure that every EL has a teacher who has received training to accommodate the additional needs of ELs in the general classroom. We've included this example in that it illustrates a shift in policy and practice across an entire state—a shift that was fundamentally compliance-driven. As of July 2015, licensure regulations require that all core-content teachers in the commonwealth of Massachusetts must obtain the RETELL endorsement to be initially licensed, retain, or advance their license. RETELL (Rethinking Equity in the Teaching of English Language Learners) is a 45-hour structured English instruction course designed to assist the general classroom teacher to meet the needs of English learners and a 15-hour course to prepare administrators for an effective implementation. Massachusetts has included administrators and teacher preparation programs in this requirement as well. During the RETELL initiative time-frame, 60,000 educators (teachers and administrators) were trained in strategies to help ELs acquire language and literacy in math, science, social studies, and English Language Arts (ELA) classes. This large-scale, professional learning endeavor and subsequent licensure regulation came as a result of a Department of Justice investigation of a claim that Massachusetts as an educational entity had failed to take appropriate action to overcome language barriers experienced by ELs. The state had not properly defined nor regulated the preparation and training that teachers and other educators must have to provide effective instruction for multilingual learners.

Full disclosure: Margarita and Shawn were highly involved in the RETELL initiative. Shawn worked at Massachusetts's Department of Elementary and Secondary Education as the RETELL coordinator, where he, his team, and colleagues developed the RETELL coursework, trained trainers, and rolled out the professional development courses needed to deliver the sessions and endorsement to the educators of Massachusetts. Margarita, as the expert witness on behalf of the DOJ, oversaw the creation, implementation, and trainings provided for the endorsement. Most evidence-based features of RETELL were based on ExC-ELL (see ExC-ELL features in Chapter 6). Additionally, some of the other authors of this book also assisted in different aspects of the RETELL initiative.

> My takeaway is that even if change for ELs occurs because of a DOJ investigation, students and their families can ultimately benefit no matter the impetus for the change.
> —Diane

Massachusetts agreed to change its policy and improve its service to ELs only after the Department of Justice investigated and became involved. The DOJ's findings held Massachusetts accountable to properly serve ELs, resulting in these changes, improving instruction for all students, and helping teachers to have a better understanding of working with ELs in their specific curriculum. This intervention by the DOJ also resulted in a change to the licensure requirements to ensure continued accountability and a serious effort to better prepare Massachusetts educators as a whole to effectively serve their multilingual learners.

At the same time, we strongly believe that educators who act from a moral imperative to improve access for all students are in the best position to shift the EL narrative. It took the commonwealth of Massachusetts's legislature and Department of Elementary and Secondary Education three years under close scrutiny by the DOJ (which continues to this day) to begin addressing compliance.

Loudoun County Public Schools in northern Virginia with 82,000 students, 16.4% of whom are ELs, launched their improvement efforts not because they were in trouble with the DOJ, but rather from a vision focused on helping ELs. Their goal is to work with the schools that have the highest percentages of ELs to attain equity and access to quality instruction. They wanted to begin with secondary schools because those ELs had so little time to become proficient and instruction had to become the catalyst for their successful graduation. Both central district administrators and school administrators made the commitment and joined resources to begin this journey. They opted for a whole-school approach to professional development that focused on ELs. The plan was to begin with a middle and a high school, gauge student and implementation progress, and if positive change was happening, they would add two more schools. Around mid-year with the pilot schools, it became apparent that by focusing on ELs, not only the ELs but also all students were improving. This was sufficient evidence to add another middle and high school. As each year progresses, they will continue to add schools, continuing with the ones that have the most ELs and moving on to the elementary schools.

QUALITY PROFESSIONAL DEVELOPMENT AS THE FIRST STEP

The Loudoun gradual approach to "whole school reform around EL achievement" is working for this district. Sometimes, approaches are either too limited, offering professional development to only a few teachers here and there. Other times, attempting to adopt an approach for hundreds of teachers depletes the resources necessary for providing on-site support such as coaching. Propitiously, Loudoun planned and funded the follow-up support system consisting of coaching all 177 teachers per year, training instructional coaches, counselors, principals, assistant principals, and key district directors, coordinators, and specialists. They purchased better materials for their newcomers and Students with Interrupted Formal Education (SIFE) and hired necessary staff who understood from the start this mission and vision, and the seriousness of a quality implementation. They accepted from a neighboring university an offer of free tuition for core-content teachers who wanted an ESOL certification. The Virginia Department of Education sponsored a parent education program to create better relationships between schools and EL parents. They are trying to cover and move beyond all the compliance issues with a systematic process, vision, and passion. The passion is evident when we visit classrooms and see the students excited, engaged, and learning, which in turn impacts the passion of the teachers and their administrators.

GOING FROM SIMPLY COMPLYING TO PROVIDING EXCELLENCE

In an ideal situation, all schools would have effective plans to cover all of the components needed to serve all ELs. Winterhaven, the exemplar school presented at the beginning of this chapter, although fictitious, illustrates what it means to move from simple compliance to excellence. The examples below from our Winterhaven creation are a compilation and based on pieces from school plans we have seen or assisted with in the interest of compliance and beyond. In reviewing this model plan, it is important to remember that equity should be at the forefront. Equity requires opportunities to participate and succeed in all aspects of the educational process: academically; social emotional well-being, curricular and extracurricular; advance placement; and as full members of the educational community.

Here are some of the notes Mr. White (the principal) and Winterhaven's committee agreed upon that needed to be in their district's three-year school improvement plan to best serve the ELs in their community. After reviewing the DOJ's "Dear Colleague" letter guidelines, look at the text in italics that shows what they added:

1. **All ELs quickly, accurately identified with instructional plans**

    Winterhaven will implement a policy to add a Home Language Survey (HLS) to its regulation process. Initial and immediate identification and placement in the appropriate program of service must start day 1, as there is a 14-day window to correctly identify and screen all possible ELs. As part of the initial enrollment and registration process, the HLS will be administered at the Family Welcome Center or at the school if students register at the school they will attend. The Home Language Survey consists of four simple questions:

    - *What language do you speak with your child at home?*
    - *What language does your child speak at home with you?*
    - *What language does your child speak with his friends?*
    - *What language did your child speak when learning how to talk?*

    Additionally, Winterhaven will have the HLS, as well as the reasoning and explanation behind this identification process, translated into the languages spoken by the new students and their families. Translators or a call-in service may need to be employed so that students and parents have assistance in understanding the benefits and be able to ask and answer relevant questions correctly. While the committee understands that at times parents do not want to admit they speak another language at home, the district will need to revisit this process often. They will need to reach out to parents and guardians to ensure accuracy of information and the importance of these additional services to the academic success of the student. Additionally, if parents opt out or waive these services, Winterhaven recognizes that it is still the district's responsibility to ensure equitable access to educational programs and to monitor the student's progress. Winterhaven will also work with the families of those who have opted out/waived services to understand that this applies only to the receipt of direct ESOL services. Winterhaven remains legally responsible to provide English language development instruction in any classroom setting and that all students identified as English learners will continue to be assessed annually until they exit ESOL status. Opting out does not negate a student's status as an English learner and that monitoring will continue for four years after exiting ESOL status.

> In Fairfax County Public Schools, Virginia, we collected and analyzed academic achievement data on ELs who had been opted out of ESOL services. We shared these data with parents upon registration and found that the number of parents who opted their children out of ESOL services declined dramatically.
> —Diane

To facilitate registration and testing, a good policy fully informs parents of the benefits and rights they have for the education of their children. Informed parents will understand the need to complete the HLS during the enrollment process and understand why the school district needs to assess their students' ELD (English language development) proficiency levels before the school year starts or as soon after registration as possible. Many districts assess the student's ELD level during the registration process. Having procedures in place for accurately identifying ELs quickly and timely is a must to ensure that each EL smoothly enters their program of service and has the opportunity to participate and succeed in the instructional day.

2. **Effective individualized language acquisition programs**

All ELs at Winterhaven will participate in general education classes with in-class ESOL teacher support or Structured English Instruction endorsed teachers. All English development direct service hours will be with highly qualified ESOL instructors based upon their English Language Development levels. The number of ESOL hours per week will meet each individual student's needs based upon their ELD levels and progress will be assessed quarterly.

When EL students are identified based on a valid and reliable ELP/ELD test, school districts must provide them with appropriate language assistance services. Language assistance services or programs for EL students must be educationally sound in theory and effective in practice; however, the civil rights laws do not require any particular program or method of instruction for EL students.

After identification, appropriate language assistance services must be provided. The program of services must be "sound in theory and effective in practice." Winterhaven has chosen to provide Sheltered English Instruction. However, there are several possible options as suggested by the "Dear Colleague" letter. Programs that have been found to be acceptable when measured against the Castañeda ruling include:

- English as a Second Language (ESOL), also known as English Language Development (ELD): Program/s of techniques, methodology, and special curriculum designed to explicitly teach ELs English. These programs must include instruction on academic vocabulary based in content instruction to facilitate ELs literacy development in speaking, listening, reading, and writing. Instruction is typically in English with minimal use of a student's home language.

- Structured English Immersion (SEI): Program/s that provide sufficient English language skills thus enabling an EL to transition to and be successful in a mainstream English-only classroom. Instruction is typically an immersion-style program in English with teachers who have ESOL or SEI certification and have demonstrated success in ensuring ELs have access to content.

- Transitional Bilingual Education (TBE) or early exit bilingual education: Program/s that develops a student's primary language early in the students' educational process, maintaining, and developing primary language skills. English language skills are introduced and over time the EL transitions into English as the primary language delivery vehicle. An ELs' primary language may be used to facilitate English development to the extent necessary.

- <u>Dual Language Program</u>, also known as two-way or developmental, is a bilingual program/s with the end goal of students developing English language proficiency in both languages: English and an additional language, typically comprised of a classroom with half of the students who speak English as a primary language and the remaining half of the class as speakers of the other language. (USDOJ/DOE, 2015)

To ensure a timely transition out of the above services, a district will need to provide appropriate and adequate direct ESOL services based on individual students' ELD levels and growth. The farther an EL needs to grow, the more direct service hours a district will need to provide; more proficient students will require less. All levels of service must be at the same or comparable service hour levels to ensure adequate and appropriate annual growth.

Any program must meet annual yearly growth as measured by an approved annual assessment. If the ELs are not making progress, the program must be revised. The "Dear Colleague" letter uses Castañeda, a previously litigated and proven gauge to measure services and instructional impact on ELs' advancement. Known as "the third prong" of the Castañeda ruling, programs that do not show adequate progress may result in staffing changes, more professional development, new instructional resources bought, or schedules reconstructed.

Caution is warranted when selecting and scheduling service hours or developing a program of service. Any program that excludes kindergarteners, fails to properly schedule ELs due to scheduling conflicts based on their EL program, supplements instruction with tutoring in place of certified ESOL instructors, fails to offer service to all ELs (i.e., students with disabilities), stops providing direct service hours based upon a high ELD level without exiting EL status, or fails to provide appropriate additional services to an EL who has not made adequate annual progress and has not exited EL status (i.e., a Long-Term English learner) has been noted as out of compliance with the EL's civil rights (USDOJ/DOE, 2015).

Keep in mind that the above information again only addresses the minimum. Instead, schools should provide individualized instructional programs with whatever support is needed for each student, regardless of language or need. For example, Winterhaven's plan is to assess growth and student needs quarterly rather than just annually.

3. **Highly qualified instructional and support staff for EL programs**

   Winterhaven School District will use the next three years to train all non-ESOL-endorsed educators in Structured English Instruction strategies, beginning year 1 with teachers and supervising administrators that currently serve ELs. Training will continue until all staff members have been trained in strategies to best serve ELs in their content or position, including but not limited to front office staff, cafeteria, and custodial staff. A review of progress and evaluation of this professional development plan will be included in the district's annual assessment. In addition to initial trainings, renew and refresh sessions will be provided for all SEI-trained educators; plus each school will convene an SEI/EL services committee and Principals Learning Communities (PLC). The SEI PLC will meet monthly to review student progress, share strategies, and evaluate current training and support plus make recommendation for revision and refinement of this process and the services provided to ESOL students.

Again, Castañeda is used as a gauge to measure adequate compliance to ensure that there are procedures in place to implement their chosen EL program. SEAs (state education agencies) must provide staff and resources sufficient to adequately implement their chosen program: highly qualified, ESOL- or SEI-certified teachers, equally trained SEI administrators to supervise, coach, and evaluate these teachers, and materials for the EL programs. Each school district must also evaluate and assess that the district has a sufficient number of highly qualified or certified teachers per EL student and that these teachers have been sufficiently trained and are able to implement the chosen program. If necessary, a school district that lacks adequate staffing to serve the EL population may require embedded teachers to attend professional development to fulfill the needed certified ratio of teacher to student.

Additionally, school districts must also provide EL students with non-teaching support staff, resources, and curricular materials, ESOL/SEI or bilingual, in sufficient amounts for ELs to successfully make yearly growth.

Some pitfalls that have been noted include the following: ESOL-endorsed teachers who do not have a complete set of skills to implement effective ESOL instruction; insufficient ESOL, SEI, or bilingually certified administrators to evaluate instruction and implementation; district or state-wide shortages of ESOL/SEI-certified or -trained teachers; and inadequate or not appropriate program materials.

Caution: Paraprofessionals, regardless of training and certification may not be permanently placed as the ESOL/SEI teacher, nor can teaching assistants or tutors. Paraprofessionals may temporarily be assigned as a stopgap measure until a highly qualified teacher is hired, trained, or certified, and only under the direct supervision of an ESOL/SEI-qualified teacher (USDOJ/DOE, 2015).

In the above-quoted materials, the words *sufficient* and *adequate* are frequently used. *Sufficient* and *adequate* will not help our ELs become excellent. It will only move them down the road of compliance. Excellence comes from hard work, determination, and a complete commitment to the process.

Winterhaven offers a great example of moving beyond the minimum as illustrated by its commitment to preparing its *entire staff* to best serve ELs and forming a dedicated PLC to regularly monitor progress and adjust practices as needed. No one becomes excellent by just complying with the bare minimum. In education, that means ensuring that ALL teachers are ready to meet the needs of whatever learners enter their rooms. Teachers need training, coaching, and funding for supplies and curriculum development. They need time to work with peers to meet the needs of their students as a team, not as individuals. The whole school must work towards the success of every student.

4. **Equitable access to all curricular and extracurricular programs for all**

Winterhaven recognizes that ELs need to have access to all curriculum, courses, and extracurricular activities to be college and career ready. This will include appropriate ESOL/ELD teacher and language support. Included in the previously mentioned process, all current and future courses, before- and after-school enrichment, or sports activities will be open to all participants regardless of their ELD levels. Teachers and staff members will be provided with the appropriate training to assist ELs in these programs.

Equitable access and participation rely on an EL's ability to attain sufficient skills in English and successfully master content regardless of the amount of service or program hours provided. Thus, proper service hours and other student services must be correctly and accurately scheduled to meet each student's individual needs. Again, we see Castañeda used as a measure of successful implementation of an ESOL/SEI program. Along with core content, extracurricular and cocurricular activities must also be accounted for, scheduled and made available. All materials, grade-level appropriate courses, curriculum, facilities, before- and after-school programs, and college or career readiness classes must be open and offered to all students regardless of EL or non-EL status.

All scheduling, course, and graduation requirements must adequately provide equitable access to courses, sufficient time to complete course work while attaining annual yearly growth toward exiting from EL status. Any program of intensive ESOL or ELD coursework must dovetail within the standard graduation or advancement schedule required of a non-EL status student.

School districts and state education agencies (SEAs) have reported that when reviewed, the DOJ and Department of Education (DOE) have assessed their design and implementation of EL programs to ensure that they are "reasonably calculated" to allow ELs to successfully acquire both English proficiency and meaningful participation in a typical instructional day. Additionally, SEAs and districts have been reviewed to evaluate compliance regarding ELs' access to grade-level curricula, materials, support programs, and assistance for proper advancement and graduation requirements. Furthermore, the DOJ has also evaluated the SEA/district's provision of equal opportunities for ELs to attend and succeed in specialized programs, curricular, cocurricular, or extracurricular with special attention to a district's process to ensure timely graduation and access to college and career readiness courses (USDOJ/DOE, 2015).

I often advocate for having a bilingual guidance counselor or team of counselors who can specialize in working with ELs and their families to ensure that ELs' placement in coursework that leads to graduation is prioritized. Your focus on having ELs take part in extracurricular programs is also integral to ELs' success and is an area that is often overlooked.

—Diane

Think about how the Winterhaven plan might move beyond "adequate and sufficient." Not only must students be allowed to attend these courses and activities, but they must also be openly recruited, advised, and guided towards these programs. In fact, courses and activities may even need to be redesigned or revamped to fit the needs and goals of ELs. Like many students, not all ELs are college bound, nor do they want to be. Many will want to have non-four-year/degree college-based careers that require a high level of technical skills and the wherewithal to be lifelong learners. Ultimately, offering appropriate programs to meet these English learners' needs in the end will benefit all students, not just ELs.

5. **Inclusive whole-school nurturing learning environment indistinguishable of program or level of service**

   As part of Winterhaven's commitment to whole-school success for ELs and all students, it also recognizes that at times ELs, newcomers, or SIFE students may need to be grouped together for targeted intensive service and instruction to help them become more proficient in English while learning the content. However, all ELs will participate with mainstream native English-speaking students most of the academic day. English language role models will help with language, literacy, and content mastery. Dually identified ELs may be in self-contained classrooms, if and only if this is the least restrictive environment and their IEP requires such a setting and an ESOL teacher will be assigned as a co-teacher.

   An ongoing assessment and review will be conducted of additional opportunities and services for newcomers or SIFE students will be invited to and encouraged to participate in before- or after-school enrichment programs to help accelerate learning. Social emotional supports and strategies will be built into all instruction so that students can learn or exhibit resiliency and other skills necessary for continued and ongoing success in school and beyond.

Of note is the "Dear Colleagues" letter and its guidelines regarding EL programs that segregate "students on the basis of national origin or EL status." Granted, some programs that reflect individualized service may mean that an EL receives instruction for a limited period, separate from his or her non-EL status peers; however, ELs are expected to be served in the least segregated program and schedule possible. Exceptional programs are those where it is impossible to distinguish between ESOL/ELD service compliance classrooms and a non-EL classroom. Again, program- or instructional-related educational justifications may apply (i.e., a dually identified EL with special education needs has an IEP requiring a self-contained classroom setting). However, this should be a rarity and not the standard. Moreover, even when justified, care must be given to ensuring that enrichment courses such as physical education, art, and music or non-curricular events—lunch, sports, assemblies—are properly and equitably scheduled for meaningful participation in a normal educational setting.

Returning to the reported items reviewed during DOJ/DOE evaluations and observations, schedules and programs are reviewed to determine whether the amount, type, and length of segregation complies with educationally sound programs aimed at achieving successful EL program implementation. The reverse is also true. When striving for excellence, scheduling and direct service hours or support should not be terminated just because an EL has achieved the chosen program's educational goals. Instead, these services need to be provided until the student has obtained native-level language proficiency. While evaluation of programs, service hours, and time in ESOL classes are required to match each student's individual ELD level and needs to successfully meet state and federal guidelines (USDOJ/DOE, 2015), excellence demands providing additional support and service to ensure that the student is successful for the remainder of his or her education and on into his or her chosen career. Winterhaven's plan shows how not only to care for the student at the moment, but also to provide lifetime skills.

6. **Indistinguishable programs and services that provide a nurturing learning environment inclusive of dually identified ELs**

    Winterhaven's Student Services department will review its processes and programs for serving all students, focusing on the needed adjustments to be able to evaluate ELs in English and in their primary language when such evaluation processes are reasonably available in the students' native language. If needed, staffing changes and adjustments will be made to provide both special education services and English language instructional services. If determined that the student's specialized educational needs are best provided in both the student's native language and English, appropriate scheduling and staffing will have to be accommodated as is reasonably possible. Winterhaven recognizes that ESOL and special education services are mutually required, that one does not supersede the other, and both amounts and types of services must conform to federal guidelines. An ESOL educator will need to serve on the student's IEP committee.

The Individuals with Disabilities Education Act (IDEA) and Section 504 of the Rehabilitation Act of 1973 (Section 504) come into review in this area of EL services. According to the USDOJ/DOE (2015), "The Department of Education's Office of Special Education Programs, a component of ED's Office of Special Education and Rehabilitative Services, administers the IDEA. OCR and DOJ share authority for enforcing Section 504 in the educational context, and DOJ coordinates enforcement of Section 504 across Federal agencies."

Any student regardless of disability or language readiness must be assured of equitable and meaningful participation in the regular curricular or non-curricular day. Process and tools must be evaluated to ensure the accurate and timely assessment of an EL who may or may not also fall under IDEA or 509 status. Students must be identified and assessed in a timely manner with all appropriate tools and materials. Districts must ensure against misidentification due to a student's ELD level or EL status.

ESOL- and IEP-mandated services hold equal sway and must be provided to the fullest extent to which the student is entitled under federal law. Parents must equally be informed of ESOL and special education services required, how such services will be implemented, and how any modifications or accommodations outlined in a dually identified EL's IEP meets the student's educational goals. As shown by Winterhaven's plan, parents need to be fully informed in a language and manner they understand regarding all of their student's needs and services.

Failing to provide ALL services whether they be ESOL or IEP related or failing to properly and timely evaluate is impermissible under IDEA and federal civil rights laws. Moreover, even if a parent waivers out of mandated services under IDEA or 504, the district is still compelled to provide all federally entitled programs and services (USDOJ/DOE, 2015).

7. **Language acquisition assistance within the general classroom setting for all learners regardless of EL status**

   Parents may choose to refuse direct service or remove their children from a school district's EL program or specific EL services within the EL program. With that in mind, Winterhaven staff members will work with parents so that they understand their child's rights, the EL services their child can receive, and the benefits of such services. All refusal of services will be documented and retained in the students' records. Winterhaven recognizes its responsibility to serve all ELs regardless of parental acceptance of direct service hours, to provide language acquisition services in all content areas, monitor student progress, and offer services again if the student is struggling. With that in mind, a three-year plan has been implemented to ensure that all educators are highly qualified to work with ELs in addition to an annual review and assessment of students' needs, success, and the program's relevance to these students and needs.

The DOJ/DOE recognizes that parents have the right to waiver or opt out of a school district's EL program or part of a program. However, school districts may not suggest that parents decline services. The decision to refuse or decline services must be voluntarily made with full knowledge. Therefore, districts are obligated to provide adequate and appropriate parent communication of the student's rights and benefits of services and possible pitfalls of declining services. Parents must be informed in a language and manner they understand. In other words, a letter home in English isn't sufficient, and even a letter home in the parent's language may not suffice either, as many may not read or write in their family language. In this regard, moving beyond compliance will mean going the extra distance to ensure that parents and students fully understand their rights and the benefits of the additional assistance, and do so in whatever language, manner—written or verbal translation—or context is needed to help parents and students become comfortable with participating in these programs. Districts will need to hire interpreters; hold informational meetings, individual meetings, and open houses; and demonstrate an open and welcoming attitude towards these students and their families.

When a district comes under review, consideration will be given to the process, procedures, documentation, and communication informing parents of their student's status, the type and scope of the program and service, the benefits of the service, and the possible consequences of failing to accept offered services.

Districts have been cited in past reviews and investigations for practices that dissuade parents from accepting a district or school's programs or for providing erroneous or misleading information to parents about programs, services, or their child's EL status. Other citations have noted noncompliance due to school personnel recommending opting out because the district had insufficient space for providing programs or higher levels of service. Quality of service and proper attention to concerns regarding the effectiveness of a district's program have also been noted as reasons for the DOJ/DOE to find a district in noncompliance. Districts, however, striving for excellence, need to implement the opposite of these policies. Staff and personnel need to be trained to be open and welcoming. School leaders, superintendents, and boards of education must regularly review, inform the community of, and promote the benefits of providing educational funding that in the end benefits all members of the community.

As noted by Winterhaven, even if parents opt out their child, the child remains classified as an EL. The school or district maintains its obligation to provide access to its educational programs, and the student must receive sufficient assistance to meet his or her English language development and academic needs. Moreover, Winterhaven's commitment to a three-year plan to ensure that all educators are highly qualified to work with ELs will increase the odds of success for these students whether or not their parents have opted out of services. Monitoring and assessment of students who have been opted out of an EL program remains a requirement until such students exit EL status. An EL who does not show annual yearly growth or demonstrates difficulty in a subject based on a language barrier must be provided with support. The student's parents must be informed of the lack of progress, and services must again be offered (USDOJ/DOE, 2015).

8. **Data documenting success and/or support of exited ELs**

    Winterhaven will monitor the progress of all EL students toward their academic, literacy, and linguistic goals ensuring that they achieve English language proficiency and master content knowledge as expediently as possible. An annual screening process will determine annual yearly progress in reading, writing, listening, and speaking, and determine eligibility to exit EL status as aligned with the state's English language proficiency standards. Winterhaven will monitor exited EL status students beyond the mandated four years to ensure each student's academic progress throughout their education, providing additional assistance as needed or requested.

Even after exiting from EL status, school and districts are obligated to monitor the academic growth in literacy and curricula plus provide adequate access to grade-level materials and programs. Annual yearly growth must be monitored and assessed in acquiring content knowledge throughout the year and appropriate steps taken when needed for those students progressing towards state and district standards.

SEAs must also monitor and assess exited ELs, ensuring that ELs are properly assessed and exited according to state and federal guidelines based on an EL's proficiency in all speaking, reading, writing, and listening plus literacy and language competency levels. Exit scores must be derived from a valid and reliable measure that meaningfully assesses a student's proficiency in all language domains, thus showing evidence that a student has attained proficiency in English.

After a student has exited EL status, federal guidelines require districts to monitor his or her academic progress for at least four years to ensure that the student was properly exited and all, if any, gaps incurred because of receiving the EL program services have been recouped. In the event a district determines that an exited EL may need additional assistance and a barrier to his or her success may result, re-testing and additional services must again be offered and acceptance or refusal should be documented. Mere compliance to the four-year requirement meets the base minimum, but the excellence model as seen in Winterhaven's plan follows through to the end regardless of the length of time and additional assistance needed.

Concerns may arise if districts or schools with recognized staffing or program exceptions exit intermediate and advanced EL students from EL status, exit students before they are proficient in all four domains with reading and writing scores specifically scrutinized, are unable to show evidence of monitoring former ELs, or do not exit ELs in a timely manner (USDOJ/DOE, 2015). Again, the excellence model works towards ensuring that all students are highly successful in all domains. This will mean more funding and training for teachers, administrators, and student support services and educating the community and policy/budget makers on the benefits of having well-educated students entering the community and work force. This will be time and money well spent.

9. **Yearly evaluations and refinement at the multiyear level analysis of programs and changing needs of EL population**

   Data will be part of the ongoing professional development and implementation process. All teachers and administrators will participate, analyze formal and informal data, and evaluate the program and whole-school involvement to plan and refine continued support and success. As part of Winterhaven's annual evaluation and revision process, the three-year professional development process will also be reviewed to ensure that all core-content teachers are receiving the needed training, coaching, planning, and support they need to meet ELs' academic language and literacy needs and expectations as outlined not just in the states' standards for annual progress but also for Winterhaven's higher benchmark standards.

As outlined in the "Dear Colleague" letter, school districts' and SEA's EL programs are monitored for successful results showing that students' needs are being met. Data sources for evaluation may include: current EL, former EL, and non-EL students and how they measure up when compared based upon a reasonable assumption that EL growth results in equity, participation, and success in a standard instructional program. As outlined by Winterhaven, a school district must evaluate its EL services and programs with the intent to modify or refine if the program's goals are not met. Winterhaven has chosen to do this as an ongoing quarterly process, while setting a high benchmark for success.

Districts, just as the DOJ/DOE will, must consider valid and reliable data to form a comprehensive comparison of how ELs, exited ELs, and their non-EL peers are performing when compared to relevant criteria over time of the program's implementation. This data and evaluation include student performance in key educational milestones (i.e., core content tests; graduation, dropout, and retention rates as measured against other ELs, exited ELs, and non-ELs). Performance of ELs and exited ELs should also be compared to that of their non-EL classmates, annually and over time, to assess trends and needed refinements.

Proper assessment and review involve each and every component addressed up to this point. ELs must be provided with sufficient time and be empowered to attain English proficiency and meaningful participation in their school's general educational program as compared to their non-EL counterparts. If a district or the DOJ/DOE deem an EL program not effective, programmatic changes must occur to rectify the deficiencies.

In addition, as stated in sections 4 and 8 above, monitoring must occur vertically from grade to grade. This monitoring aids districts in reviewing and assessing any possible remediation of academic content-area deficits and whether ELs are progressing according to state and federal guidelines towards advancement, graduation, or college and career readiness alongside their non-EL peers. Additional care should be taken to monitor and evaluate any possible gaps between ELs and non-ELs participation in co-curricular classes such as advanced placement, special education services, or extracurricular activities as compared to their non-EL peers (USDOJ/DOE, 2015).

10. Documentation of successful communication with limited English proficient parents

Winterhaven is revisiting its parent involvement activities, curriculum nights, open houses, report cards, official notifications, and parent conferences to ensure that parents of all students will feel welcome, comfortable, and well informed. For ELs and their families this will involve hiring and having available translators and translated forms in the languages of their students' parents.

The DOJ/DOE (2015) define EL parents or guardians as those whose "primary language is other than English and who have limited English proficiency in one of the four domains of language proficiency (speaking, listening, reading, or writing)." Districts and SEAs are obligated to communicate with an EL parent in the language that he or she understands so he or she is able to reasonably comprehend his or her student's rights and acceptance or denial of services. The DOJ/DOE continues by stating that essential information "includes but is not limited to information regarding: language assistance programs, special education and related services, IEP meetings, grievance procedures, notices of nondiscrimination, student discipline policies and procedures, registration and enrollment, report cards, requests for parent permission for student participation in district or school activities, parent-teacher conferences, parent handbooks, gifted and talented programs, magnet and charter schools, and any other school and program choice options."

In addition to identifying ELs attending their schools, districts must also have a process to determine what ELs' parents' language needs are, including those of parents or guardians whose children may not be ELs but they themselves are ELs or are limited in their English ability. Many school districts use the HLS to gather this information. Teachers and staff need to become masters of sussing out if parent communication requires oral and/or written communication in something other than English. A parent may communicate in a language, but they may not be literate to the point of reading and writing in that language. In addition, the educational system has many highly specified processes and terms that parents will need assistance comprehending, thus the need for translation assistance beyond the written word. Translations of district and school forms in languages that are common for the school's attendance area should be readily available, with alternates for those who do not read well enough in any language. For parents who speak rarer or less common languages, a generic letter explaining in those languages the process by which a parent may use translation or interpretation services should be provided. The DOJ/DOE cautions against web-based automated translation programs but understands the need to do so in some instances. The translated document must convey the intended meaning of the English language document, and such translations should be reviewed by an individual qualified to do so. Furthermore, a student's Family Educational Rights and Privacy Act (FERPA) rights must be retained while using any automated translation system. Additionally, when retaining the services of translators or volunteers, they must have sufficient knowledge in both English and the family's language and appropriate knowledge of educational or service-related terms or concepts. Finally, since these translators and volunteers are equally held to the confidentiality mandate of FERPA, as such, they should also receive the appropriate training to maintain confidentiality.

> I would also suggest that districts share forms commonly used with each other to model what collaboration can look like to show how it would benefit ELs and their families and to also reduce each other's workload.
> —Diane

Pitfalls to avoid as reported by the DOJ/DOE (2015) are relying on students, siblings, and other unqualified persons to translate or interpret; failing to provide translation or an interpreter at student services meetings (i.e., IEP, parent-teacher, or disciplinary conferences); failing to provide timely notification of school programs, services, and activities; or failing to contact the EL's parent.

Winterhaven's commitment to providing a sufficient number of qualified translators and revisiting its current parent involvement activities to ensure that all families feel welcome and included in the life of the school is but another example of moving beyond compliance.

TYING IT ALL TOGETHER

Yes, this will be a process. Yes, it may take time and there will even be setbacks. Nevertheless, starting with proper identification of the ELs in your school or district, individualizing their instructional programs, and providing highly qualified staff and equitable access to all curricular and extracurricular programs is the ethical thing to do. Continuing the process by making sure there is an inclusive whole-school nurturing learning environment for all ELs and their peers shows that all students are important. Be sure to document not only the compliance pieces, but also the growth and success of all ELs, exited ELs, and those who graduate and move on to other things. Establish, refine, and hold the district, teachers, and students accountable with yearly evaluations, multiyear analysis of programs and change with the needs of the ELs to always move towards that goal of excellence. Last, but, as they say, by no means least, make sure to share all of this support, care, success, and growth with your staff, the students, their parents, and the community.

THE CALL FOR ACTION

As seen above in Winterhaven's planning notes, extensive evaluation of existing services and programs to ensure that they meet they meet the needs of a rapidly changing student body is required. English learners are a population

Not only are ELs here to stay, but we can also learn and benefit so much from their presence if we provide them an equitable and excellent education experience!
— Diane

that is here to stay and deserves equitable and effective instruction and a positive educational experience. All educators, schools, districts, and departments of education must review their current programs and services, making changes as needed, not just for compliance, but to ensure that all students receive an excellent education. This typically involves extensive professional development for teachers, administrators, and in some cases, support staff. The establishment of ESOL committees, PLCs, annual evaluation involving all stakeholders, and yearly refinements is a necessity to meet the changing needs of the population.

Schools, districts, and DOEs have guidance from the DOJ to help implement these changes, but it is our position that we must always look beyond what is adequate and sufficient. Massachusetts is an example of how an entire state has started the process of moving to compliance. Loudoun County Public Schools in Virginia is an example of moving beyond compliance by developing a proactive plan and committing to increase capacity to serve ELs. Winterhaven, while only created to be an example, shows the viability of looking beyond compliance to excellence. (See Chapter 6.)

Wherever you are in this process—under scrutiny for failure to comply, realizing that you need more, gearing up to move beyond compliance, or somewhere in the middle—you have taken the first step by reading this chapter and the others in this book. Now that you have completed this chapter, review what your district does, and fill in the chart below with your ideas or thoughts on what you want to research further or share with your leaders to help your school or district move forward.

---

1. Quickly and accurately identify ELs' instructional plans

For compliance, we already . . .
_____
_____
_____

For excellence, we need to do . . .
_____
_____
_____

---

2. Effective individualized language acquisition programs

For compliance, we already . . .
_____
_____
_____

For excellence, we need to do . . .
_____
_____
_____

---

3. Highly qualified instructional and support staff for EL programs

For compliance, we already . . .
_____
_____
_____

For excellence, we need to do . . .
_____
_____
_____

4. Equitable access to all curricular and extracurricular programs for all

For compliance, we already . . .

_____

_____

_____

For excellence, we need to do . . .

_____

_____

_____

5. Inclusive whole-school nurturing, learning environment indistinguishable by program or level of service

For compliance, we already . . .

_____

_____

_____

For excellence, we need to do . . .

_____

_____

_____

6. Indistinguishable programs and services that provide a nurturing learning environment inclusive of dually identified ELs

For compliance, we already . . .

_____

_____

_____

For excellence, we need to do . . .

_____

_____

_____

7. Language acquisition assistance within the general classroom setting for all learners regardless of EL status

For compliance, we already . . .

_____

_____

_____

For excellence, we need to do . . .

_____

_____

_____

8. Data documenting success and/or support of exited ELs

For compliance, we already . . .

_____

_____

_____

For excellence, we need to do . . .

_____

_____

_____

9. Yearly evaluations and refinement at the multiyear level analysis of programs and changing needs of EL population

For compliance, we already . . .

_____

_____

_____

For excellence, we need to do . . .

_____

_____

_____

10. Documentation of successful communication with limited English proficient parents

For compliance, we already . . .

_____

_____

_____

For excellence, we need to do . . .

_____

_____

_____

Summary and Conclusions

Compliance with an EL's civil rights should be part of any class, program, school, district, or state's unstated objective. All children have the inalienable right to a well-crafted, well-designed, challenging, and supportive education.

Unfortunately, this does not seem to be universally applied. In response to this unevenness, part of the education system of the United States includes those who are charged with protecting these rights and holding all accountable, whether the need arises from intentional or unintentional failure to serve children. For those reading this book, hopefully you are one of the intentional ones who recognize the need to properly educate our children and ensure a healthy and strong future for all of us. If you are reading this because you have found yourself in the situation of needing to make changes, we hope that we have provided enough support and examples to help move you on your way. For more resources, an internet search will provide many.

The USDOJ/DOE is intentionally quoted heavily within this chapter, as they have provided exceptional guidance to both help disabuse faulty thinking and more importantly ensure that even the least of us is properly cared for. However, the guidance provided by the USDOJ/DOE is, as we have mentioned earlier, the minimum needed for compliance. This challenge is to go beyond compliance to excellence. What does that look like? Perhaps it doesn't have distinguishing factors. Perhaps the most distinguishing thing about excellence is that it isn't distinctive, but rather expected, demanded, and supported without hesitation, agenda, or political aspirations. It is simply done since it is the right thing to do for any and every child. This chapter is but a small part of the information available to educators of ELs. A simple internet search will provide more than enough resources for any school leader, whatever your role is.

In the realm of the DOJ/DOE, when compliance is met, the word *adequate* frequently appears. However, is *adequate* the level to which we should aspire for our children? Margarita and I challenge you to help carry the load and move beyond compliance to excellence. We applaud your hard work.

"There can be no keener revelation of a society's soul than the way in which it treats its children."

—Nelson Mandela

References

Goldenberg, C. N. (2010). Improving achievement for English learners: Conclusions from recent reviews and emerging research. In G. Li & P. A. Edwards (Eds.), *Best practices in ELL instruction*. New York: Guilford.

Kanno, Y., & Cromley, J. (2015). English language learners' pathways to four-year colleges. *Teachers College Record*, 1–46.

Maxwell, L. (2012). Raising Latino achievement seen as 'demographic imperative.' *Education Week, 31*(34), 4–5. Retrieved from https://www.edweek.org/ew/articles/2012/06/07/34overview.h31.html

Migration Policy Institute. (2015, July 8). *The limited English proficient population in the United States.* Retrieved from https://www.migrationpolicy.org/print/15316#.W1tz0fZFy7c

Migration Policy Institute. (2018, February). *Growing superdiversity among young U.S. dual language learners and its implications.* Retrieved from https://www.migrationpolicy.org/research/growing-superdiversity-among-young-us-dual-language-learners-and-its-implications

Núñez, A.-M., Rios-Aguilar, C., Kanno, Y., & Flores, S. (2016). English learners and their transition to postsecondary education. In M. Paulsen (Ed.), *Higher education: Handbook of theory and research* (Vol. 31, pp. 41–90). New York: Springer. doi: doi.org/10.1007/978-3-319-26829-3_2

Olsen, L. (2010). *Reparable harm: Fulfilling the unkept promise of educational opportunity for California's long-term English learners.* Long Beach, CA: Californians Together. Retrieved from http://www.californianstogether.org/

United States Department of Education. (2018a). *Every student succeeds act.* Retrieved 2018 from https://www.ed.gov/ESSA

United States Department of Education. (2018b, April). *LEAs fact sheet 2018 final.* (Office of English Language Acquisition, Ed.) Retrieved July 2018 from https://ncela.ed.gov/files/fast_facts/LEAs_Fact_Sheet_2018_Final.pdf

United States Department of Education. (2018c, April). *The condition of education.* Retrieved 2018 from https://nces.ed.gov/programs/coe/indicator_cgf.asp

United States Department of Justice and United States Department of Education. (2015, January 7). Dear colleague letter on English language learners. Washington, DC: U.S. Department of Justice Civil Rights Division and U.S. Department of Education Office for Civil Rights. Retrieved 2018 from https://www2.ed.gov/about/offices/list/ocr/letters/colleague-el-201501.pdf

chapter three

From Watering Down to Challenging

TONYA WARD SINGER
AND DIANE STAEHR FENNER

PREMISE

Ensuring access to rigorous and intellectually rich learning opportunities is essential for raising multilingual learner achievement. It is essential to disrupt inequitable outcomes with high expectations, strategic scaffolds, and collective efficacy to ensure programs and instruction accelerate, not remediate, learning.

VIGNETTE

Imagine a fifth-grade science class in which ESOL teacher Ms. Perry co-teaches with Mr. Leonardo, a fifth-grade classroom teacher. Over the past two weeks, students have been learning through many hands-on activities how plants get the materials they need for growth chiefly from air and water. Ms. Perry has been previewing the science concepts and academic vocabulary with the ELs, adding in supports in their home languages, so ELs feel prepared to engage in classroom discussions. Ms. Perry and Mr. Leonardo have integrated several graphic organizers into their instruction and have been chunking the grade-level text so that ELs can engage with the complex science text and content concepts. Now it's students' turn to write an essay, using evidence from two texts to support an argument that plant matter comes mostly from air and water, not from the soil.

This vignette vividly describes an authentic co-taught class for ELs. It illustrates true integrated instruction and hopefully will help our readers think differently about what co-teaching for ELs should actually be.
—Maria

During their scheduled planning meeting, Ms. Perry suggests ways to group students for the task so that one EL with emerging English proficiency can discuss the academic concepts with a peer who is fluent in his home language before applying those ideas to write in English with sentence frames. The teachers strategically pair the other six ELs, who have higher English proficiency, with fluent English speakers to do the task. During the lesson, all thirty students engage in extended partner discussions about the best text evidence to use to support their arguments. They refer to the text they have annotated and collaborate to paraphrase important ideas from the two texts into the graphic organizer in preparation for writing their essay.

THE URGENCY

To excel with rigorous academic content, English learners need access to rigorous academic learning experiences. Engagement in daily opportunities to listen, speak, read, and write about grade-level content topics, concepts, and complex texts is essential for learning both grade-level content and the academic language of school.

Unfortunately, however, many English learners across the nation are routinely pulled out of core content, tracked into lower-level courses (Arias, 2007; Gandara & Orfield, 2010), and/or given only simplified texts and low-level tasks instead of access to what they need to thrive academically and build the academic language for career and college success. As a result, many ELs experience a "watered-down" curriculum that remediates, rather than accelerates, their content and language learning. When ELs are tracked into lower-level courses, they lose access to grade-level content and miss opportunities to learn the academic language that is central to rigorous tasks and texts. By high school, such tracking can result in students missing the courses they need to access higher education, or lacking the credits they need to graduate, causing them to "time out" by becoming too old to qualify for public school.

Even in the optimal program design in which ELs have both access and embedded supports to successfully engage with rigorous core learning and additional language support services, there is another challenge: empowering every teacher with strategic pedagogy to be effective with ELs. By every teacher we mean EVERY teacher, not just EL, bilingual, or ESOL specialists. ELs spend the majority of their instructional time in core classrooms and thus learn best when every general education teacher has the mindset and efficacy to serve ELs. Of equal importance are administrators understanding the issues and leading with the high expectation that every teacher challenges his or her ELs in a strategically supportive environment.

It's an urgent imperative that every teacher knows how to effectively scaffold content and language learning in the context of rigorous academic learning. Default practices of lowering expectations or simplifying texts and tasks for ELs may seem like a support in the moment, but over time these practices add up to significant gaps in ELs' opportunities to learn content and language. Simplified texts, for example, "offer no clue as to what academic language sounds like or how it works" (Fillmore & Fillmore, 2012, p. 2). ELs need to work with complex texts to build the meaning-making skills essential for working with such texts and the academic English proficiency to excel across the curriculum. ELs need opportunities to engage in high-level thinking tasks to thrive with such tasks throughout their lives, not be put on a path of simplified, watered-down learning toward failure.

Scholars and practitioners already have the knowledge and skills to advance the achievement of ELs. Schools *can* and *do* disrupt inequitable EL outcomes by providing English learners with access to high-level content and language learning with quality teaching and strategic supports. For example, an Education Trust-West analysis of 276 districts serving 100+ ELs found that the highest performing districts share mindsets of expecting excellence from ELs and valuing EL assets, and design programs and teaching to ensure ELs' access to rigorous coursework. These districts "avoid the mistake of over-simplifying their instruction and materials with the intent of helping ELs" (Education Trust-West, 2014, p. 25).

While many educators have what they believe are good intentions in providing simplified instruction and materials for ELs, these practices are actually highly detrimental to ELs' equity and eventual success. Decades of acting on "good intentions" in this manner have given rise to some alarming patterns of disparity, for example:

- Low EL graduation rates. Nationwide, in the 2013–14 school year, 82.3% of all students graduated, while only 62.6% of ELs graduated (NCELA, 2018). There were six states in which fewer than 50% of ELs graduated during that same time frame.

- ELs in some EL programs performing at a lower level than ELs who opted out of support services. (Callahan, Wilkinson & Mueller, 2008)

- Underrepresentation of ELs in Gifted and Talented programs. While 2% of ELs were enrolled in Gifted and Talented programs, 7% of non-ELs were enrolled (U.S. Department of Education, Office for Civil Rights, 2014).

- High percentage of Long-Term ELs (LTELs) in many school systems. For example, in CA, one of the few states to track Long-Term EL data, 74% of ELs in secondary schools are Long-Term ELs who have been in U.S. schools for six or more years yet don't have the English proficiency to reclassify to fluent.

Again, we need to reinforce that these data are not a reflection of EL competency. When ELs are offered appropriate supports and challenges by educators who share high expectations and value the inherent assets of their students, they are capable of achieving at very high levels. Educators can and do disrupt these data trends when we collaborate to shift from watering down EL instruction to challenging ELs with assets-based teaching and strategic supports.

Watering down often happens as a default, despite the best intentions of educators and administrators working hard for ELs to succeed. We invite readers into humble inquiry into ways we can get stuck, and specific actions we can take courageously together to shift our mindsets, programs, and practices. Watering down happens for a variety of reasons including the following three we emphasize in our calls-to-action throughout this chapter:

1. **Mindsets about ELs.** Low expectations and deficit thinking about ELs can lead to program design and/or instruction that remediates rather than accelerates content and language learning (Singer, 2017; Staehr Fenner & Snyder, 2017; Walqui, 2011). Even with the very best program design, ELs will rise or fall to the level of individual teachers' expectations. Assets-based thinking and high expectations are foundational in leading the shift from watering down to challenging ELs.

2. **Program design.** With the good intention of providing EL supports, oftentimes the design of EL programs themselves creates barriers to EL achievement. For example, if ELs are placed into low-level classes or routinely pulled out of core learning for isolated language services, their instructional schedule sets them up for watered-down instruction. (When ELs are given a one-size-fits-all pathway to placement that doesn't account for their diverse prior schooling experiences, academic strengths, and proficiency levels in English and other languages, they are scheduled to stagnate by program design.)

3. **Strategic scaffolding in everyday teaching of ELs.** The caliber of everyday teaching in core classrooms and aligned EL services makes or breaks EL achievement. It's not enough to simply ask for high expectations and put ELs in challenging courses. We must also support teachers with relevant, job-embedded professional learning that helps them make high-level learning accessible without watering down expectations—a feat requiring a nuanced interplay of effective culturally relevant teaching, essential mindsets, and acumen to build language with academic learning.

Shifting from watering down to challenging requires courageous collaboration across all roles and levels of our schools, districts, and states. It requires humble inquiry and critical questioning about what isn't working in current mindsets as well as equitable programs, policies, and practices so we can remove barriers that hinder the progress of our ELs and realize the true potential of every child.

THE VISION

As we see in the fifth-grade classroom featured in our opening vignette, it is indeed possible for ELs to excel in challenging content while they

Mindsets about ELs are critical. Changing mindsets about ELs is often difficult to accomplish. I often wonder what is the best way to accomplish this.
—Maria

The idea of courageous collaboration is so very powerful—it reminds me of what Richard DuFour (2003) called true collaboration, which involves faculty and staff using collaboration as a catalyst to change practice. This type of collaboration includes deep and honest talk among teachers to identify common challenges both as individuals and as a team.
—Maria

simultaneously acquire academic language. Our vision from watering down to challenging consists of three components: (1) shifting all educators' mindsets so that they operate from an assets-based perspective and set high and attainable expectations for ELs, (2) positioning ELs for success by creating programs and schedules that facilitate ELs' access to challenging content, and (3) ensuring all teachers use (and lose) scaffolds strategically to appropriately support and challenge ELs.* Courageous collaboration, built upon a framework of humility, curiosity, and openness to keeping the focus on our students, is necessary across all three components in order for them to be fully realized.

Shifting all educators' mindsets. Our vision first involves teachers as well as administrators operating from an assets-based perspective of ELs and setting high expectations for ELs. Gone are the days of putting ELs in the back of the classroom with a computer program while other, more fluent students work on challenging content and interact with their peers. ESOL teachers or EL specialists being regarded as the only teachers whose responsibility it is to teach ELs is a remnant of the past. We've witnessed such classrooms where ELs are excluded from meaningful instruction and interaction with their peers and have found that this deficit-based practice usually results from teachers not believing that ELs can acquire challenging content as well as not having a toolkit of effective strategies and scaffolds to draw from. In addition, this practice can result from teachers not being afforded meaningful collaboration with their peers to constantly receive and give support to one another in order for their ELs to thrive. While teachers need to have high expectations for their ELs, they should also be cognizant of the length of time it may take for ELs to acquire English and recognize the dynamic strengths inherent as ELs acquire proficiency in English. Using "I can" language objectives that emphasize next-level language learning for ELs according to their proficiency levels, such as WIDA's Can-Do Descriptors (https://wida.wisc.edu/teach/can-do), is one way for teachers to recognize the linguistic assets ELs bring in reading, writing, listening, and speaking and that teachers can build upon at each level of English proficiency.

All educators who touch ELs' lives in a school or district must recognize they are all teachers of language as well as content (Staehr Fenner & Snyder, 2017). Further, it falls on all educators to shift the narrative from falling into the deficit think trap of noting the challenges ELs may bring to instead beginning with a sense of their students' strengths and abilities. In the words of author M. K. Asante (2008), "when you make an observation, you have an obligation." This grounding mantra especially applies to EL education. We believe that when an educator notices that a colleague is focusing on an EL's deficit, the onus is on that educator to actively shift the narrative to focus on ELs' assets and, further, to also offer solutions and support.

For example, an EL specialist who is aware of a grade-level teacher struggling with ELs who aren't comprehending grade-level text may share how those ELs may come with a strong foundation of oral language in their home language and also offer to provide that teacher specific, tangible supports for that student. Such support could be in the form of a teacher encouraging a Spanish-speaking EL to draw from her knowledge of cognates to figure out unknown words, strategies for drawing from students' background knowledge, or integrating a graphic organizer so that those ELs can acquire academic language and content simultaneously (Staehr Fenner, 2014; Staehr Fenner & Snyder, 2017). Similarly, an administrator who overhears teachers expressing frustration at teaching newcomers grade-level content can offer time for content teachers and ESOL teachers to collaborate on lesson planning or on observing each other's instruction to gain new strategies to support their ELs. We believe that small changes in shifting the narrative to an assets-based mindset about ELs at the individual teacher-to-teacher or administrator-to-teacher level can create a groundswell of positive changes at the school or district levels, paving the way for high expectations of ELs and, with them, higher EL achievement and equity.

This vision is also one in which ELs' assets are recognized and are brought to life through their teachers' assets-based perspective as well as high expectations, which then translate to ensuring ELs' meaningful access to challenging content. As Gándara notes (2016), ELs are especially resilient and tend to come from families with strong beliefs in the positive impact of education success. Considering these assets instead of focusing on perceived EL deficits can foster positive learning outcomes. Our vision of an assets-based mindset as the basis for all EL learning cannot come to fruition without courageous collaboration, which must be prioritized, supported, and modeled by administrators.

Programming and scheduling to benefit ELs. In addition to a shifting mindset that ensures a focus on assets of and high expectations for ELs, purposeful, informed programming and scheduling must be in place for ELs to thrive and their teachers to draw from their own full professional expertise and strengths. The Every Student Succeeds Act (2015) mandates a report every two years of the number and percentage of "ELs who have not yet attained English language proficiency within five years." This report helps bring ELs' progress to the spotlight and holds schools and districts accountable for all their ELs, especially schools with newer and growing populations of ELs who may not have paid attention to their ELs' acquisition of English and academic success. Further, the Office of English Language Acquisition's English learner Toolkit states that school districts "must limit the segregation of ELs to the extent necessary to reach the stated goals of an educationally sound and effective program" (U.S. Department of Education, Office of English Language Acquisition, 2017, Chapter 5, p. 1). Programs must have language support services in place to not only limit segregation but also ensure ELs are fully integrated into their schools.

Ample research has shown that ELs in dual language programs reach proficiency in English at higher rates than ELs not in dual language programs (e.g., Steele et al., 2017; Collier & Thomas, 2017). In addition, the number of dual language programs is increasing across the nation (U.S. Department of Education, Office of English Language Acquisition, 2015). Ideally, districts should provide dual language programming when student demographics warrant the inclusion of such programs, but we recognize this ideal may not always be immediately attainable. Within the realm of what is possible within educators' sphere of influence, educators do have the agency to make programmatic decisions that will position their ELs for success with challenging content (Staehr Fenner, 2014). For example, we suggest co-teaching programs over solely pull-out, isolated instruction of ELs, which regularly takes them out of their core classes (Dove & Honigsfeld, 2018). However, shifting from a watering down to a challenging framework does not end with choosing a program. Within the programs chosen for ELs, schools must carefully create schedules that are conducive to maximizing their ELs' learning and increasing their access to challenging content including the same college and career options available to fluent English speakers.

Our vision for program design is one in which schools and districts think strategically and engage their creativity to determine: (1) how they provide ELs language support services and (2) how they schedule ELs within those programs. We envision program design and scheduling being a collaborative, inclusive process so that voices of diverse students, families, teachers, support staff, and administrators are all heard and that all of these stakeholders are at the table when these important decisions are made. As we share our vision, we also recognize that staffing roles will have an effect on how these programs and schedules are realized, but we wish to emphasize our vision is for systems to be in place that facilitate all ELs' equity, excellence, and achievement.

In order for programming and scheduling to be effective, schools must have a structure in place so that teachers can work together in a systematic and ongoing way and share their expertise with one another (Staehr Fenner & Snyder, 2017). When these systems and structures are in place, teachers' use of strategic scaffolds and supports for ELs will have a greater impact.

All scheduling for ELs should be designed to ensure that ELs have full access to the required time per day for all content-area instruction, as well as appropriate supports for them to engage with this instruction in order to ensure they receive the same opportunities that fluent English speakers have in accessing core content. In terms of scheduling,[†] we recommend the following:

- ELs should always be integrated meaningfully into whole-group core instruction and never removed from core instruction for separate language support services.

- ELs' participation in specials (e.g., art, physical education, etc.) must be regarded as crucial as a way for them to acquire academic and social language across all areas as well as develop skills and interests outside the core content areas.

- Master schedules must be developed with common, recurring planning time for grade-level or content teams, and this planning time needs to include an ESOL or bilingual teacher, when such a position exists in the school or district.

- Administrators must hold co-planning time sacred and must also provide the support, structure, and guidance for EL-specific supports and planning to be realized.

Scheduling decisions should be tailored to the size of the EL population in a given school. Figure 3.1 outlines suggestions for scheduling ELs based on the size of the population.

FIGURE 3.1 EL Scheduling Considerations Based on Size of EL Population[‡]

Size of EL Population	Description	Suggestion for Scheduling ELs
Small	Approximately 10% ELs or fewer	Cluster the few EL students together with one classroom or content teacher who has either ESOL certification or successful experience teaching ELs. ELs should not be "sprinkled" over numerous teachers.
Medium	Approximately 11–30% ELs	Cluster the EL students together with 2 or 3 teachers, who have either ESOL certification or successful experience teaching ELs.
Large	Approximately 31% ELs or greater	Elementary level: Hire grade-level teachers with dual certification in ESOL and general elementary education. Secondary level: Hire content teachers with dual certification in ESOL and content areas.

STRATEGIC IMPLEMENTATION OF SCAFFOLDS AND SUPPORTS

We know that teachers can "keep rigor of tasks and texts high while providing appropriate scaffolds and supports to engage ELs in building concepts, skills, and language to thrive on a path toward college and career success. When a student struggles, a teacher who expects excellence knows the struggle is temporary, and the student has the capacity for growth" (Singer, 2018, p. 29). Further, instruction in academic language and language skills helps build a bridge so that ELs can access challenging, grade-level content (Staehr Fenner & Snyder, 2017). A meta-analysis of research on educating ELs in PreK–12 by the National Academies of Sciences, Engineering, and Medicine (2017) found multiple promising and effective practices for educating

ELs. These practices include developing academic language during content instruction; providing visual and verbal supports to make core content comprehensible; and capitalizing on students' home language, knowledge, and cultural assets.

In order to provide this type of support that will enable ELs to access core instruction and grade-level content, teachers and administrators need to have a sense of what scaffolds are, know how to use them and when to remove them, and be involved in ongoing professional learning opportunities to hone their skills in supporting ELs. A scaffold is a temporary support a teacher provides to students that allows the students to perform a task they would not be able to perform on their own (Gibbons, 2015; National Governors Association for Best Practices, CCSSO, 2010). Scaffolds can be grouped into three main categories: materials and resources, instruction, and student grouping (WIDA, n.d., as cited in Staehr Fenner & Snyder, 2017). In our work with teachers, we have found that most think of scaffolds only as materials and resources (or things that are provided to students), including graphic organizers, visuals, and sentence frames. We envision teachers expanding their scaffolding repertoire to include instructional scaffolds (or things the teacher does to support students), such as pre-identifying and pre-teaching vocabulary, building background knowledge, and modeling tasks for students. Finally, it is our hope that teachers also provide scaffolding through the ways in which they group students, such as flexible grouping so that students with the same home language can support each other during instruction or structured pair work (Staehr Fenner & Snyder, 2017).

Effective scaffolds for ELs intentionally address the language demands of tasks. Teachers analyze the academic language demands of the tasks in which they are asking students to engage in order to align specific scaffolds with tasks (e.g., sentence starters for supporting an argument). In collaboratively planning lessons, teachers should consider creating an academic language objective and mapping scaffolds to students' English language proficiency levels.

Effective scaffolds also ensure access to rigorous learning. When selecting and developing materials, teachers should consider how they may need to enhance texts and materials given to students so that ELs can access them, for example by providing them video clips in students' home languages or adding a graphic organizer to help students comprehend texts in English. Finally, teachers should always reflect on the efficacy of their lessons and may need to rethink how they scaffold instruction for ELs. We encourage teachers to collaborate and observe one another's lessons to ensure they are in a cycle of continuous improvement and inquiry.

As with the previous two components of our vision, collaboration is essential to support the integration of scaffolds and supports. We suggest drawing from Edwards's (2011) framework of distributed expertise to foster effective collaboration. This framework underscores that "building and using common knowledge is an important feature of the relational expertise required for working across the practice boundaries on complex tasks" (p. 33). When all types of teachers successfully collaborate by determining which strengths each type of teacher brings to the task of designing and implementing instruction for ELs, they are able to better support ELs' acquisition of academic language and content knowledge.[§]

WHAT THIS LOOKS LIKE: MASON CREST ELEMENTARY SCHOOL

Mason Crest Elementary School in Annandale, Virginia, embodies all three elements of our vision. Brian Butler, the former co-principal of Mason Crest—a Title 1 school whose students speak more than thirty language at home—writes: "The responsibility to ensure that every single student learns at high levels cannot be placed on the shoulders of an isolated teacher. To be frank, that practice is a recipe for failure. It has to be a coordinated, purposeful, and embedded process of adult professional development and learning" (Butler, in Buffum & Mattos, 2015, p. 52).

Mindsets. Grade-level teachers as well as core content teachers, ESOL, and special education teachers develop lessons collaboratively to ensure that all students, including ELs, are supported during instruction. In this way, the mindset has been established that all teachers have something beneficial to bring to their context and teachers leverage each others' expertise. This mindset affirms that teachers approach lesson planning from a strengths perspective, ensuring that ELs' assets provide a central focus of instruction.

Program and Schedule. One way that Mason Crest ensures that all teachers are responsible for ELs' success is through creating an effective, inclusive master schedule. DuFour and DuFour (2012) implore principals to be creative to provide time for teachers to collaborate without losing significant amounts of instructional time. Butler (2015) suggests that there need to be specific structures in place in a school's master schedule to provide teachers uninterrupted time for teamwork and collaboration. At Mason Crest, Butler invited teams to participate in developing the instructional block schedule, ensuring representation from core content, ESOL, special education, specials classes, library, gifted and talented, and technology. Three "nonnegotiables" outlined the master schedule development: (1) two hours of daily uninterrupted language arts instruction, (2) ninety minutes of daily uninterrupted mathematics instruction, and (3) one hour of common planning time at least four days per week. ESOL and content teachers co-teach and flexibly group students so that teachers can leverage their expertise and also so that most ELs aren't pulled from their content classes. Teachers are also provided times to observe each other using an observation form or checklist.

Scaffolds. During their common planning time, teachers use a common lesson planning format for every content area with integrated scaffolds for ELs and other students who may need extra support. Lessons begin with linking to prior knowledge, then deliver new content, provide guided practice differentiated for different students' strengths and needs, and offer an opportunity for students to reflect on new content and make a connection to future learning. As an extra support to ELs, an academic language goal is included in each lesson to help ELs access grade-level content.

THE CALL FOR ACTION

To disrupt inequitable outcomes for ELs, we must transform our mindsets, our programs, and our practices. Shifting from watering down to challenging ELs is not a technical challenge with a quick-fix solution to implement at scale, but an adaptive challenge that requires we collaborate deeply to unpack what isn't working and transform our approaches to realize the true promise and potential for every child. It truly takes every shift detailed in this book to move our systems from the old paradigm of EL education to one in which every EL builds on their cultural and linguistic assets to excel with rigorous academic learning in every classroom every day.

Three specific areas of action we emphasize in this chapter are

1. Mindsets—Collaborate to Raise Expectations for ELs

2. Program Design—Ensure Access to Rigorous, Grade-Appropriate Learning

3. Instruction—Scaffold Strategically Without Lowering the Bar

In this next section, we emphasize the why and the how with specific actions you can take right away to move from theory to action.

ESSENTIAL ACTION: COLLABORATE TO RAISE EXPECTATIONS FOR ENGLISH LEARNERS

Why? Students rise or fall to the level of teacher expectations. Research clearly indicates a strong correlation between teacher expectations and student achievement as well as a correlation between teachers' racial biases and expectations of students of color (Gershenson, Holt, & Papageorge, 2015; Peterson, Christine, Osborne, & Sibley, 2016). When we have high expectations, we can help students grow toward those expectations. When we have low expectations for students, we limit the impact of our teaching to that low level (Singer, 2018, p. 29).

How? We raise expectations for ELs in the context of also shifting other mindsets about ELs that are the emphasis of other chapters in this book. Read Chapter 1, "From Deficit-Based to Assets-Based," and Chapter 8, "From Monolingualism to Multilingualism," to build a strong foundation in the shared agreement that children's multilingualism is not a disability or detriment, but rather an asset in a global world and a strength they can build on daily as they learn content and English. (Read also Chapter 4, "From Isolation to Collaboration," and Chapter 9, "From Nobody Cares to Everyone/Every Community Cares," to build shared ownership among ALL educators for the success of ELs.) From this assets-based perspective of shared agency, collaborate across all roles to get specific about what we mean by *high expectations* so administrators, teachers, and students all have clarity about the goals they are trying to achieve.

It's not enough to morally agree on high expectations for ELs; we make this theory a reality when we collaborate to make our expectations visible to ourselves and our students. Here are specific job-embedded professional learning activities you can take with a colleague, a team, a school, or district staff to make high expectations a reality. The following activities are easy to facilitate at your school site either with the entire site together seated in teams, in team collaboration time, or as a two-person activity for teachers co-teaching who serve ELs in the core.

HOW TO COLLABORATE TO CLARIFY AND CALIBRATE EXPECTATIONS

Teacher clarity about our goals is critical for achieving them (Hattie, 2012). Making expectations visible together is a powerful way to calibrate expectations to align with grade-level standards and competencies essential for career and college success. Choose a site-wide specific area of emphasis, and then within teams collaborate to clarify together the following:

- What are our content goals for student learning? What aspects of language must students understand and use to excel with these goals?

- What are my success criteria in content and language?

- How will students demonstrate success?

- What does success look like?

See Figure 3.2 for collaboration tasks aligned to each question.

Tips for Administrators to Make These Job-Embedded Professional Learning Activities Possible and Powerful:

Structure Time for Collaborative Job-Embedded Professional Learning. Calibrating expectations only happens when you structure time for this work. In the Mason Crest example, one non-negotiable was that all staff receive one hour of common planning time at least four days per week. Go-to strategies to make time for job-embedded professional learning include (1) moving logistical communication out of staff meetings and into digital communication so staff meetings can be used to improve teaching and learning, and

FIGURE 3.2 Job-Embedded Professional Learning to Clarify and Calibrate Expectations

Questions	Teacher Collaboration Tasks to Clarify and Calibrate Expectations
What are our goals for student learning? What aspects of language must students understand and use to excel with these goals?	Collaborate to choose the standard(s) that most closely align with your priority goals. Important tips: *Prioritize and synthesize* 1–3 standards at the intersection of your goal. For example, if your local initiative is to elevate academic conversations about academic texts, choose both a listening/speaking standard that details expectations for conversations, and a priority content standard such as making and justifying inferences from a text. *Expect Beyond the Standards* Don't limit yourself to what's written in the standards if your goal goes beyond academic standards. For example, if your top priority is to build students' agency as self-directed learners, collaborate to define together what that means. *Identify Aligned Language Standards* Use your local language proficiency standards (e.g., WIDA) to identify language objectives that align with your specific goal. Align these to the success criteria as an excellent reference to differentiate across proficiency levels.
What are our success criteria for content and language?	Using the priority standard(s) or goal identified above, collaborate to write student-friendly success criteria in the form of "I can" statements. Make sure to include all expectations represented in the standards. When a standard is vague or states a goal that you know from experience requires many sub-goals to master, co-create those sub-goals in the form of "I can" statements.
How will students demonstrate success?	Co-design active engagement tasks through which students will demonstrate success with the goal. A task is what students will say and do (e.g., listening, speaking, reading, and/or writing) to demonstrate success and/or instructional needs with the specific goal. It should be an opportunity for students who thrive with the goal to demonstrate their success, and also a great task for you to gather formative data about what instruction students need. Reflect together: • What will students need to do at the end of the year to demonstrate their success with this goal? • If we use this task now, will it give us insight into what they already know and can do specific to our goal? • Does our task align with the grade-level expectation (and not a watered-down sub-skill related to the goal)?
What does success look like?	Collaborate to create (or chose from exemplary student work) an exemplar of what success looks like with your goal and your success criteria. Simply choose the task you planned above and collaborate to write a model response. Reference both your content and language success criteria to ensure the exemplar demonstrates success with both your expectations for content and language. Reflect, does this exemplar reflect our shared understanding of what success will look like when students excel with this goal?

Source: Singer (2017).

(2) schedule regular collaboration time for job-alike teams by creating an early release schedule, aligning prep blocks of job-alike colleagues, and/or strategizing ways to use your resources creatively to create collaboration time beyond the instructional day.

Focus and Align This Work with Priority Initiatives. These activities can be used to calibrate expectations about ANY goal, but no one has time to do this for EVERY goal. These are most powerful when you focus on a very ambitious and urgent goal as a school that aligns with your top priority initiatives and data-driven needs. A school-wide focus helps teams go deep, rather than be scattered to scratch the surface of many competing initiatives. Lead the work of calibrating expectations with a very specific focus relevant to your top priority goals for student growth. Build from your shared vision to align all collaboration to raise expectations to very specific learning outcomes for students that are your top priority to move together. For example, in a school focused on increasing the caliber of peer-to-peer academic conversations with high-level thinking tasks, each team should focus on calibrating expectations about academic conversations with high-level tasks. In a secondary school focused on academic argument, each team should focus on specific standards (e.g., content and language) and high-level tasks that integrate the expectations for academic argument with their content learning goals.

Team Strategically. When facilitating these activities with many educators, make sure each team shares a common goal for supporting ELs and ideally a common grade-level or content area. For example, team job-alike colleagues such as teachers who teach the same grade level (e.g., third grade) or same content area (e.g., secondary English) together. Also have ESOL/EL specialists, literacy specialists, content specialists, intervention specialists, and other specialists or leaders integrate with a team focused on a grade-level or content-area goal, so teams benefit from cross-role sharing of expertise in clarifying the intersection of content and language learning expectations.

Build From High Expectations to Inquiry for Impact. These activities are a natural starting point for data-driven, job-embedded professional learning through which teams engage in continuous improvement to realize an ambitious goal. With that said, don't stop with clarifying expectations. Next have teams co-plan, co-teach, co-assess, and co-analyze student work as a basis for refining instruction until ELs, and all students, achieve the goal.

ESSENTIAL ACTION: DESIGN EL PROGRAMS TO ACCELERATE, NOT REMEDIATE

Effective programs for ELs ensure both access to rigorous content learning and aligned language development essential for success. Moving from "watering-down" to challenging is not just about improving the quality of instruction for ELs in each classroom. It also requires that we look critically at how we design our programs for ELs, including answers to the following questions:

- What are our policies and practices for hiring and staffing classrooms that serve ELs? Do all staff who serve ELs have high certification or training as well as the mindset to be effective with ELs?

- How do we identify ELs? When an EL is identified, what services do they receive?

- What are our policies for placement of ELs into services? What success criteria determines entry into and exit from EL services?

- Do our placement policies and EL services create unnecessary segregation or track EL students in ways that hinder their success with challenging content or academic language?

- How do we monitor progress over time to ensure the services we design for support actually result in higher levels of academic and language learning for ELs?

- What are our criteria for reclassifying to fluent-English proficient? Do we analyze our data to see where students who have not reclassified within a reasonable time frame need the extra support? Does this data analysis drive the supports students receive?

There is no one approach to EL program design, and the approach that's right for each district will vary according to local resources, EL population, and staffing. As we detail in our vision and in Chapter 8, dual immersion programs have a strong track record as the most effective program model for ELs even when measuring impact via standardized assessments in English. The added benefit is ELs and participating fluent English speakers become biliterate in two languages. The most powerful programs by design build from elementary to secondary and qualify students for a seal of biliteracy on their high school diploma, a recognition now official in many districts and also in 36 American states.

The vast majority of schools and districts, however, are working within the English contexts and have the dual challenge of providing access to rigorous content WHILE students learn the language used for content instruction. Monolingual English programs can also be successful when intentional about creating high challenge, high support environments for ELs. No matter your program design, collaborate in inquiry about the impact of instruction on ELs. Analyze student growth data and disaggregate EL data to identify your impact. If ELs aren't thriving, reflect with key stakeholders: How can we change our programs and practices to ensure ELs succeed?

Dare to ask tough questions about policies and practices for assessment, placement, scheduled supports, and curriculum so that you can unpack together any possible barriers to EL achievement. To ensure your programs are not watering down by design, especially look for the following barriers.

Unnecessary Segregation:

- Do your program practices and policies lead to segregation of ELs and/or removal from core learning?

- Are ELs tracked into low-level courses, or scheduled into a multiyear path of lower-level learning?

- Do placement policies and practices result in inequitable placement of ELs into low-level secondary classes, or exclusion from courses they need to graduate with access to higher education?

Supports Replace Access to Core:

- Do EL services in your context result in ELs doing low-level, skill-based activities? "There is a particular danger in teaching diverse youth and particularly ELs by only focusing on discrete tasks, basics, vocabulary, mechanic and language errors, minimizing attention to content knowledge development" (Athanases & Oliviera, 2014, p. 286).

- Is English language taught as discrete skills in isolation from the linguistic demands of academic tasks and texts? "One of the biggest roadblocks to learning is (ELs) never get a chance to work with complex texts" (Fillmore & Fillmore, 2012, p. 2).

  Inequitable Staffing: Do ELs learn from teachers with mindsets and qualifications to effectively teach ELs?

  Culturally Irrelevant Curriculum: Do our materials, texts, and pedagogy affirm students' linguistic, cultural, and racial identities, or do they devalue or demotivate ELs and students of color?

Involve students and parents as partners in co-evaluating your programs. Seek to understand EL students' perspectives and experiences, whether positive or negative, with the school community, with rigorous classes, and with the level of supports for language and content learning. When researcher Shawna Shapiro interviewed high school ELs, she found many wanted and appreciated challenging curricula. One student "described how her ELL English teacher had talked constantly of her academic future: 'The teacher was always reminding us . . . 'You need this in college. These are the kind of things they're gonna ask you.' This student was proud to report that her ELL class was actually harder than the mainstream English class she took in her senior year" (Shapiro, 2014, p. 400). Another student critiqued ELL exclusion from high-level math, "Students of color are, like, they're in Algebra I, and below that. . . . You have seniors that are taking ELL math. That's not right" (p. 396).

It is courageous work to lead changes in program design as humans get comfortable with business as usual. Collaborate with all stakeholders to ensure multiple perspectives are at the decision-making table. Collaborate across departments, not in a silo of only the educators with *EL* or *bilingual* in their job title. Ensuring every student excels is everybody's business. Every teacher and every leader and every stakeholder in our school community is part of the solution. Unify around the compelling vision that every student deserves access, opportunity, and excellence. Use your data including the perspectives of EL students and families to establish a compelling urgency for change.

ESSENTIAL ACTION: SCAFFOLD STRATEGICALLY WITHOUT WATERING DOWN

Even with the optimal program design, it's possible for ELs to experience watered-down learning via over-scaffolding in everyday teaching. Scaffolds, when used as temporary supports to help students excel in new ways, are an essential part of raising expectations in schools. By contrast, when scaffolding practices are based on deficit perspectives about students of color and ELs (Walqui, 2011), they can become a life sentence for low-level work. How we use scaffolds determines whether ELs stagnate or thrive. To scaffold strategically, we must shift from seeking to scale "silver bullet" solutions, such as adopting "one-size-fits-all" EL strategies and training teachers with a prescriptive approach, to implement those teacher actions with fidelity no matter what. To scaffold strategically, we must be flexible and responsive to students' ever-changing assets and needs. This involves a focus on high-level goals, our students, and the ever-changing "just right" instruction between where students are now and where we want them to be.

We support strategic scaffolding collectively when we build a culture promoting courageous inquiry about our impact. *Impact* is the key word. No strategy or scaffold, no matter how many experts or research studies support it, is the right fit for the right student every time. If we think that using a specific strategy is the end goal for effective EL teaching (e.g., using sentence frames), we can arrive there quickly and continue with false confidence that we are doing the right thing while blindly unaware about the actual impact our scaffold is having on students' thinking, language use, and self-directed learning. Administrators can use an observation checklist that focuses on teacher scaffolding and celebrate positive shifts in teacher action—without clarity about whether those teacher actions are positively or negatively impacting the results we seek. Avoid this common mistake by shifting your focus from nouns (e.g., *curriculum* and *strategies*) as the solution, to verbs as the essentials we must master to raise rigor and access for every learner. See Figure 3.3. for six essential verbs to teach for equity and EL achievement.

FIGURE 3.3 Six Essentials for EL Excellence

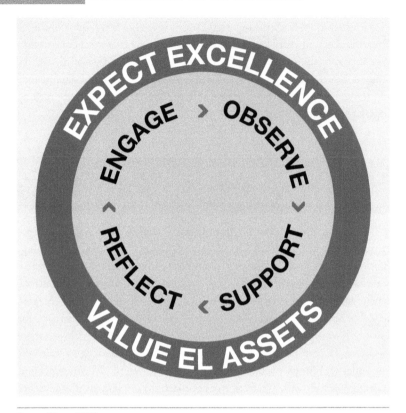

Source: Singer (2018).

We must courageously shift at every level of the school system from expecting compliance with a set of teacher actions to leading a culture of learning in which we set ambitious goals and collaborate to:

1. **Value:** Ensure a strong sense of belonging for all students, and make intentional connections to assets students bring to learning.

2. **Expect:** Clarify expectations, using the activities in Figure 3.2 (see p. 59).

3. **Engage:** Engage students in rigorous tasks aligned with our goals.

4. **Observe:** Gather formative data about students' assets and prior knowledge with our goals, and also instructional priorities for next-level learning.

5. **Support:** Choose and lose scaffolds as appropriate to specifically help students build on their assets to progress towards our ambitious goals.

6. **Reflect:** Reflect on the impact of our scaffolds and teaching. Did every learner engage? Did my scaffolds support student thinking and self-directed learning, or get in the way? What shifts will I make to my teaching to ensure all learners excel?

These six verbs are core to effective teaching with high expectations and strategic scaffolds, and even more powerful when we collaborate with collective efficacy to enact these verbs in a cycle of collaborative teacher inquiry.

Collaborative teacher inquiry comes in many forms with many names (e.g., PLCs, Data Teams, Observation Inquiry, Lesson Study, Co-Teaching), but in any manifestation, encompasses these essential activities: We co-expect when we collaborate to calibrate expectations (use the activities in Figure 3.2). We co-engage when we co-plan or co-teach instruction. We co-observe when we collaborate to analyze student work, or to observe students in the classroom to identify assets, needs, and the impact of our teaching. We co-reflect when we reflect on the data before us and, rather than blaming factors beyond our control, have the courage to ask ourselves: what will we change about our instruction and practices and policies to ensure every EL succeeds?

Strategic scaffolding requires all of these six verbs in synthesis. We build our collective capacity to scaffold strategically when, in the context of high expectations and asset mindsets about ELs, we collaborate to analyze student work specific to our goals, and co-reflect to refine our impact. Co-analyzing expressive language (speaking and writing) especially gives us insight into student thinking, conceptual understandings, confusions, and also language use. Here's the flow to collaborate in the process of using data to reflect and refine scaffolding together:

Co-Engage. Collaborate to plan how students will actively engage. Have students do a task aligned to your goals with the minimum level of scaffolds essential to understand and participate in the task. If teachers only have time to collaborate outside of task, each does this step in a classroom, then brings student work samples (e.g., writing or video of conversations) to share. When teachers can be in classrooms together, such as in co-teaching (Dove & Honigsfeld, 2018) or peer observation inquiry (Singer, 2015), gather observation data during the lesson as one person facilitates the task and others observe.

Co-Analyze. Collaborate to analyze student work. With written response or video, you may opt to score with a rubric, and then collaborate to calibrate how you score so that you come to shared agreement about each level of learning. Another method is to cluster work in categories (1) at grade level, (2) approaching grade level, and (3) far below, and then analyze each cluster for strengths and instructional needs. No matter how you handle it, be sure you use the success criteria you developed for your goal to analyze the work.

With observation data, use a non-evaluative protocol such as observation inquiry (Singer, 2015) to collaborate to describe what you observed without judgement, organize the data, and make generalizations about the data aligned to your success criteria and goals.

Co-Support. Collaborate to build from this analysis to co-plan the next level of instruction for each identified level of performance in the class. Consider both which supports and scaffolds you will add to meet specific identified needs, and which supports and scaffolds you will remove to increase rigor and students' self-directed learning.

Be intentional about using effective supports for ELs that don't lower the challenge of the task, such as the following:

- Concisely build background in concepts, content, and/or language to equitably position ELs with their fluent English-speaking peers (Staehr Fenner & Snyder, 2017).

- Draw on home language assets and students' funds of knowledge (Moll, Amanti, Neff, & Gonzalez, 1992) such as providing them video clips in students' home languages.

- Structure peer conversations in English and/or primary language that call for high-level thinking about complex content in support of deeper learning.

- Support access to complex texts (e.g., chunk, annotate, structure peer conversations, use graphic organizers, and/or teach language structures) rather than simplify the texts.

- Provide just-right, just-in-time feedback aligned to your content and language goals.

While there are times we may provide extensive scaffolds to address a specific student need that do have the collective impact of watering down a task, make sure this is a temporary state. Be intentional to build from the successes of a scaffolded moment to increase rigor and/or remove scaffolds in subsequent lessons.

Co-Reflect. Collaborate to reflect on what the data show us about how our supports impacted instruction. How did our instruction impact student learning for all students? How did it impact learning for ELs at different proficiency levels in the classroom? How did our scaffolds specifically impact students' thinking and academic language use? What shifts will we make to our instructional choices and scaffolds to build from where students are now to higher levels of achievement?

Co-Value. Collaborate with a shared commitment to value multilingual students' linguistic strengths, cultural assets, identities, life experiences, and communities. Asset mindsets about ELs are especially important when using data to co-reflect together. Educator mindsets make or break our capacity to use data to refine our teaching. Notice, when an EL struggles, do we blame the student, the EL status, the families? Or do we self-reflect to ask courageously, what will we change about our instruction to ensure our ELs succeed? Commit to shared ownership, asset mindsets, and high-expectations, and then help one another translate those theories into actions in the moment by reframing blaming or other deficit discourse about ELs to self-reflection and shared agency for change.

Tips for Leaders to Scale This Shift

Lead a Culture of Learning that values reflective data-driven practice over implementation of specific strategies at scale. Don't expect every teacher to use the same specific supports for ELs; instead foster a school-wide culture of setting high expectations and being in inquiry about impact. This means that in classroom walkthroughs, you are not checking off specific strategies a teacher uses (e.g., Think-Pair-Share), but instead focusing on what students are saying and doing as evidence of the task, their learning, and language use. Focus your classroom "look fors" on student learning. Notice, what is the task? How does it align with grade-level expectations? Notice, what are students saying and doing? Who participates? Who doesn't? What assets with content and language do ELs demonstrate in these tasks? What challenges do they demonstrate? Discuss together what you observed students saying and doing. Ask questions to foster teacher reflection and agency to adapt as needed to help students move toward your shared vision for student success.

Integrate, Don't Silo Professional Learning. Align and synthesize initiatives to focus on an urgent, shared goal so that data-driven collaborative inquiry can be the central work of your school(s). Build teacher agency and efficacy for ELs *within* this context. Notice this is not a one-shot siloed workshop on EL strategies. Engaging in collaborative inquiry to co-clarify expectations, co-engage, co-analyze, co-support, and co-reflect is relevant to everyday teaching for ALL students. Within the context of this rigorous, data-driven collaboration, build teacher efficacy for ELs by deeply examining the intersection of content and language in your goals, in your analysis of student work, and in planning strategic scaffolds to reach every child. Get specific and humble about which scaffolds work and don't work so you can continuously refine teaching to ensure ELs thrive. When you build the capacity of core teachers to serve ELs in this context, it's relevant, it's job-embedded, and it builds their agency to serve ELs as they differentiate to reach each unique individual they teach every day.

Summary and Conclusions

We all have the ability to make transformative shifts in our schools and our teaching so that ELs access challenging, grade-appropriate learning with strategic supports that ensure full access to college and career success. To do so, we must look at EL achievement through a systems perspective in which we thoroughly examine the system in which ELs are educated, instead of placing blame on individual ELs, and suggest making changes to the system to move from one that operates from a watered-down mindset to one that challenges ELs in a supportive environment. We recognize that enacting changes in the way in which we approach and carry out educating ELs will require effort and dedication from the entire staff and community; equally, we offer that the rewards for this type of courageous collaboration will be great not only for ELs themselves but also for their educators and their community. To help you get started on your journey, Figure 3.4 provides a set of reflection questions for you and your colleagues to reflect on where you are with the three components we've outlined in this chapter and determine your next steps to implement the three components of our framework, so that all ELs can receive challenging instruction within a system that puts them on a path to success.

FIGURE 3.4 Self-Reflection Questions and Next Steps

Component	Self-Reflection Questions	Next Steps
1. Mindsets About ELs	Does our school operate from an assets-based perspective about ELs? Y / N Do all administrators and teachers have and communicate high expectations for their ELs? Y / N	
2. Program Design	Is our program designed in a way that ensures ELs' access to rigorous, grade-appropriate learning? Y / N Is our program designed in a way that encourages ELs' integration with fluent speaker peers? Y / N Are ELs scheduled in a way that is conducive to them receiving core content instruction and specials classes with their peers? Y / N	
3. Strategic Scaffolding in Everyday Teaching of ELs	Are all teachers supported with relevant, ongoing job-embedded professional learning so that they provide supports for ELs to successfully engage with grade-level content? Y / N Does our school/district culture emphasize a shared commitment to continuous learning based on clear outcome goals for ELs over and above compliance? Y / N Do teachers and administrators prioritize ongoing collaboration among teachers to strategically support ELs with both content and language learning? Y / N	

References

Arias, M. B. (2007). PICS: The educational implications of linguistic isolation and segregation of Latino English language learners (ELLs). Retrieved from https://civilrightsproject.ucla.edu/legal-developments/court-decisions/the-educational-implications-of-linguistic-isolation-and-segregation-of-latino-english-language-learners-ells

Asante, M. K. (2008). *It's bigger than hip hop.* New York, NY: St. Martin's Press.

Athanases, S. Z., & de Oliveira, L. C. (2014). Scaffolding versus routine support for Latina/o youth in an urban school: Tensions in building toward disciplinary literacy. *Journal of Literacy Research, 46*(2), 263–299. Retrieved from http://journals.sagepub.com/doi/pdf/10.1177/1086296X14535328

Buffum, A., & Mattos, M. (2015). *It's about time: Planning interventions and extensions in elementary school.* Bloomington, IN: Solution Tree Press.

Butler, B. K. (2015). Collaborating in the core. In A. Buffum & M. Mattos (Eds.), *It's about time: Planning interventions and extensions in elementary school* (pp. 51–77). Bloomington, IN: Solution Tree Press.

Callahan, R., Wilkinson, L., & Muller, C. (2008). School Context and the Effect ESOL Placement on Mexican-Origin Adolescents' Achievement. *Social science quarterly, 89*(1), 177–198. doi:10.1111/j.1540-6237.2008.00527.x

Collier, V. P., & Thomas, W. P. (2017). Validating the power of bilingual schooling: Thirty-two years of large-scale, longitudinal research. *Annual review of applied linguistics, 37,* 203–217.

Dove, M. & Honigsfeld, A. (2018) *Co-Teaching for English learners: A guide to collaborative planning, instruction, assessment and reflection.* Thousand Oaks, CA: Corwin Press.

DuFour, R. (2003). "Collaboration lite" puts student achievement on a starvation diet. *Journal of Staff Development, 24*(4), 63–64.

DuFour, R., & DuFour, R. (2012). *Essentials for principals: The school leader's guide to professional learning communities at work.* Bloomington, IN: Solution Tree Press.

Education Trust West (2014) The Language of Reform: English Language Learners in California's Shifting Landscape. Retrieved from https://west.edtrust.org/wp-content/uploads/sites/3/2014/11/ETW-Language-of-Reform-Report.pdf.

Edwards, A. (2011). Building common knowledge at the boundaries between professional practices: Relational agency and relational expertise in systems of distributed expertise. *International Journal of Educational Research, 50*(1), 33–39. doi:10.1016/j.ijer.2011.04.007

Every Student Succeeds Act. (2015). Every Student Succeeds Act of 2015, Pub. L. No. 114-95 § 114 Stat. 1177 (2015–2016).

Fillmore, L. W., & Fillmore, C. J. (2012, January). *What does text complexity mean for English learners and language minority students?* Paper presented at the Understanding Language Conference, Stanford, CA: Understanding Language. Retrieved from http://ell.stanford.edu/sites/default/files/pdf/academic-papers/06-LWF%20CJF%20Text%20Complexity%20FINAL_0.pdf

Gándara, P. (2016, November 30). *Educating immigrant students and emergent bilinguals in an anti-immigrant era.* American Educational Research Association Centennial Lecture Series. Brooklyn, NY: Brooklyn Museum.

Gandara, P., & Orfield, G. (2010). *A return to the "Mexican room": The segregation of Arizona's English learners.* Los Angeles, CA: University of California Los

Angeles, The Civil Rights Project. Retrieved from http://files.eric.ed.gov/fulltext/ED511322.pdf

Gershenson, S., Holt, S. B., and Papageorge, N. W. (2015). Who believes in me? The effect of student-teacher demographic match on teacher expectations. Upjohn Institute Working Paper 15-231. Kalamazoo, MI: W.E. Upjohn Institute for Employment Research. https://doi.org/10.17848/wp15-231

Goldenberg, C. (2013, Summer). Unlocking the research on English learners. *American Educator, 37*(2), 4–11. Retrieved from https://www.aft.org/sites/default/files/periodicals/English_Learners.pdf

Hahnel, C., Wolf, L., Banks, A., and LaFors, J. (2014). *The language of reform: English learners in California's shifting educational landscape.* Education Trust-West https://west.edtrust.org/resource/the-language-of-reform-english-learners-in-californias-shifting-education-landscape/

Hattie, J. (2012) *Visible learning for teachers: Maximizing impact on learning.* Thousand Oaks, CA: Corwin.

Los Angeles Unified School District. (2018). Designated ELD Resources. Retrieved from https://achieve.lausd.net/cms/lib/CA01000043/Centricity/domain/22/el%20sel%20master%20plan/master%20plan%20toolkit/Chapt%204%20Scheduling%20EL%20and%20Classroom%20Composition.pdf

Moll, L. C., Amanti, C., Neff, D., & Gonzalez, N. (1992). Funds of knowledge for teaching: Using a qualitative approach to connect homes and classrooms. *Theory Into Practice, 31*(2) 132–141. doi: 10.1080/00405849209543534

National Academies of Sciences, Engineering, and Medicine. (2017). *Promoting the educational success of children and youth learning English: Promising futures.* Washington, DC: The National Academies Press.

National Clearinghouse for English Language Acquisition. (2018). National- and State-Level High School Graduation Rates for English Learners. Retrieved from https://ncela.ed.gov/files/fast_facts/OELA_FF_HS_GradRates.pdf

National Governors Association for Best Practices, Council of Chief State School Officers (2010). Common Core State Standards for English language arts and literacy in history/social studies, science, and technical subjects. Appendix A: Research supporting key elements of the standards. Glossary of key terms. Retrieved from http://www.corestandards.org/assets/Appendix_A.pdf

Office of English Language Acquisition (OELA). National and state level high school graduation rates for English language learners. NCELA: https://ncela.ed.gov/files/fast_facts/OELA_FF_HS_GradRates.pdf

Olsen, L. (2010). Reparable harm: Fulfilling the unkept promise of educational opportunity for California's long term English learners. Californians Together. Retrieved from https://www.californianstogether.org/product/reparable-harm-fulfilling-the-unkept-promise-of-educational-opportunity-for-californias-long-term-english-learner/.

Peterson, E., Christine, R., Osborne, D., & Sibley, C. (2016, April). Teachers' explicit expectations and implicit prejudiced attitudes to educational achievement: Relations with student achievement and the ethnic achievement gap. *Learning and Instruction, 42,* 123–140. https://www.sciencedirect.com/science/article/pii/S095947521630010X

Seal of Biliteracy Map downloaded https://sealofbiliteracy.org/

Shapiro, S. (2014). "Words That You Said Got Bigger": English Language Learners' Lived Experiences of Deficit Discourse. *Research in the Teaching of English, 48*(4), 386.

Singer, T. (2015). *Opening doors to equity: A practical guide to observation-based professional learning.* Thousand Oaks, CA: Corwin.

Singer, T. (2015, October 1). Seven ways to raise expectations for all students. [Blog post]. Retrieved from https://tonyasinger.com/seven-ways-to-raise-expectations-for-all/

Singer, T. (2018). *EL excellence every day: The flip-to guide for differentiating academic literacy.* Thousand Oaks, CA: Corwin.

Singer, T. W. (2017). Job-embedded professional learning to collaborate to calibrate expectations. From consultation resources by www.tonyasinger.com.

Staehr Fenner, D. (2014). *Advocating for English learners: A guide for educators.* Thousand Oaks, CA: Corwin.

Staehr Fenner, D., & Snyder, S. (2017). *Unlocking English learners' potential: Strategies for making content accessible.* Thousand Oaks, CA: Corwin.

Steele, J. L., Slater, R. O., Zamarro, G., Miller, T., Li, J., Burkhauser, S., & Bacon, M. (2017, April). Effects of dual-language immersion programs on student achievement: Evidence from lottery data. *American Educational Research Journal, 54*(1), suppl.

SupportEd. (n.d.) Best practices in scheduling for English Learner education. Retrieved from http://getsupported.net/wp-content/uploads/Best_Practices_In_Scheduling_For_EL_Education.pdf

U. S. Department of Education, Office for Civil Rights. (2014). *Civil rights data collection, Data snapshot: College and career readiness.* Retrieved from http://www2.ed.gov/about/offices/list/ocr/docs/crdc-college-and-career-readiness-snapshot.pdf

U.S. Department of Education, Office of English Language Acquisition. (2015). Dual language education programs: Current state policies and practices, Washington, D.C. https://ncela.ed.gov/files/rcd/TO20_DualLanguageRpt_508.pdf

U.S. Department of Education, Office of English Language Acquisition. (2017). *English Learner tool kit* (2nd Rev. ed.). Washington, DC: Author.

Walqui, A. (2011). The growth of teacher expertise for teaching English language learners: A socio-culturally based professional development model. In T. Lucas (Ed.), *Teacher preparation for linguistically diverse classrooms* (pp. 160–177). New York, NY: Routledge.

Notes

* See also Calderón & Slakk, Chapter 6, for more information on moving from language to language, literacy, and content.

† Adapted from an infographic at https://getsupported.net/wp-content/uploads/Best_Practices_In_Scheduling_For_EL_Education.pdf.

‡ Adapted from an infographic at https://getsupported.net/wp-content/uploads/Best_Practices_In_Scheduling_For_EL_Education.pdf.

§ For more information on this topic, please see Chapter 4 by Dove and Honigsfeld.

chapter four

From Isolation to Collaboration

MARIA G. DOVE AND
ANDREA HONIGSFELD

PREMISE

Educators who learn to collaborate in a manner that effectively pools their knowledge, skills, and dispositions are best equipped to engage and advance the achievement of their culturally and linguistically diverse students.

VIGNETTE

Right now, there is a teacher somewhere in the United States who is trying to differentiate instruction for his English learners (ELs), and he is unsure of the impact his efforts are making on student learning. In a neighboring state, there is a teacher who is racking her brain about how to fairly assess an EL's work and how to accurately report the progress of a student who has yet to attain proficiency in English. In an adjacent town, there is a teacher who has a number of English learners who are or have transitioned to being former ELs, yet he is not quite sure if these students still need support. In the same school, there is a teacher who has figured out ways on his own to effectively engage English learners through a great deal of trial and error, yet that information remains in the confines of his own class. Down the hall, there is a principal who is responsible for meeting the needs of a large influx of English learners yet feels unprepared to support her staff and the community through this change.

What if these educators began to team together to develop curricula, lesson plans, and assessments for the sake of culturally and linguistically diverse students and work collaboratively with their school administrators to meet these challenges? Although it may appear to be a simple, practical remedy, systemic collaboration calls for an integral change and a cultural shift within the entire school community. A shift for successful change first and foremost requires developing the intrinsic motivation of all concerned to shape whole-system reform and maintain its sustainability. Genuine change also depends on specific actions and supports that require shared meaning and capacity building for it to take hold (Fullan, 2016).

THE URGENCY

One of the most important aspects of human experience is how we live, work, and play within a vast array of social networks (Christakis & Fowler, 2009); yet, we still find teachers and school administrators frequently working in isolation from their colleagues. While schools face an inordinate number of instructional challenges, our longstanding norm of working on our own often prevents us from tapping into the brilliance of our colleagues. Elmore (2004) notes that within a given school, teachers often develop innovative ideas and instructional practices in their own classrooms that are rarely shared. Consequently, these innovations make little impact in other classes within the same school. In the course of our professional collaboration, the authors of this chapter began to wonder how teachers might be inspired to harness their individual expertise, open up their classroom doors, and meaningfully interact with one another. How might administrators capitalize on the collaborative potential of their faculty? How might collaboration counteract the isolation experienced by teachers and school leaders alike and improve the learning outcomes for diverse students such as English learners (ELs)? The answers to these questions have become the central themes of our work together (Dove & Honigsfeld, 2018; Honigsfeld & Dove, 2010, 2015, 2019).

The urgency for this shift—from working in isolation to collaborative school practices for the sake of English learners—is that the status quo—privatization of practice—simply isn't working. This urgency can be framed by recognizing that we are ill-equipped to serve children of immigrants—more than half of whom are identified as English learners in U.S. schools—who continue to be an increasing part of student populations nationwide (National Center for Education Statistics, 2018). We continue to fail the children who are most in need of our support. A significant number of long-term English learners (LTELs) were born in the United States, and, despite having spent six or more years in U.S. schools, have yet to exit, are quite likely to drop out, and, should they graduate, are unlikely to attend college. In many parts of the United States (and much of Canada), general educators assume that most ELs are immigrants, although in fact, the vast majority (in the United States at least) are U.S. born. The reality of so many LTELs in the school system may be an even greater cause for alarm than our lack of preparedness for increasing numbers of immigrants, in that it is such a clear indicator of systemic failure.

Additionally, disparities in academic achievement between culturally and linguistically diverse students and other student groups demonstrate the need to further address the way in which ELs are taught and assessed (Calderón, Slavin, & Sanchez, 2011). Although school decision makers may establish policies, new curricula, and other innovations at a rapid pace, educational environments change slowly (Weixler, Harris, & Barrett, 2018).

Ineffective instructional practices, deficit mindsets, and low-expectation curricula remain unaltered in many classes where English learners are taught, and by the same token, school cultures—especially if working in isolation continues to be the norm—are slow to change as well (Honigsfeld & Dove, 2019). At the same time, Darling-Hammond and Richardson (2009) note, "research points to the effectiveness of sustained, job-embedded, collaborative teacher learning strategies" (p. 52).

From this, it would seem that a logical solution to our inability to adequately meet the needs of our ELs begins with the initiation, continuation, and preservation of networking opportunities in schools to tap into the on-site expertise and know-how of veteran as well as novice teachers and administrators. Yet, Christakis and Fowler (2009) further posit that "human beings are and always have been subject to an analogous set of constraints that determine what kinds of social-network structures work and endure" (p. 216). In most cases, it is the culture set in a school environment that hinders the shift from working in isolation to pursuing collaborative practices—joint planning, teaching, assessment, and reflection—in schools. Schmoker (2006) calls it the "system we place our teachers in, with its isolation and lack of constructive feedback" (p. 16) that often perpetuates the lack of understanding as well as the development of essential tools and strategies to meet the needs of culturally and linguistically diverse pupils.

Consequently, an even greater sense of urgency stems from the need for the organization, implementation, and development of overall strategies for true systemic collaboration to take hold. Supovitz's (2006) case study concerning learning communities revealed the difficulty of such collaborative practices being effectively established district wide in that "the possibilities created by professional learning communities—rigorous inquiry into the problems and challenges of instructional practice—seemed only to be occurring in pockets of the district" (p. 174). Although learning communities and other kinds of teacher collaboration can be powerful approaches for instructional change, developing collaborative cultures requires "transforming the *culture* of schools and the systems within which they operate" (Fullan, 2016, p. 119). Cultural transformation is a difficult undertaking that requires time and consistent attention from both teachers and school leaders. Fullan emphasized that it is not an innovation or a program that we should be working on; instead,

I think it is important to underscore the value of collaboration between language specialists and content teachers, teachers and school leaders, as well as between school leaders and the community in creating unity of spirit, mission, and vision that is inclusive of multilingualism and multiculturalism.
—**Margo**

establishing and nurturing a new school culture that is built upon collaboration, capacity building, and the collective professional capital members of the school community contribute to the essence of the learning environment. Thus, it would appear that focusing on the human resources available and tapping into the collaborative expertise at hand are the best and most logical solutions to support the successful outcomes of English learners.

THE EVIDENCE

English learners and the language development specialists who are designated to work with them tend to operate on the margins, apart from the *mainstream*, or general education students and teachers for part of each day. Gandara and Orfield (2010) note that English learners may be "triply segregated in the schools to which they are assigned: by ethnicity, by poverty, and by language" (p. 4). When English learners participate in pull-out or stand-alone classes whether for a short interval or for several periods a day, they may be separated not only from their English-speaking peers but also from the core curricula as well (Dove & Honigsfeld, 2018). Many ELs do not have access to the rigorous curriculum, aren't given opportunities to engage in academic conversations around challenging content, and become disengaged and demotivated. In addition, the norm of teacher isolation may further reinforce student isolation. To counter the effects of these negative experiences, Gandara and Orfield suggest organizing instruction "in ways that can mitigate, not exacerbate, this segregation for students who are learning English" (p. 4). Successful integration strategies include grouping language learners in and outside the classroom with English-speaking peers as much as possible to recognize and support language acquisition as a socio-cultural process (Walqui & van Lier, 2010).

What supports our claim that teacher collaboration must replace teacher isolation? We will tackle this challenge by offering both research-based evidence from the extant literature and practitioner-based findings from our field-based work. It has been recognized that "the long-standing culture of teacher isolation and individualism, together with teachers' preference to preserve their individual autonomy, may hinder deep-level collaboration to occur" (Vangrieken, Dochy, Raes, & Kyndt, 2015, p. 36), and teacher isolation has been documented as an obstacle to teacher learning, teacher efficacy, and student achievement (Fullan, 2016; Hattie, 2018; Little, 1982).

In her seminal work, Warren Little (1982) focuses on the differences between more effective and less effective schools and concludes that the more effective ones had a greater degree of collegiality. She also identified unique characteristics of collegiality (or collaboration) in schools where teachers participate in the following activities:

1. Teachers engage in frequent, continuous, and increasingly concrete and precise talk about teaching practice.

2. Teachers are frequently observed and provided with useful critiques of their teaching.

3. Teachers plan, design, evaluate, and prepare teaching materials together.

4. Teachers teach each other the practice of teaching. (pp. 331–332)

Several decades ago, Lieberman and Miller (1984) reported that "self-imposed, professionally sanctioned teacher isolation" (p. 11) is the norm. More recent research indicates that teachers only spend approximately 3% of their time in collaboration with others as they carry out their day-to-day work (Mirel & Goldin, 2012), and many continue to work in isolation from each other. Elmore (2000) emphasizes the isolation of teaching as a vocation, suggesting, "individual teachers invent their own practice in isolated classrooms, small knots of like-minded practitioners operate in isolation from their colleagues within a given school, or schools operate as exclusive enclaves of practice in isolation from other schools" (p. 21). On the other hand, collaboration allows teachers and administrators to build a learning community to support both professional and student learning.

> What we lose sight of as educators, at times, is that learning is a social activity and that collaboration promotes socialization among participants in the teaching–learning process.
> —Margo

Collaboration appears to run through both seminal and current research on teachers' impact on student learning. Central to these studies is the way they define teacher collaboration. See Figure 4.1 for a summary of key perspectives on teacher collaboration. Many emphasize the importance of collaboration as an essential skill for bringing about much-needed educational and social change. Finally, some research indicates that collaboration may hold a possible answer to improved teacher and student learning.

FIGURE 4.1 Key Findings and Assertions About Teacher Collaboration

Researchers	Key Findings and Assertions About Collaboration
Smith & Scott (1990)	"Collaboration depends inherently on the voluntary effort of professional educators to improve their schools and their own teaching through teamwork." (p. 2)
Little (1990)	Joint work is "teachers' decisions to pursue a single course of action in concert or, alternatively, to decide on a set of basic priorities that in turn guide the independent choices of individual teachers." (p. 519)
Colton, Langer, & Groff (2015)	"A culture of collaboration, although slow to develop, is worth its weight in gold when it comes to discovering responsive teaching approaches for struggling learners." (p. 21)
Moolenaar, Sleegers, & Daly (2012)	"Teacher interaction offers opportunities to experience the team's ability to promote student learning and to build consensus around shared goals and expectations for students." (p. 253)
Hargreaves & Fullan (2012)	"Teaching like a pro is not about yet more individual accountability, but about powerful collective responsibility." (p. 23)
Burns & Darling-Hammond (2014)	"More than any other policy area, actions that support collaborative learning among teachers appear to hold promise for improving the quality of teaching." (p. v)

(Continued)

FIGURE 4.1 **(Continued)**

Researchers	Key Findings and Assertions About Collaboration
Hattie (2015)	"Collaboration is based on cooperativeness, learning from errors, seeking feedback about progress and enjoying venturing into the 'pit of not knowing' together with expert help that provides safety nets and, ultimately, ways out of the pit. Creative collaboration involves bringing together two or more seemingly unrelated ideas, and this highlights again the importance of having safe and trusting places to explore ideas, to make and to learn from errors and to use expertise to maximise successful learning." (p. 27)
Fullan & Quinn (2016)	"Deep collaborative experiences that are tied to daily work, spent designing and assessing learning, and built on teacher choice and input can dramatically energize teachers and increase results." (p. 63)
Donohoo (2017)	"For collaboration to be productive, fostering collective efficacy, leading to changes in beliefs and practice and ultimately, increasing student achievement, it has to be purposefully organized. To reach the level of joint-work and to ensure teams avoid the pitfalls of groupthink, structures and processes need to be in place that promote and require interdependence, collective action, transparency, and group problem solving in search of a deeper understanding." (p. 39)

One of the most compelling pieces of evidence in support of teacher collaboration has emerged from Hattie's (2018) work, which documented a groundbreaking discovery of the importance of collaborative expertise as well as recognizing the power of collective efficacy. He also claims that the greatest barrier to students' academic achievement is within-school variability. For this reason, meaningful teacher collaboration—sharing successful instructional strategies, examining student data, and reflecting on effective teaching practices, and so on—is key. When teachers collaborate and form high functioning teams, the whole is greater than the sum of its parts, and their collective efficacy—their belief in their collaborative effectiveness—is increased (Eells, 2015; Knowapple, 2015). Donohoo (2017) concludes that certain enabling conditions contribute to higher collective teacher efficacy, one of which is through increased network membership. "By breaking down the isolation of the classroom, teachers' feelings of effectiveness and satisfaction are increased as a result of relationships built through networks" (p. 59). When transferred to the context of working with multilingual learners, teachers' collective efficacy indicates the shared belief—a new frame of reference—that together they can achieve success with ELs.

Collaborative practices are a new direction for many teachers, and they can be viewed as both complex and challenging. In our research and observation in numerous school districts, we have found that for successful collaboration for the sake of ELs, guidelines and procedures must be developed, implemented, and maintained in order to cultivate the transition from working in isolation to collaborative partnerships. The development of collaborative practices may have a more or less direct instructional or noninstructional focus. Yet, these practices work best when there is a core focus on learning fostered by collaborative inquiry as a catalyst for action, a commitment to purpose, and goal attainment (DuFour, DuFour, Eaker, & Many, 2006), and a shared vision as well as "strongly held convictions that all students in their charge can become capable and productive citizens" (Dove, Honigsfeld, & Cohan, 2014, p. 2).

THE VISION

We travel a great deal together to schools and districts throughout the country, and one of our common habits to pass the time is to jointly complete a *New York Times* crossword puzzle—generally the Monday edition. Sometimes there are easy answers prompted by the puzzles clues, and sometimes we are at a loss to figure them out. Sometimes we blurt out the answer at the same time; at other times, we complement each other because of our diverse cultural backgrounds and experiences. However, our goal is always the same—to finish the puzzle before we arrive at our destination. By the same token, our vision for creating pathways for teacher collaboration is similar in many ways. At times, the solutions to common challenges will be effortless, and on occasion, resolving certain dilemmas will not be easy—but our vision is unwavering—to make teacher collaboration a genuine, sustainable practice for the support of all learners. Blankstein (2013) offers a powerful explanation of what a vision is and how it differs from a school's or district's mission:

> Whereas the mission statement reminds us why we exist, a vision paints a picture of what we can become. . . . A school's vision should guide the collective direction of its stakeholders. It should provide a compelling sense of where the school is headed and, in broad terms, what must be accomplished in the future to fulfill the school's purpose. Every decision made, every program implemented, every policy instituted, and all goals should align with this vision. (p. 94)

We have also found that school leadership must have a clear vision and targeted focus for teacher collaboration to be successful; however, "we strongly believe that to truly obtain stakeholder buy-in, all members of the school community must have a voice in shaping its vision and mission, particularly when diverse learners are at stake" (Dove et al., 2014, p. 5). Further, our vision for teacher collaboration fosters an inclusive, assets-based culture for learning that is deeply rooted in respect for all viewpoints among stakeholders, shared decision-making, and instructional and noninstructional practices that support the growth and development of all students.

COLLABORATIVE PRACTICES

Instructional collaborative practices allow teachers to align teaching objectives, materials, learning strategies, and assessment so that ELs can be supported academically in a cohesive manner. These activities require an ongoing commitment as a part of shared beliefs and overall mission for ELs.

Joint planning. ELs need both access to the mainstream curriculum and assistance from particular teaching and learning strategies to make academic material comprehensible. When English language development (ELD) specialists and content teachers plan together, they can assure that ELD lessons contain pertinent academic subject matter and content lessons are presented with strategies aimed at reaching ELs. Collaborative planning is also a nonnegotiable prerequisite within the collaborative instructional cycle consisting of co-planning, co-teaching, co-assessment, and reflection.

Curriculum mapping and alignment. To ensure instructional content and practices for ELs are consistent with content standards and learning outcomes for all students, and to ensure that English language development is integrated with content instruction, mapping and aligning the ELD and core content curricula is an essential practice. It helps ELD teachers to draw from academic content appropriate language-learning opportunities to support ELs' understanding of the general education curricula. Additionally, curriculum frameworks can guide general education teachers how to differentiate instruction for ELs according to their levels of language proficiency.

Parallel teaching. Even if instruction is conducted in separate classrooms, ELD and core content teachers plan lessons together that include similar content and language concepts to foster continuity and congruence with ELs' teaching and learning. In this way, even if ELs are instructed in pullout or stand-alone classes for language instruction, there is cohesiveness in the instructional delivery for ELs and, therefore, less fragmentation of the development of content, concepts, and skills.

Co-developing instructional materials. This shared practice promotes the use of differentiated learning; it supports all teachers in their efforts to adapt content for ELs and can lighten individual workloads. Co-developing materials is preceded by team discussions about learning targets, lesson content, instructional delivery, development of appropriate student activities, and the needs of individual learners. Next, teacher teams identify the necessary scaffolds that should be in place to allow all students access points to the content and language presented in the lesson. From this planning, teachers then can determine the adjustments to the content of the lesson, the process of the instructional delivery, and/or the assessment in which students can demonstrate what they learned. Once these determinations are made, teaching teams can divide up the work of material preparation.

Collaborative assessment of student work. Teachers examine student work together not only to determine areas of instruction that need further clarification and reinforcement but also to identify teaching practices that need improvement. ELD and content teachers also may have different viewpoints on the progress of ELs as they each focus on different aspects of student academic growth and language or literacy development. Co-assessment may also include co-developing assessment tasks (what students will be expected to do) and assessment measures (what criteria and tools will be used to assess whether students have met the academic and linguistic targets set for them).

Co-teaching. Within the context of a single classroom, both the ELD and content teacher are equal instructional partners who combine their expertise and talents to make instruction comprehensible for ELs. In a co-taught class, students experience instruction that integrates content attainment and language and literacy development, thus receiving carefully designed, scaffolded opportunities for simultaneously working on grade-appropriate core content goals and language acquisition targets. Additionally, for co-teaching to be effective, both teachers must share the responsibility of planning, implementing, and assessing instruction for all students in the class.

Additionally, noninstructional activities also are an important aspect of collaborative practices, and engagement in these enterprises can have a great impact on student outcomes. These practices include (a) creating opportunities for joint professional development, (b) encouraging collaborative inquiry or individual teacher research to collect data on an intervention, (c) preparing for and conducting joint parent-teacher conferences, and (d) planning, facilitating, or participating in other extracurricular activities, such as family literacy programs, enrichment activities, field trips, and so on. Supporting the entire faculty in developing an ownership of serving ELs by planning, participating in, and evaluating these collaborative activities significantly contribute to successful instructional practices.

> As we noted in the assessment chapter, collaborative teams that center their attention on assessment *for* and *as* learning see how ongoing, descriptive, and timely feedback can enhance learning opportunities for both English learners and their teachers.
> —Margo

CASE STUDIES

To illustrate the shift from isolation to collaboration, we offer three case studies that exemplify success stories of classrooms, schools, and districts that made this shift as well as discuss the power of building and participating in professional learning networks (PLNs).

Beaverton Public Schools, Beaverton, OR

Among many other school districts whose transformation we have either supported or witnessed, Beaverton Public School in Oregon stands out. Beaverton School District is the second largest school district in the state of Oregon with a population of a little over 40,000 students, 13% of whom are ELs. Beaverton School District is representative of over 100 different languages and is one of the most culturally and linguistically diverse districts in the state. Under the leadership of Toshiko Maurizio and Sarita Amaya, the district began to examine their service delivery mode for English learners in 2015.

Through systematic assessment of how teachers deliver the state and federally mandated language development program, the district initiated a comprehensive approach to co-teaching training throughout the year, a district collaborative co-teaching guide for implementation had been developed, and collaborative co-teaching schools were able to access up to eight hours of collaborative planning time each month to support school building efforts. Sustained professional development and intentional teacher pairing led to building capacity districtwide. Teams made school visits to see the different co-teaching models in action; they used early release Wednesdays for collaborative planning and assessment and accessed additional hours to attend conferences and plan outside of their regularly scheduled workdays. The commitment and dedication were evident. Education Northwest, in conjunction with the Beaverton School District Multilingual Department, conducted a comprehensive three-year study about the various program models implemented in the district and concluded that co-teaching has a positive impact on student learning. More specifically, the study affirmed that when students only received co-teaching services implemented with fidelity (including co-planning and co-assessment), they performed higher on a range of literacy assessments (ELPA21 reading, writing, listening, and Smarter Balanced English language arts) than students who also participated in pull-out and push-in services (defined as in-class instruction without collaborative planning) (also cited in Honigsfeld & Dove, 2019).

Comsewogue High School, Port Jefferson Station, NY

Comsewogue High School has approximately 1,200 students: 28% are language minority students, and 5% are English learners. The leadership for this school—from the superintendent of schools to the building leadership team—has been supportive of co-teaching and collaborative practices for the sake of English learners for almost nine years. All English learners are placed in classes that include an English-as-a-new-language (ENL) teacher and a core content teacher. English language arts, mathematics, social studies, and science are all co-taught for the sake of ELs. One particular teaching team, Joel Sutherland and Lia Pantanelli, have forged a collaborative partnership in which they have overcome their individual apprehensions about teaching a mixed group of ELs and English proficient students in one algebra class and have over time acquired each other's set of teaching strategies to provide language and content instruction for all their students.

In a recent interview, Joel described their collaboration as a "weird mix in the beginning." He was unaccustomed to sharing the decision-making in what he considered to be his class. However, through their ongoing communication and getting to truly know one another both professionally and personally, Joel and Lia developed a strong partnership. Joel believes that he and Lia share a common purpose to get their ELs to work at the level the learning targets demand. He clearly expressed how much he relies on Lia to bring the students to where they need to be academically and linguistically.

Lia's greatest misgivings stemmed from her lack of confidence in her ability to teach algebra alongside Joel and not having the respect of the English-speaking students. She explained to us how she sat with Joel every day, two periods per day on her free time, to learn the content to be able to properly support the students in algebra. Over time, she grasped the material well enough to feel confident in teaching the content.

Together, they have built a long-standing teaching team in which they regularly co-plan lessons, develop materials and resources for instruction, and continuously assess the progress of their students through formative and summative assessment strategies. Through their commitment to working collaboratively, they have created a supportive classroom atmosphere in which their students grow academically and linguistically, without even having to be aware of which teacher is certified to teach which subject.

P.S. 69 Vincent D. Grippo School, Brooklyn, NY

An elementary school with a strong visual and performance arts curriculum in the Sunset Park area of Brooklyn, P.S. 69 Vincent D. Grippo School has over 800 students enrolled; 90% of the students are Asian, and 60% of the students are English learners. In a unique program that uses a seven-day rotation schedule, this school offers students multiple opportunities to develop their talents in the arts from the first through fifth grades. Jaynemarie Capetanakis, principal, also views the arts-infused curriculum as one of the many opportunities students have to develop their English language proficiency.

Ms. Capetanakis has established a collaborative culture at the school, in which peer coaches meet regularly with grade-level teachers to plan lessons, scaffold curriculum, and support instruction for the sake of all students. Although class sizes are often above 30 students, the program instituted for supporting ELs combines a three-way teaching strategy in which two ELD or ENL teachers co-teach with a grade-level teacher to reduce student–teacher ratios and provide scaffolded instruction according to students' language proficiency.

In one first-grade class we visited, the teaching team divided students into three groups for instruction. Each group of students was engaged in a hands-on activity with one of the three teachers using various types of fruit—making applesauce, a fruit salad, and an apple pizza. The learning target was basically the same for each group—to use transition words to explain their steps in the process. Yet, the grouping of students was done strategically so that one group of students completed the task verbally with prompting from one of the teachers, another group responded both verbally and in writing with scaffolded sentences supports, and the third group wrote the steps in the procedure independently.

This type of three-way teaching requires a great deal of time to determine appropriate, differentiated learning targets, to develop scaffolded materials, to negotiate shared class space, and to coordinate on-going formative and summative assessment procedures. Yet here, the school culture supports teachers to continuously collaborate for the academic improvement of all students. Moreover, the collaborative efforts of the school leaders and faculty combined created a language-rich curriculum and a school environment where ELs as well as all students can thrive.

PROFESSIONAL LEARNING NETWORKS (PLNS)

One most powerful way teachers have escaped their isolation is establishing and expanding their professional learning networks, also referred to as PLNs. Social media platforms such as Twitter and Facebook have broken down silos for tens of thousands of educators. Through professionally oriented Facebook groups and Twitter chats, educators were provided a newly-found opportunity to connect with other across geographic boundaries. Some notable ways educators globally connect and share best practices, challenges, and possible solutions is through online chats.

Katie Toppel and Tan Huyn initiated #EllChat_BkClub in November 2016 with an online book club discussing one of our books, *Collaboration and Co-teaching: Strategies for English Learners* (Honigsfeld & Dove, 2010). As authors, we have connected with our many readers across the United States and beyond and firsthand witnessed the power of participating in Twitter chats and connecting with others nationally and internationally through the power of social networks. Katie Toppel, an avid online chat contributor, reminds us,

> Being a language specialist can be a very isolating role and my typical professional development at work rarely applies directly to language development or ELs. By connecting to an enthusiastic, knowledgeable, and passionate PLN of language teachers, including experts and published authors in the field via Twitter, my personal professional growth has been supercharged. #EllChat_BkClub involves an international network of language teachers who all provide expertise and contextual differences that have helped me grow as a teacher, leader, and professional.

Tan Huyn affirms that he is a better teacher because of the network he has built through Twitter and reflects on the past three years of #EllChat_BkClub online events that featured 20 books and engaged over 100 educators worldwide. He identifies the greater impact of these informal collaborative professional learning opportunities as follows:

We have had club participants that have brought these texts into their school to do a school-wide book study, participants have gone on to present at state-level conferences based on the books, and readers who are now sharing from their knowledge on their own blogs. All this innovation, excitement, and collaboration just from an informal book club on Twitter.

THE CALL FOR ACTION

The path from isolation to collaboration is rarely an easy and simple one to follow. We have found that it may present special challenges for some to break out of the egg-carton model—a metaphor that vividly evokes the image of an egg carton with one egg in each designated spot representing one teacher in each classroom. The egg carton may be comfortable and safe; leaving it may lead to discomfort, unforeseen challenges, and maybe even conflict. Our decade-long exploration of collaboration and co-teaching for the sake of ELs has taught us that paradigm shifts are particularly challenging for educators who have thrived doing it alone! Yet, collaboration can no longer be optional—something we do when we feel like it or when we find time for it. Collaboration is the ultimate call for action—action to disrupt the status quo and join forces with others for an equitable, fair, and just educational system for all. To demonstrate, let's consider what changes must take place on three levels—the micro-, meso-, and macro-levels—and how each strand will ultimately be intertwined with the others.

On the micro-level, individual teachers must take a bold step that leads them right to their classroom doors to let others in or to step out of their own classrooms to invite new perspectives for instruction. Each individual can take on the status quo as an interrupter or disruptor while also serving as community builder. Individual teachers can foster collaborative efforts in one class, thereby sowing the seeds that support the growth of a collaborative school culture and providing opportunities to influence one another, one team at a time.

On the meso-level, educators must initiate and maintain teams that embrace collaborative approaches to the teaching-learning cycle. In this approach, teams of teachers—grade level, content area, ELD specialists, educators of students with disabilities, and administrators—work in tandem to write accessible curricula, to promote collaborative decision-making, to share innovative, effective professional practices, and to foster a genuine understanding of language-minority students.

On the macro-level, educators must ensure strong school and community collaborations—building partnerships among all stakeholders. These partnerships ensure students have support from their home, school, district, and community, and they provide the school community with access to resources, facilities, and programs that otherwise they may not have. See Figures 4.2 and 4.3 for practical ideas for collaboration and professional learning.

FIGURE 4.2 Collaboration Opportunities for Teachers

Practice	Activities
Collegial circles	Teachers meet on a regular basis to discuss common questions, share concerns, and offer solutions to common problems and appropriate instructional techniques.
Peer observations	All teachers of ELLs are provided opportunities to visit one another's classes to observe the teaching-learning process and ELL outcomes in the classroom.
Collaborative coaching and mentoring	Teachers support each other's practice through a framework of modeling effective instruction and providing ongoing, student-centered classroom assistance for one another.
Research and development	Teachers collaboratively study and review research related to an instructional approach for ELLs and plan and implement lessons based on their studies.
Collaborative inquiry (action research)	This is a more in-depth exploration of an overarching concept that deals with ELLs' language acquisition or instructional needs—also known as teacher research or action research.
Lesson study	Teachers jointly plan a lesson in response to a preestablished study question or goal. Through repeated lesson observations and discussions, teachers revise the lesson as it is re-taught and observed in each new class.
Professional-learning communities (PLCs)	PLCs create a structure for improving schools by establishing and enacting a collaborative school culture and a collective purpose for learning.
Professional-learning networks (PLNs)	PLNs take advantage of social media and function as online communities for learning.
Collaborative-learning teams (CLTs)	CLTs—through shared goals, regular meetings, and an organized approach—are vehicles for teachers to engage in professional learning focused on effective instruction.

FIGURE 4.3 Organizational Options for Collaborative Models of Professional Development on Three Levels

Participants	Practices	Activities
Whole school staff	Research and development	All school members delve into literature about a specified topic; teachers design their own resources alone or in small groups and share them on a specially designated school website (e-board).
School staff organized into smaller study groups	Collaborative inquiry (or variations on it, such as independent study groups, collegial circles, lesson study groups, etc.)	Individual groups set procedures typically consisting of • Identifying the issue • Examining the data • Reviewing the literature • Determining and implementing a course of action
Individual faculty volunteer to participate in partner groups	Peer observations, collaborative coaching, and mentoring	Each two-person team independently determines the focus of professional improvement.

Summary and Conclusions

We propose four core principles of teamwork to provide the foundation for the day-to-day collaborative work in support of English learners (Cohan, Honigsfeld, & Dove, 2020). They are common purpose, shared mindset, supportive environment, and diverse team membership. When educators effectively collaborate, they share a common goal of empowering English learners' in their academic, linguistic, and social-emotional development; they share ownership of the challenges and joy of educating all children and believe that together they can do better than they would alone; they transform each classroom and the entire school community to be a positive, highly supportive learning environment; and finally they seek out to engage with diverse members of the larger school and neighborhood community.

References

Blankstein, A. M. (2013). *Failure is not an option: 6 principles that advance student achievement in highly effective schools.* Thousand Oaks, CA: Corwin.

Burns, D., & Darling-Hammond, L. (2014, December). *Teaching around the world: What can TALIS tell us.* Stanford, CA: Stanford Center for Opportunity Policy in Education. Retrieved from https://edpolicy.stanford.edu/publication/pubs/1295.

Calderón, M., Slavin, R., & Sanchez, M. (2011). Effective instruction for English learners. *The Future of Children. 21*(1), 103–127.

Christakis, N. A., & Fowler, J. H. (2009). *Connected: How your friends' friends' friends affect everything you think, feel, and do.* New York, NY: Bay Back Books.

Cohan, A., Honigsfeld, A., & Dove, M. G. (2020). *Team up, speak up, fire up! Educators, students, and the community working together to support English learners.* Alexandria, VA: Association for Supervision and Curriculum Development (ASCD).

Colton, A., Langer, G., & Groff, L. (2015). *The collaborative analysis of student learning: Professional learning that promotes success for all.* Thousand Oaks, CA: Corwin.

Darling-Hammond, L., & Richardson, N. (2009). Research review/teacher learning: What matters? *Educational Leadership, 66*(5), 46–53.

Donohoo, J. (2017). *Collective efficacy: How educators' beliefs impact student learning.* Thousand Oaks, CA: Corwin.

Donohoo, J., Hattie, J., & Eells, R. (2018). The power of collective efficacy. *Educational Leadership, 75*(6), 40–44.

Dove, M. G., & Honigsfeld, A. (2018). *Co-teaching for English learners: A guide to collaborative planning, instruction, assessment, and reflection.* Thousand Oaks, CA: Corwin.

Dove, M. G., Honigsfeld, A., & Cohan, A. (2014). *Beyond core expectations: A framework for servicing the not-so-common learner.* Thousand Oaks, CA: Corwin.

DuFour, R., DuFour R., Eaker, R., & Many, T. (2006). *Learning by doing: A handbook for professional learning communities at work.* Bloomington IN: Solution Tree.

Eells, R. J. (2011). Meta-analysis of the relationship between collective teacher efficacy and student achievement. Doctoral dissertation. Retrieved from http://ecommons.luc.edu/cgi/viewcontent.cgi?article=1132&context=luc_diss

Elmore, R. (2000). *Building a new structure for school leadership.* Washington, DC: The Albert Shanker Institute.

Elmore, R. F. (2004). *School reform from the inside out: Policy, practice, and performance.* Cambridge, MA: Harvard University Press.

Fullan, M. (2016). *The new meaning of educational change.* New York, NY: Routledge.

Fullan, M., & Quinn, J. (2016). *Coherence: The right drivers in action for schools, districts, and systems.* Thousand Oaks, CA: Corwin.

Gandara, P., & Orfield, G. (2010). A return to the "Mexican Room": The segregation of Arizona's English learners. *UCLA: The Civil Rights Project/Proyecto Derechos Civiles.* Retrieved from https://escholarship.org/uc/item/7m67q3b9

Hargreaves, A., & Fullan, M. (2012). *Professional capital: Transforming teaching in every school.* New York, NY: Teachers' College Press.

Hattie, J. (2015). *What works best in education: The politics of collaborative expertise.* London, UK: Pearson.

Hattie, J. (2018). Collective Teacher Efficacy (CTE). Retrieved from https://visible-learning.org/2018/03/collective-teacher-efficacy-hattie/

Hattie, J., & Zierer, K. (2018). *Ten mindframes for visible learning: Teaching for success.* New York, NY: Routledge.

Honigsfeld, A., & Dove, M. G. (2010). *Collaboration and co-teaching: Strategies for English learners.* Thousand Oaks, CA: Corwin.

Honigsfeld, A., & Dove, M. G. (2015). *Collaboration and co-teaching for English learners: A leader's guide.* Thousand Oaks, CA: Corwin.

Honigsfeld, A., & Dove, M. G. (2019). *Collaboration for English learners: A foundational guide to integrated practices* (2nd ed). Thousand Oaks, CA: Corwin.

Knowapple, J. (2015). *Equity leaders must work themselves out of a job: What collective efficacy has to do with educational equity.* Retrieved from http://corwin-connect.com/2015/12/equity-leaders-must-work-themselves-out-of-a-job-what-collective-efficacy-has-to-do-with-educational-equity/

Langer, G. M., & Colton, A. B. (2005). Looking at student work. *Educational Leadership, 62*(5), 22–26.

Lieberman A., & Miller, L. (1984). *Teachers, their world, and their work: Implications for school improvement.* Alexandria, VA: Association for Supervision and Curriculum Development (ASCD).

Little, J. W. (1982). Norms of collegiality and experimentation: Workplace conditions of school success. *American Educational Research Journal, 19,* 325–340.

Little, J. W. (1990). The persistence of privacy: Autonomy and initiative in teachers' professional relations. *Teacher College Record, 91,* 509–536.

Mirel, J., & Goldin, S. (2012, April 17). Alone in the classroom: Why teachers are so isolated. *The Atlantic.* Retrieved from https://www.theatlantic.com/national/archive/2012/04/alone-in-the-classroom-why-teachers-are-too-isolated/255976/

Moolenaar, A., Sleegers, P., & Daly, A. (2012). Teaming up: Linking collaboration networks, collective efficacy, and student achievement. *Teaching and Teacher Education, 28,* 251–262.

National Center for Education Statistics. (2018). *English language learners in public schools.* Retrieved from https://nces.ed.gov/programs/coe/indicator_cgf.asp

Schmoker, M. (2006). *Results now: How we can achieve unprecedented improvements in teaching and learning.* Alexandria, VA: Association for Supervision and Curriculum Development (ASCD).

Smith, S. C., & Scott, J. L. (1990). *The collaborative school: A work environment for effective instruction* (Report No. ISBN-0–86552–092–5). Eugene, OR: University of Oregon. (ERIC Document Reproduction Service No. ED316918)

Supovitz, J. (2006). *The case for district-based reform.* Cambridge, MA: Harvard Education Press.

Vangrieken, K., Dochy, F., Raes, E., & Kyndt, E. (2015). Teacher collaboration: A systematic review. *Educational Research Review, 15,* 17–40.

Walqui, A., & van Lier, L. (2010). *A pedagogy of promise. Scaffolding the academic success of adolescent English language learners: A pedagogy of promise.* San Francisco, CA: WestEd.

Weixler, L. B., Harris, D. N., & Barrett, N. (2018). Teachers' perspectives on the learning and work environments under the New Orleans school reforms. *Educational Researcher, 47*(8), 502–515. Retrieved from https://doi.org/10.3102/0013189X18787806

chapter five

From Silence to Conversation

IVANNIA SOTO AND
TONYA WARD SINGER

PREMISE

If all classrooms actively engage all students in conversations that value all voices, schools will realize deep shifts in student learning, motivation, and capacity for collaboration in a global world. A collective focus on how our classroom conversation practices impact English learners is imperative to transforming teaching for equity.

VIGNETTE

Ms. Elena's seventh grade English students are reading and discussing the poem *Bilingual/Bilingüe* by Rhina Espaillat. Ms. Elena asks her class of 32 students the text-dependent, open-ended questions: What is the author's message of the poem? What is the theme? She has students re-read with these questions in mind and annotate in preparation for the discussion. Compare the following two scenarios for the discussion that follows:

A. Ms. Elena asks the questions again to the whole class, 32 students who are all seated in rows facing the front. Five students raise their hands to share ideas. Each says one idea, and the teacher responds with a comment or asks for another volunteer. Not one of the six English learners in the class speaks.

B. Students are strategically seated in tables of four for productive collaboration. Ms. Elena has students discuss the theme with "elbow" partners. As partners engage in discussion, the teacher listens to check for understanding and listen to students' evolving academic conversation skills. She hears students making inferences about the theme and sees them reread and point to the text as they justify their thinking with specific evidence. Students participate in extended conversations through which they listen and respond to one another to build up ideas together.

Scenario A is the default approach to classroom discourse in many classrooms. The teacher does most of the talking and calls on students to be part of a teacher-directed conversation. Sixteen percent of the students participate, and 84% are silent. The five doing the talking are those most confident with the goal of the lesson and the language central to the task. All six ELs are silent. The students who most need to benefit from this lesson don't participate, and their inaction gives the teacher no formative data to understand why.

Scenario B, by contrast, engages 100% of students, both ELs and non-ELs, as active participants in the discussion. In addition, it requires academic conversation skills including taking turns, building up ideas together, listening to one another, asking questions, and explaining thinking with text evidence. It provides a low-stress opportunity for every student to express and develop ideas with a single listener before speaking in front of the larger group. After talking with partners in scenario B, students then form a circle to share ideas, and hear from other perspectives in the larger group. There is a rich exchange of ideas from multiple points of view. For example, some students who have experience being multilingual share their personal connections to ideas in the poem, leveraging their linguistic and cultural assets to help monolingual speakers in the classroom deepen their understandings about the nuanced relationships between ideas in the poem.

Shifting classroom discourse from scenario A to scenario B is one of the most essential transformations schools must make to be effective with ELs. Students learn language by using language, and ELs learn the academic language of school by using the academic language of school. Students learn best in welcoming, low-stress environments in which they belong and have a voice (Hammond, 2015).

> Ivannia and Tonya powerfully show us the importance of language acquisition happening through active engagement. In my own work, I often liken this process to riding a bicycle or swimming. You cannot acquire these skills without getting on the bicycle or being in the pool.
> —Andrea

THE URGENCY

We know this, and yet there is a knowing-doing gap. Across the nation, ELs are more often than not silent in classrooms. A nationwide study found that ELs spent 2% of their classroom day engaged in academic talk (Arreaga-Mayer & Perdomo-Rivera, 1996). It's easy to envision how this happens when scenario A is repeated across classrooms, across content areas, year after year. Silence is a natural outcome when the norm is as Nystrand (2006) observed in secondary classrooms—an average of 14 to 52 seconds of discussion time per instructional period. A shift from silence to conversation benefits all students (Hattie, 2012), and structured talk with intentional equitable practices to increase ELs' active learning of rigorous academic content and language (Bunch, Kibler, & Pimentel, 2013) is an imperative to break down the wall to EL success.

Given the importance of academic talk to build language, EL silence at scale is a recipe for stagnation. It is a prescription for ELs not advancing in language, in content, or in the rigorous learning essential for access to college and career opportunities. Furthermore, a normalcy of EL silence perpetuates an inequitable power dynamic between students whose voices shape the classroom community (often by default monolingual and white) and students without voice (often ELs and/or students whose cultural, linguistic, racial, ethnic, or gender identities are undervalued in the school community). EL silence is not just about ELs; it reflects a default norm of white English speakers dominating classroom discussions in racially, culturally, linguistically diverse classrooms. This is a discourse dynamic that must change for equity within and beyond schools.

In our globalized world we can do better. In a world economy that prioritizes collaboration, communication, and problem solving, we must do better to prepare all students to engage in active, collaborative conversations. We must prepare students to listen to people with perspectives different from their own and collaborate across differences of language, race, and culture.

Transform EL silence into EL conversations with a simple shift: instead of calling on individuals, use strategies to structure student-to-student discourse in every classroom every day. Lead the change by building a shared vision for dynamic peer conversations in every lesson, building teacher capacity to facilitate conversations, and using observation data strategically in your collective efforts to amplify active participation and dynamic discourse among ELs, and all learners in every lesson every day.

THE VISION

In our vision, all students are engaged in peer conversations in every lesson every day. ELs and fluent English speakers all have multiple opportunities to discuss academic texts, tasks, and ideas to build thinking, build language, and build collaboration skills in community with other learners.

Academic conversations are essential for ELs to build oral academic language (August & Shannahan, 2006; Zwiers & Soto, 2016), and have many benefits for all students including the following:

Benefits of Peer Conversations

Partner and small-group conversation structures have all of the following advantages over calling on individuals:

- Increase the percentage of students who actively engage
- Increase opportunities for students to talk
- Increase opportunities for students to deepen thinking

(Continued)

(Continued)

- Foster academic language development by having all students *use* language to articulate thinking about academic concepts and topics
- Create a low-risk opportunity for ELs to participate
- Create a low-risk opportunity for introverts to participate
- Create a low-risk opportunity for students who may struggle
- Foster collaboration
- Increase your opportunities to listen to students to gather formative data during your lessons

Source: Singer (2018, p. 48).

Shifting from silence to conversation necessitates a sustained, systemic focus. More specifically, it requires enhancing the capacity of *all* educators to promote academic language development of English learners. The following section will focus on a case study of capacity building in two southern California school districts that employed *EL Shadowing*—a unique form of professional learning. By engaging in EL Shadowing and committing to a multiyear focus on academic language development, educators at Whittier Union High School District (Whittier, CA) and Morrison Elementary School (Norwalk, CA) disrupted long-standing linguistic inequities.

> Walk in someone else's shoes . . . the classic proverb is brilliantly translated into a teaching practice here! Spending a sustained amount of time with clear focus and purpose gives ELL Shadowing its unique power as a professional learning tool.
> —Andrea

Using ELL Shadowing as a Systemic Catalyst for Change From Silence Into Conversation

EL Shadowing is an ethnographic research project in which educators experience a day in the life of an EL. Participants pay particular attention to EL students' opportunities for academic oral language production and active listening. Observation cycles take place during five-minute intervals, periods when teachers observe the same student across two or more content areas for comparison. Focusing on one EL student for two hours enables teachers to observe and examine the language struggles and inequities in access and engagement that many ELs experience, including a lack of opportunities for oral language expression and/or the visible disengagement right before the observers' eyes. Shadowing ELs in other classrooms leads many teachers to an *ah-ha* moment in which they reflect on what they, themselves, need to change to ensure equity and access for ELs. For example, after one EL Shadowing experience in District J of the Los Angeles Unified School District, one teacher realized, "The person talking the most is learning the most, and I'm doing the most talking in my classroom." This is a perfect example of how EL Shadowing can disrupt language inequities while enhancing empathy for ELs among teachers.

Watching the dynamics of classroom conversations while focusing on one subgroup of students helps teachers notice subtle yet pervasive inequities, such as ELs and students of color being called upon less frequently, and being given the answer rather than giving them the opportunity to solve the problem themselves (Soto-Hinman & Hetzel, 2009). Observing students via shadowing allows teachers to see such inequities at a level of specificity and immediacy that promotes a sense of an urgency in making improvements.

While EL shadowing is a powerful "jump start" in teachers' journeys, it is only the first step. As is argued in a number of chapters in this book, educational systems must commit to a systemic professional learning plan to promote EL achievement including focused professional learning on shifting from EL silence to conversation. For example, many school districts begin by using high-impact, research-based strategies that benefit ELs (e.g., Think-Pair-Share), and more collaborative structures (e.g., Reciprocal Teaching), which will be described in the section below.

Systemic Shadowing and Academic Language Development Implementation: Whittier Union High School District

Whittier Union High School District (WUHSD) is a 9–12 urban district located in the city of Whittier (population 80,000) about 10 miles from downtown Los Angeles, CA. The district is comprised of five comprehensive high schools, two alternative schools, and one continuation school serving a total of 13,000 students. Students enter the district at Grade 9 from five local feeder districts. The racial make-up of the district is about 88% Latinx, with single-digit percentages of African American, Asian, and white students. About 72% of all WUHSD students qualify for free-reduced lunches. Although the district as a whole demonstrates moderate academic success, there are individual schools with higher populations of students in need.

One in ten WUHSD students is an EL, and 95% of these are students who have received all required English Language Development (ELD) services but have still not been redesignated as fluent in English. They are called Long Term English learners (LTEL) and typically receive no additional services after finishing the required coursework. Whittier's student population also included Standard English learners (SEL)—students whose home languages are variations of Standard English, for example, African American and Chicano English. These students have never received language services at school and need specific instruction in academic English in order to improve their performance, as do LTELs. The professional development efforts described in this case study have been found to strengthen instruction in a manner that benefits both LTELs and SELs, although the focus of this chapter is limited to ELs.

District-level professional development in WUHSD began with EL Shadowing. Again, shadowing is an especially powerful starting point as it creates an urgency for change on behalf of ELs within a system and allows educators to realize that they must change their instructional practices in order to meet the academic language development needs of this group of students. Once shadowing has been completed, and the aggregate data for the percentage of academic oral language output has been analyzed (typically between 5–10% of an EL's school day), teachers can be introduced to the use of three ALD strategies that require academic oral language and develop academic language development skills (Soto, 2012).

We propose introducing the following strategies one at a time, over several months, so that teachers have time to build efficacy. The strategies include Think-Pair-Share with an emphasis on academic speaking, active listening, and consensus; the collaborative approach to the Frayer model for academic vocabulary support and building background knowledge; and Reciprocal Teaching for academic group discussions and literacy support. Not only are each of these strategies research-based, but they also provide rich opportunities for academic conversations and academic language development. These strategies are also user-friendly and simple for both teachers and students to learn, as well as for educators to see results, which causes them to want to go deeper with additional strategies. After each strategy is introduced in a workshop, teachers implement the strategies in their classrooms and bring back student work samples they analyze and use for reflective next steps. Only after engaging in such reflections do teachers move onto the next strategy. The reflection not only encourages accountability for implementation of the strategy but also provides an opportunity for teachers to measure the impact of their efforts. A typical shadowing and ALD professional development year 1 cycle might look as follows:

Date	ALD Focus Area
August/September	• EL Shadowing (shadow between days 1 and 2, or all together as part of day 1) • Introduction to Think-Pair-Share/planning for implementation
October	• Shadowing debrief • Think-Pair-Share reflection using student work samples • Introduction to Frayer model/planning for implementation
November/December	• Frayer model reflection using student work samples • Introduction to Reciprocal Teaching/planning for implementation

It is important to note that these ALD professional efforts are typically enacted over the course of several years. Again, an overarching principle of this book is that large-scale, systemic improvements on behalf of ELs won't be enacted through what Singleton calls "random acts of equity (2018). In year 2, depending on district need and/or focus areas, they may choose to focus on more sophisticated academic discourse structures or how to use the three ALD strategies to scaffold writing with ELs.

In addition to the cycle above, 10 teachers in WUHSD, from across all five comprehensive high schools, completed an Academic Language Development certification program in year 3. ALD Certification teachers were videotaped while using Think-Pair-Share, the Frayer model, or Reciprocal Teaching in their classrooms. They shared these videos with each other, thus learning from each other, and also reflected on their next steps, much like the National Board Certification process. ALD Certification teachers have also opened up their classrooms to other teachers and assisted in sharing best practices with their peers. At the district level, WUHSD highlighted EL and Standard English learner instruction, as well as EL Shadowing, in both of its major three-year planning documents: the Local Control Accountability Plan and the ELL Master Plan.

Teacher Reflection on ALD Strategy Implementation

As mentioned briefly before, part of the ALD professional development series is accountability for trying out each of the ALD strategies and bringing back student work samples. After teachers have tried out a strategy in the classroom setting, they reflect on how the implementation went and what possible adjustments can be made with each strategy. After a student work sample is shared with the entire group, with a focus on noticings and wonderings, teachers share their student work sample with each other to receive feedback in smaller groups. The smaller group conversations about implementation of the strategy with colleagues allow teachers to share best practices. More importantly, sharing student work samples in a climate of support and trust helps keep these conversations student-centered: from their analyses and discussion, teachers are better able to determine areas of student need as well as their potential next steps.

Below is a Frayer model student work sample from a math teacher in WUHSD. The Frayer model is a vocabulary development strategy that allows teachers to teach words that are associated with a target word or concept. After building sufficient background knowledge around a Tier 2 (high frequency words that intersect different content areas, such as *analyze*) or Tier 3 (words that are specific to a particular discipline) word, teachers lead students through a process of discussing examples of the word, non-examples of the word, a visual, and a definition. Notice that the graphic organizer below is enumerated and should be completed counterclockwise. When first implementing the Frayer model, the teacher should facilitate a discussion around each of the sections of the graphic organizer (examples, non-examples, visual, and definition), but should be sure to gradually release each quadrant for student-to-student discussion after a couple of whole class examples are elicited. In this way, each student should have a partner and class discussion about examples and non-examples first; then students draw their visual and describe it to teach other, and finally students can work with each other to come up with their own definition of the word. Even though students are working on vocabulary development, they are still having academic conversations about each step in the Frayer model process. The power of the strategy is that students learn key concepts alongside of the key word and that students come up with their own definition, which is more likely to be retained than a dictionary definition. Oftentimes, when students look up words in a print or digital dictionary, they do not understand the archaic language, as using a dictionary is a skill in itself. In this way, the Frayer model process allows for efficient and effective vocabulary development, instead of teaching one word at a time, which also requiring academic oral language.

FIGURE 5.1 Student Work Sample for Frayer Model in Math With Academic Discourse About Each Quadrant

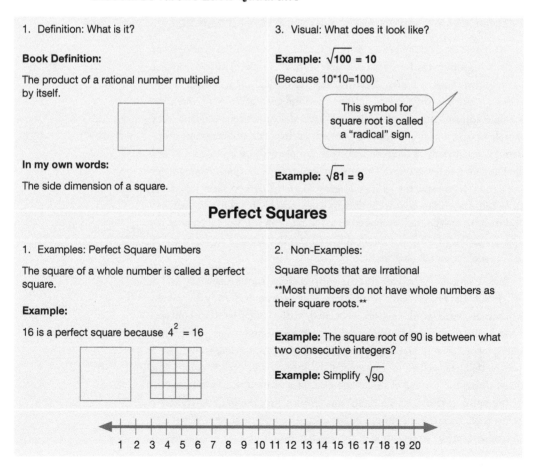

1. Definition: What is it?

Book Definition:

The product of a rational number multiplied by itself.

In my own words:

The side dimension of a square.

3. Visual: What does it look like?

Example: $\sqrt{100} = 10$

(Because 10*10=100)

This symbol for square root is called a "radical" sign.

Example: $\sqrt{81} = 9$

Perfect Squares

1. Examples: Perfect Square Numbers

The square of a whole number is called a perfect square.

Example:

16 is a perfect square because $4^2 = 16$

2. Non-Examples:

Square Roots that are Irrational

Most numbers do not have whole numbers as their square roots.

Example: The square root of 90 is between what two consecutive integers?

Example: Simplify $\sqrt{90}$

1 2 3 4 5 6 7 8 9 10 11 12 13 14 15 16 17 18 19 20

Systemic Shadowing and ALD Implementation: Morrison Elementary School

Morrison Elementary School is a school in Norwalk, California, with 39% of the school's student population comprised of ELs, and an additional 75% of students living in poverty—demographics that mirror the same language needs of many of the schools with similar populations of students in the Los Angeles area. This school has been recognized for many accolades, including being a 2012 Golden Bell Award recipient and receiving the Title I Academic Achievement Award every year since 2011. After noticing that despite these awards many of their ELs were still struggling, the school decided to focus their professional development efforts around the needs of their ELs. As demonstrated by the chart below, the rate of growth for the EL subgroup between 2008–2011 was actually higher than that of the overall population, with an overall growth of 60 points over the three-year time period. This growth was during the same time period that ELD and ALD were systemically implemented.

Through focused professional development, which began with EL Shadowing, the school was able to focus on the urgency and need for creating more opportunities for academic talk throughout the school day. Shortly after the EL Shadowing experience, Morrison Elementary School began study groups around the texts *Scaffolding Language, Scaffolding Learning* (a foundational work that informed the development of EL Shadowing is derived) by Pauline Gibbons (2002), and *The Literacy Gaps: Building Bridges for ELLs and SELs* by Ivannia Soto-Hinman and June Hetzel (2009). These study groups allowed the staff to further build background knowledge around the linguistic and cultural needs of ELs. That foundational base was then accompanied by establishing a well-supported daily curriculum of dedicated English Language Development, as well as ALD scaffolding support throughout content area subjects each day. These reform structures have allowed the school to make consistent and effective progress with ELs over time. The systemic changes are also positively noted by the API growth above: EL API-850 and overall API-856.

In addition to EL Shadowing, teachers received professional development on how to embed ALD strategies, including Think-Pair-Share, the aforementioned Frayer model, and Reciprocal Teaching throughout the school day, so that ELs also received scaffolding support during content area instruction. As previously discussed, the Think-Pair-Share strategy is a way to structure and amplify academic oral language development and active listening. Additional information on how to implement effective Think-Pair-Shares appears in the following *Call to Action* section. Reciprocal teaching is a way to reinforce both good reader habits of summarizing, questioning, predicting, and connecting, while also requiring student academic dialogue via structured group roles. The Reciprocal Teaching graphic organizer allows for both individual and group accountability during discussions, as each student must not only complete his or her own role, but then also listen carefully in order to synthesize what the group members have shared. In this way, teachers are teaching not only productive group work and collaboration, but also the two most under-developed domains of listening and speaking. It is important to note that each of these Reciprocal Teaching roles should be modeled and practiced with the whole group before students can be expected to be successful with Reciprocal Teaching on their own. ELs will also benefit from meeting in expert groups—all of the summarizers together—before being expected to share out with their home group (when all four different roles are together).

Below is a Reciprocal Teaching lesson outline by a teacher at Morrison Elementary School named Jennifer Murrey, who became the school's Reciprocal Teaching expert.

Reciprocal Teaching Lesson 1: "Global Warming"

Focus: Identify causes and effects. We had read a similar article during shared reading, so it helps for the connecting part.

- **Day 1:** Define objectives (students can identify what causes global warming and what the effects of global warming are on Earth).
  - ○ Look at/discuss text features and make predictions (both with their partners and then whole group).
  - ○ Read paragraphs 1 and 2. After each paragraph, discuss with the group the main idea. Write the main idea on a Post-it note when consensus is reached.
  - ○ Share out with the whole group to make sure they have come up with the main idea.

- **Day 2:** Review what we learned yesterday. Finish reading paragraphs 3 and 4. After each paragraph, discuss with the group the main idea. Write the main idea on a Post-it note when consensus is reached.
  - ○ Students are given roles and task cards to begin their jobs.

- **Day 3:** Finish roles with task cards.
  - ○ Students share with group, then whole class.
  - ○ Make sure objectives have been met.

As teachers at Morrison Elementary School learned each of these strategies—Think-Pair-Share, Frayer model, and Reciprocal Teaching—they implemented them in their classrooms and analyzed student work products from these strategies by grade level each month. Each of these strategies, as well as the EL Shadowing process, is outlined further in the book *ELL Shadowing as a Catalyst for Change* (Soto, 2012), which includes video footage of teachers from Morrison Elementary School modeling use of the strategies.

Each of these examples emphasizes the need to create multiple opportunities for speaking and listening *throughout* the school day. Since ELs make personal meaning through discourse and the foundation of literacy is academic language, such opportunities are key to an EL's academic success. We use and recommend the *10-minute rule*: don't talk *at* students for more than 10 minutes, at which point required partner talk or other collaborative structures are introduced. Moreover, it should be obvious that such opportunities for student-to-student collaboration must be carefully planned for alignment with standards, learning intentions, and success criteria. The following Call to Action section includes additional information on how maximize the use of academic conversations.

THE CALL FOR ACTION

Shifting from EL silence to EL conversations is one of the most essential shifts to make to ensure the success of our language-learning students. Engage every student in academic conversations with peers in every lesson, every day. As evidenced by the previous case studies, this is a win-win-win shift as it benefits all students, benefits ELs, and benefits teachers by providing daily formative data about student thinking, learning, and language use.

In this section, we emphasize three areas for action to make this shift:

1. Replace Hand Raising with Effective Conversation Structures and Scaffolds

2. Make Conversations Routine in Everyday Teaching

3. Use Observation Data to Continuously Improve Classroom Conversations. For each we begin with essential shifts for teachers to make within the classroom, and then make recommendations for instructional leaders to effectively lead this work for collective change.

ESSENTIAL ACTION: REPLACE HAND RAISING WITH EFFECTIVE CONVERSATION STRUCTURES AND SCAFFOLDS

All teachers need to learn and use effective conversation structures and scaffolds to engage students in talking to one another rather than *only* raising hands to talk one at a time to the group.

For structures, Think-Pair-Share, introduced in the previous section, is a natural starting place to make conversations routine in the classroom. At a glance, this strategy has us ask a question, provide think time, then have partners discuss their ideas. As a final step, a teacher calls on individuals to share or report their idea or their partner's idea. There are many variations to this strategy and layers of scaffolds (like sentence frames or word banks) a teacher can choose to support students' language use or their critical-thinking and self-direction. For example, for pairs that need more guidance, it helps to model, guide, and structure every step. As students become more used to

This reminds me of a second-grade class I used to visit as an instructional coach. I was most impressed to see several Socratic circles running at the same time around the classroom, facilitated by students. Similar to a Socratic seminar used in secondary context, each child came well-prepared to the conversation with text annotations ready for discussion and scaffolded sentence frames available to support the interaction.
—Andrea

everyday partner conversations, these become as routine and easy for a teacher as asking students to "take out a piece of paper."

In addition to Think-Pair-Share, there are many other strategies to build upon your tool kit. One powerful variation to calling on individuals at the "share" step is to use the Build Ideas Ball Toss (Singer, 2018) to make the discussion student-led and encourage students to listen closely to build on one another's ideas.

Build Ideas Ball Toss at-a-Glance: After discussing a question with partners, students stand in a circle with the whole class. The teacher asks the same question partners discussed to invite students to bring their ideas to this whole-group setting and to hear new ideas from others. First, toss a ball to the first student who wants to share. All students turn to listen to the student holding the ball. After that student speaks, any student who wants to respond to the speaker (e.g., by asking a question, adding ideas, agreeing or disagreeing) raises a hand. The speaker, not the teacher, chooses who speaks next, and tosses the ball to that person.

The discussion follows with these guidelines, and often there is a long silence after one student speaks before another raises a hand. This silence is rich "think time" for ELs and all students who want to deeply listen and process their ideas. The teacher doesn't fill the space because this isn't expected—students are looking to each other, not the teacher, to see who will speak next. Students drive the conversation, and the teacher takes a back seat, except to listen and help with redirection if needed.

Some conversation structures like Think-Pair-Share and Build Up Ideas Ball Toss can be used in any context. Other strategies are specific to the context and task, such as Reciprocal Teaching protocol we described earlier in this chapter, a powerful routine for engaging students in collaborating to make meaning from texts through specific roles and protocols for academic conversations.

From partners to small groups to up-and-moving activities, there are many possible ways to structure peer conversations. Don't be daunted by the options, as the goal isn't to use as many as possible. The goal is to actively engage students in conversations in which they are more focused on the topic, the task, and the conversation than the actual structure you use. Start with Think-Pair-Share and make it routine because partner conversations engage the most students and are the easiest to manage. When you master partner conversations and seek variety, add other conversation structures to your tool-kit only as they help you engage your students productively in collaborative peer conversations to build equitable discourse in your classroom community and achieve rigorous content and language learning goals.

In addition to structures for how students converse (e.g., Think-Pair-Share), learn to use scaffolds to help ELs make effective language choices in academic conversations. (For a more extensive discussion on the use of scaffolds, refer to Chapter 3—"From Watering Down to Challenging.") Using partner or small-group structures for peer-to-peer conversations is important, but this alone doesn't ensure all ELs actively engage. It is important teachers also learn to strategically use (or lose) scaffolds that help ELs of all proficiency levels build on what they know and can do to engage with increasingly high-levels of success with the concepts and academic language of content tasks. Scaffolds that especially support academic language use during peer conversations include the following:

- **Linguistic Frames** (aka response frames, sentence frames). A linguistic frame is a partially completed sentence students say then complete with their own idea(s) in a conversation. For example, a teacher asking students to make and justify inferences may provide the frame "I infer _____ because _____" or a series of frames such as "I infer _____. One detail that shows me this is_____."

- **Word Banks**. A word bank is a group of words, often of the same part of speech, that students can use to complete a task. For example, when asking students to describe a character, a teacher may teach and post a word bank of character trait adjectives (e.g., courageous, fearful, generous, selfish, kind, mean) that students can use to express their ideas.

Use or lose linguistic frame(s) and word bank(s) as they are appropriate for the students and the task, as these are language scaffolds that should be internalized and eventually taken away. There is no one way to implement these scaffolds that will work for all ELs because ELs are not a monolithic group: they bring to conversations a wide range of prior knowledge, experiences, and proficiency levels in English and other languages. An emerging EL, for example, often benefits from a teacher providing a single linguistic frame along with a word bank of words (with pictures when possible) that can be used to complete the sentence. Modeling, gestures, and guided choral practice help emerging ELs use the frame and word bank to communicate ideas with a partner relevant to the classroom conversation. In this highly structured example, students then practice using the frame and word bank to express their own sentences orally using Think-Pair-Share. The substantial guidance and supports in this approach are optimal to help an emerging EL move from silence to conversation, and yet would hinder a conversation for more proficient speakers of English.

ELs with expanding-to-bridging English proficiency levels (and most fluent speakers) often benefit from having a range of linguistic frames (e.g., Based on _____, I infer _____) and prompts (How do you know? What's your evidence) posted as options to help extend the conversation and encourage an academic register. Posting multiple frames, including a simple sentence a teacher or peer can model and practice with an emerging EL, is one effective strategy to offer differentiated scaffolds in a diverse, multilingual classroom.

No matter the scaffolds you use, always watch and listen to students in conversation to see who participates, how they collaborate in conversation,

I so appreciated this explanation. Scaffolds—though the name itself suggests that they are temporary—may easily be misused with the best of intention.

—Andrea

and hear how they use language. Teachers can use power walks, in order to monitor and ensure that conversations remain on topic, or to answer questions. Notice if the scaffolds you provide seem to interfere with student thinking or natural discourse. Notice if they build on students' use of academic language or keep the sentences and vocabulary they have been using as a default for a long time. To get a good assessment of what students can do without your scaffolds, try structuring a peer conversation with the minimum scaffolds needed for students to engage. Watch and listen to see what students can already do on their own. Build on the strengths you observe to celebrate effective language choices, and address the needs by planning following modeling and strategic scaffolds to help students at all proficiency levels engage and use language with increasing levels of sophistication and self-direction.

Tips for Leaders to Scale This Shift

Build capacity of all teachers to structure conversations in the classroom, and use effective scaffolds to ensure ELs at all proficiency levels productively engage. The two case examples earlier in the chapter provide good illustrations of how sustained professional learning can promote the use of conversation structures across an entire school and system. This section includes more general leadership actions that can be applied in multiple settings to build a culture of continuous improvement focused on student impact. A first step is often having teachers learn and practice specific conversation structures and scaffolds, but do not stop here. Build time for teachers to collaborate to apply their learning to their specific lessons and curriculum to make peer conversations routine in everyday teaching. Use the protocols for Job-Embedded Professional Learning to Clarify and Calibrate Expectations in this book's Figure 3.2 (page 59) to build shared teacher clarity about what successful peer conversations look like. Then collaborate to co-plan active engagement, co-observe conversations (or co-analyze transcriptions of conversations), and then co-reflect to refine teaching and scaffolds for impact.

Lead change with a focus on student learning, not the scaffolds. Scaffolds are a means to the end. They are not the destination. When students arrive at the destination without scaffolds, that is something to celebrate. A common leadership misstep with EL scaffolds is to attempt to implement scaffolds at scale with checklists and walkthroughs focused on teacher actions alone. With scaffolds such as linguistic frames and word banks, it's critical these supports are not the goal you strive towards as a school. The goal you strive toward is all students actively engage in peer conversations in every classroom, every day. The goal is that all students use high-level thinking and academic language to express unique ideas that deepen their learning and collaboration across the curriculum. Keep the goal of impacting students at the center of your shared vision and build a community of learning and reflection through which teachers continuously use data to choose and lose scaffolds as appropriate to ensure ELs and all students succeed.

ESSENTIAL ACTION: MAKE CONVERSATIONS ROUTINE

Learning how to do a strategy is only the first step; applying conversation strategies to everyday teaching is a critical action to make academic conversations routine. One powerful and simple action teachers and schools can take collectively is to plan academic conversation tasks aligned to core curriculum. Administrators, make time for teachers to collaborate to plan academic conversations into everyday teaching. Teachers, use this time to collaborate to plan high-level conversation tasks that align with your core content goals and curriculum.

Here are examples of what this might look like in different content areas:

In reading, choose a text students will read (or you will read aloud to students), and identify the points before, during, and after the reading in which you will have students engage in a peer discussion to anticipate, read to understand, and revisit a text to analyze, infer, or draw conclusions. High-level thinking tasks often elicit the best conversations as they do not require a single "right answer" but invite the sharing of diverse perspectives, and elaboration with evidence and explanation. Write or choose at least one high-level question about a text that is text-dependent, open-ended, and aligned to goals you want to emphasize (e.g., theme illustrated in the opening of this chapter).

In mathematics, a rich opportunity for peer-to-peer conversations is after students sketch out a solution to an open-ended problem with many possible solutions. Have partners discuss: How did you solve the problem? Why? To invite more negotiating, ask them, Which approach to solving the problem would you use to teach another student? Why?

One easy approach to planning conversations is to insert a large self-stick note into the text, the teacher's edition, or lesson plan. On that note, (1) write the conversation prompt or question, (2) write the structure you'll use for the discussion (e.g., Think-Pair-Share), and (3) write the scaffolds you'll provide to support and extend academic language use (e.g., linguistic frames or word banks).

Tips for Leaders to Scale This Shift

Lead with a shared vision for academic conversations: Change initiatives are most powerful with a shared vision and sense of urgency (Kotter, 2012). Make conversations a priority and use your precious time in staff meetings with the leadership team and with teacher collaboration to collectively realize this powerful shift. Make time for teachers to plan academic conversations aligned to their curriculum.

Look for and listen to conversations in classrooms: Make conversations the focus of your informal classroom walkthroughs and your conversations with teachers about instruction. In walkthroughs, notice when students are engaged in extended conversations and take notes on the task, the scaffolds, and what you hear students say and do. Share success stories back with the staff so they can celebrate the shifts happening across the school.

Align all initiatives: Promoting the routine implementation of academic conversations is not "just another initiative." Rather, think of it as one of those "things that make the other things work!" If you have many competing initiatives in your school and district, seek ways to synthesize and align so you can focus and go deep in your work to strengthen academic conversations. For example, one elementary school has a new math adoption and is in a district that is emphasizing higher-level thinking in all professional learning. Don't add one more thing to the plate! Instead, focus on improving academic conversations in math aligned to higher-level thinking tasks. It's a natural place to start that is relevant and aligned to what you are already doing. This gives you more time to go deep as the work you do planning, listening to, and analyzing student conversations will help teachers strengthen their teaching of math and their use of high-level thinking tasks. Win-Win-Win!

ESSENTIAL ACTIONS: USE OBSERVATION DATA TO CONTINUOUSLY IMPROVE

Learning strategies and integrating conversations into lesson plans is a great start, but alone will not lead to the ultimate shift from silence to conversation for ELs. Sometimes our conversations don't go as planned. Students are still silent. Or some students dominate and others are quiet. Students speak, but perhaps only in words and phrases using social language not the academic language of school. Sometimes every student engages in talking, but no one seems to be listening or few understand the rigorous task. For true transformations, we must use the formative data our student conversations provide us to reflect and refine our teaching so every EL, and every student, succeeds.

Listen to students as they engage in conversation to gather formative data about students' strengths and needs with the content, language, and conversation required for the task. Use that data to reflect and refine your scaffolds and approach to structuring conversions.

Collaborative conversations are a rich source of formative data about content understandings, confusions, language use, student thinking, and more (Singer & Zwiers, 2016). Use data of successes to raise rigor, remove scaffolds, and release responsibility to students to drive their own academic conversations. Use data of challenges to increase modeling and linguistic supports. As a teacher, use data in the moment every single day.

For example, use this three-step "Engage, Observe, Support" sequence (Singer, 2018) to use observation data to determine the optimal level of modeling and support your students need in this moment to take their conversations to the next level:

1. Engage students with the minimum scaffolds necessary to ensure they feel comfortable and know what to do.

2. Observe to gather formative data about the assets they bring to the conversation task in terms of content understandings, language, and conversation skills.

3. Add or remove scaffolds as appropriate to foster increased participation, student thinking, and academic language use.

In addition to using observation data in the moment to refine your own teaching, collaborate with colleagues in a cycle of inquiry about your impact. First, clarify your vision for academic conversations with a teaching partner, co-teacher, or in collaborative teams, by using the protocols in Figure 3.2 (p. 59) to identify success criteria for effective conversations. Next, plan a task and try it with your students. Finally, analyze conversations together. You can do this by easily by filming conversations on your phones and/or by transcribing a few select student conversations to co-analyze together. Take notes on what students say and how student interact. Analyze where students are in relation to your goals and then reflect and refine your approach to help them continue to grow their oral language and conversation skills across the curriculum.

Open classroom doors to even deeper collaboration to shift classroom conversations with co-teaching (Dove & Hongisfeld, 2018), lesson study, or observation inquiry (OI) (Singer, 2015). Many teams use OI to build collective teacher efficacy to transform their classrooms from EL silence to EL success in rigorous, academic conversations.

For example, at San Miguel Elementary School in Northern California, a team of kindergarten teachers collaborated using Observation Inquiry (Singer, 2015), a design for collaborative professional learning. They applied this process to solve the problem-of-practice that their ELs and students in poverty struggled to engage in partner discussions and rarely used text evidence in their conversations about texts read aloud. Of the school's students, 17% were ELs and 39% were eligible for free or reduced-priced lunch. Through OI, San Miguel's teachers noticed that most classroom conversations were between the teacher and the very few students who raised their hands to speak. Students doing the most talking often represented the school majority: white, fluent English speakers ineligible for free or reduced-price lunch.

The team decided to address this problem by structuring high-level partner conversations about texts they read aloud with intentional visual and linguistic scaffolds. They applied their theory to plan partner conversations for a specific read-aloud text and then watched as one team member taught the lesson. During the lesson, observers each focused on a pair of students (pre-selected to focus on ELs and students eligible for free or reduced-price lunch) and wrote detailed notes on how they participated and what they said. After the lesson, the team collaborated to analyze their data with the following five steps:

1. Describe specific observations without judgment.

2. Organize observation data to find connections and themes.

3. Make generalizations.

4. Build on successes and brainstorm ways to address challenges.

5. Apply learning to set goals and plan the next lesson to observe together.

Between October and February, the team met four times to repeat this process with a new read-aloud text in a different teachers' classroom. With each lesson, the team refined their approach to asking questions, structuring conversations, and using scaffolds. As student conversations, thinking, and academic language use evolved, the team continuously raised the rigor of tasks and released responsibility to foster increased student initiative. Through 12 total hours of OI collaboration, every teacher on the team shifted from first trying partner conversations as a new strategy to skillfully integrating conversations and strategic EL scaffolds into their daily read-aloud routine.

OI is not specific to a grade level or content area. It is simply a protocol that helps teachers collaborate using observation data to build their collective efficacy and transform teaching together. Through the shared ownership and risk-taking in the OI process, teams shift from only learning strategies or talking about structuring conversations to actually co-planning, co-observing, co-supporting, co-reflecting, and refining teaching until all students productively engage in academic conversations to deepen academic language and literacy learning. Such an instructional shift across *all* classrooms does not happen through workshops alone. Research on professional learning tells us that, although workshops help most participants gain understanding, fewer than 10% of participants apply the learning from one-shot workshops to their teaching (Joyce & Showers, 1995). It takes sustained opportunities for practice and continuous evaluation of one's impact to actually change instruction in meaningful ways. Working with a coach or participating in collaborative professional learning designs such as OI are effective means to solving the "knowing-doing gap."

Tips for Leaders to Scale This Shift

Value Conversation Data. Highlight conversation data in your data conversations at the school. Use conversation data in your cycles of continuous improvement, not just results from pen-to-paper or computer-driven assessments. If you say you want academic conversations, and then only seek, analyze, and hold teachers accountable for high-stakes assessment data, there will be a gap between vision and action.

There are many ways to engage a whole staff in using conversation data to drive the shift from EL silence to dynamic academic conversations in every lesson every day. The EL Shadowing Protocol we describe earlier in this chapter is powerful for building a shared understanding of who is doing the talking in classrooms and specifically how ELs participate or are silent (Soto, 2012). Shadowing helps you see the current state of oral participation in classrooms and establish a shared urgency to change practice. You can also repeat the protocol after making changes to identify and celebrate successful shifts in discourse across an entire school. In addition to gathering school-wide information via Shadowing, engage teachers in collaborating to use their observation of conversations in their own classrooms to continuously refine their teaching. When release time is an option, use the OI protocol to engage teams in continuous inquiry about impact. When teams only have time to meet outside of classrooms, engage teams in co-analyzing conversations (transcribed or filmed) with a shared rubric to identify strengths and needs. Observation data is essential for identifying and shifting the hard-to-quantify skills we value like academic language use, discourse skills, and student collaboration. More significantly, observation data is essential for seeing who speaks and who is silent, and collaborating to ensure equity and opportunity for voice in all classrooms across a school.

Be in Inquiry About Equity. Look to see who is talking in a classroom and who is not talking in a classroom. Compare data by EL status, by language group, by race and ethnicity, by socio-economic level, by gender. What trends do you notice? What inequities exist? What factors within a school's control could be influencing those inequities in participation? What shifts in teacher mindsets, classroom cultures, and/or instructional actions will be most effective to shift those trends so ALL students have equal voice in your learning community?

> Sustained teacher collaboration helps with any of the specifics recommended in this chapter!
> —Andrea

Summary and Conclusions

Although the shift from silence to conversation may strike some readers as fairly straightforward and basic, we believe that its implications for the future are revolutionary!

Student-centered classrooms and student voices can engage and motivate everyone within a system. The systemic implementation of collaborative conversations will create equitable classroom conversations from which all students will benefit. Oftentimes in classrooms, we hear only the voices of students of privilege who already have a strong academic identity and have been well-served by schools. Strategies like Think-Pair-Share, where students are required to stop and think about their responses before they share them, allow everyone to participate. When we don't provide adequate wait time, or time for students to think about and/or write down their responses before they share them, everyone in the classroom suffers, as we'll only hear from the same voices. Even our gifted or precocious students need time to stop and think about their responses before they share them out in order to make sure that they are sharing their best thoughts and not their first thoughts. Similarly, ELs often need that additional wait and think time to process both language and content. With the assistance of an intentional or linguistic model during partner or Think-Pair-Share conversations, ELs can also begin to produce more sophisticated language.

All students also benefit from student-centered classrooms in that multiple perspectives will be heard and validated. While working in pairs or teams may feel awkward at first, collaboration and working with others are fundamental skills that are required in most careers in which our students will enter. When we hear the same voices again and again, we tend to hear the same ideas (what author Chimamanda Ngozi Adichie calls "The Danger of a Single Story"), which closes us to opportunities for creativity and innovation. When students are taught *how* to collaborate, they will solve problems and think critically about ideas together. This means that during collaborative conversations students have to be taught *how* to come to consensus. They need to be taught that their ideas can and will be strengthened by sharing them with others. Students must then strategically be taught how to be democratic about sharing out ideas with the whole class. The teacher can do this by teaching and modeling how to come to consensus, as well as justifying why they came to that consensus decision. Some options for consensus are: (1) sharing their own idea with the whole class, and not just because the student is precocious; (2) sharing their partner's idea with the class, and not because he or she is shy; (3) comparing and combining ideas because there were similarities when sharing; or (4) arriving with a whole new idea as a result of the conversation, and/or because the conversation led them in a new direction. These options must be modeled, practiced, and reinforced in order for true consensus to occur.

In order for group work to be equitable and democratic, it is essential that group work norms be in place. Students must trust each other and practice working with each other often. Trust can be built by having a classroom discussion about the importance of group work, the advantages of becoming a democratic classroom, as well as allowing everyone to have a voice, and being willing to take language and cognitive risks with each other. One way to get there is to have students co-construct group work norms with the teacher—a practice that offers students voice and choice as well as collective ownership. It is also essential that when first practicing productive group work, each student has a role, so that one person does not complete all of the work for the group. This will also assist with groups eventually becoming interdependent and self-regulating, which can happen with enough group work time and practice.

Classrooms with equitable and democratic structures such as the ones described above produce students with those same values. Just imagine what could happen to our society if we all engaged in and practiced equitable and democratic partnerships and groups every day. We would create leaders who were capable of listening and working collaboratively with each other! All students, including ELs, will rise to the level of our expectations. If, as educators, we consistently model and reinforce equitable and democratic conversations in the classroom setting, our students will begin using them with and beyond the classroom to speak, listen, and collaborate for a better world.

References

Arreaga-Mayer, C., & Perdomo-Rivera, C. (1996). Ecobehavioral analysis of instruction for at-risk language-minority students. *The Elementary School Journal, 96*(3), 245–258. doi:10.1086/461826.

August, D., & Shanahan, T. (2006). *Developing literacy in second-language learners: Report of the National Literacy Panel on language-minority children and youth.* Mahway, NJ: Laurence Earlbaum and Associates.

Bunch, G. C., Kibler, A., & Pimentel, S. (2013, April). *Realizing opportunities for English learners in the Common Core language arts and disciplinary literacy standards.* Paper presented at 2013 Annual Meeting of the American Educational Research Association. Retrieved from https://ell.stanford.edu/sites/default/files/events/Bunch-Kibler-Pimentel_AERA_2013-04-08.pdf

Gibbons, P. (2002). *Scaffolding Language, Scaffolding Learning.* Portsmouth, NH: Heinemann.

Hammond, Z. (2015). *Culturally responsive teaching and the brain: Promoting authentic engagement and rigor among culturally and linguistically diverse students.* Thousand Oaks, CA: Corwin.

Hattie, J. (2012). *Visible learning for teachers: Maximizing impact on learning.* New York, NY: Routledge.

Joyce, B., & B. Showers. (1995). *Student Achievement Through Staff Development: Fundamentals of School Renewal. 2nd ed.* White Plains, N.Y.: Longman.

Kotter, J. (2012). *Leading change.* Boston, MA: Harvard Business Review Press.

Nystrand, M. (2006). Research on the role of classroom discourse as it affects reading comprehension. *Research in the Teaching of English, 40,* 392–412.

Singer, T. (2015). *Opening doors to equity: A practical guide to observation-based professional learning.* Thousand Oaks, CA: Corwin.

Singer, T. (2018). *EL excellence every day: The flip-to guide for differentiating academic literacy.* Thousand Oaks, CA: Corwin.

Singer, T., & Zwiers, J. (2016, April). What conversations can capture. *Educational Leadership, 73*(7). Retrieved from http://www.ascd.org/publications/educational-leadership/apr16/vol73/num07/What-Conversations-Can-Capture.aspx

Singleton, G. (2014). *Courageous Conversations About Race.* Thousand Oaks, CA: Corwin Press.

Soto, I. (2012). *ELL shadowing as a catalyst for change.* Thousand Oaks, CA: Corwin.

Soto-Hinman & Hetzel (2009). *The Literacy Gaps: Building Bridges for ELLs and SELs.* Thousand Oaks, CA: Corwin Press.

Zwiers, J., & Soto, I. (2016). *Academic language mastery: Conversational discourse in context.* Thousand Oaks, CA: Corwin.

Zwiers, J., & Crawford, M. (2011). *Academic conversations: Classroom talk that fosters critical thinking and content understandings.* Portland, ME: Stenhouse.

chapter six

From Language to Language, Literacy, and Content

MARGARITA ESPINO CALDERÓN
AND SHAWN SLAKK

PREMISE

Every content teacher in a school is a language, literacy, and content teacher. Every school goes from teaching language in isolation to teaching language and literacy in the context of all subject areas. ELs benefit from integrated, well-designed content, language objectives, and meaningful, challenging, and motivating instruction rich with content. This is content that is clearly designed and explicitly modeled to provide background and a foundation upon which to practice and apply newly acquired language and literacy skills. Teaching academic language, discourse, reading comprehension, and academic writing is achieved by implementing empirically tested strategies in all core content areas in elementary and all core content classrooms in secondary schools.

VIGNETTE

Ivan—I don't know why I didn't do good on my test. I'm a good student. I study hard. I always did. I was in a bilingual program in first and second grade and then to third grade in all English. That was hard! But, my third-grade teacher said I was a nice attentive boy and she let Samuel translate for me and we sat in the back all the time. She passed me to the fourth grade because I was a nice boy and studied hard. My fourth-grade teacher also said I was a well-behaved boy, but my grades weren't very good. She passed me to fifth grade anyway. That teacher asked Francisco to sit in the back with me and help me. We always finished our worksheets; we worked quietly, stayed out of trouble, but we didn't pass the big test. The good thing is that they sent us to middle school anyway! They said we could catch up with our English there.

The Student's Plight. Ivan is an eighth-grade student who is still labeled as Limited English Proficient (LEP) as per federal guidelines. Through his elementary school years, he was provided ESOL in either pull-out or push-in modes (see Chapter 10 on the different models and the challenges with each). His story—one that is all too common—is about being relegated to the back of the bus to keep out of trouble. He learned to comply with this and was rewarded by being passed from grade to grade.

What is missing for students like Ivan? Active and successful participation in all core content areas that depends upon use and comprehension of the content presented in English, and, if the student is in a Dual Language program, in another language as well. When English is the sole language of instruction, then students have no other option than to become proficient in the academic vocabulary and discourse protocols of math, science, social studies, electives, as well as English language arts. Students must also have the required literacy skills to read and comprehend dense materials in all the content areas to meet this proficiency goal. When instruction is in two languages (e.g., Spanish and English; Arabic and English; Mandarin and English), students need to be equally proficient in both languages. Both languages can be developed simultaneously, even on the same day, not one before the other (Slavin & Cheung, 2005). We also know from research (Calderón & Carreón, 2001) that both languages can be developed at grade level from the onset and have a greater impact on students' academic achievement. In brief, a rigorous systematic instruction in all subjects seemed to be missing for Ivan and other Long-Term English learners. Our collective belief in this book is that every educator should be committed to multilingual instruction. See Chapter 8 regarding the merits of multilingualism for details.

What is missing for teachers today? If we know what works, why are teachers feeling disenfranchised just as Ivan did? Core content teachers feel left out, and ESOL/ELD teachers feel overwhelmed with huge workloads. Yet most school structures are not set up for their collaboration, as in Ms. Anderson's case:

> *Ms. Anderson—This is my fourth year as an ESOL teacher at this middle school. I am not pleased with the gains my students make in the subject areas. I try to work with the pre-algebra and biology teachers, but we rarely coincide on a schedule. I have a caseload of 60 ELs. I pull them out of language arts, some from math, and some from history. The history teacher says they don't understand anything anyway. The science teacher lets me come in and help the 6 ELs that are in that class. As much as I try, I cannot give those 6 ELs quality time. I don't speak Urdu or Farsi, and only a little Spanish. I keep asking the principal to hire another ESOL teacher, but each year it is the same answer: we don't have the budget.*

The Teacher's Plight. Ms. Anderson's conundrum shows the plight of many ESOL/ELD teachers who have to provide services to small and large numbers of ELs, at different grade levels, for different subjects, with different core content teachers, without adequate materials and very tight schedules. Sometimes they have to pick up students for a pull-out class from four or five different classrooms, teach, and take students back to class in record-breaking 30-minute timetables. ESOL/ELD teachers are typically the adults that EL students turn to for moral support, translations, advocacy, and family connections. They participate in IEP meetings, EL performance assessment teams, and are most likely the person who district EL specialists or project administrators go to at a school.

What is missing in these schools? All teachers need adequate preparation to teach their culturally and linguistically diverse students in their respective content areas if all students are expected to succeed academically (August, et al., 2008; National Academies of Sciences, Engineering, and Medicine, 2017). The fundamental problem has been that content teachers have not been expected to integrate language and literacy development into their content areas. As a result, content and language are divorced from one another. Language is the domain of the ESOL/ELD teacher, and content is the realm of content teachers, and they have been separated by non-pedagogical reasons. This separation is contrary to everything we know about promoting EL achievement.

In spite of research panels and evidence-based practices, language-literacy-content instruction for English learners and learners in ESOL or sheltered English or Dual Language Programs is still disjointed and not as effective as it could be (National Academies for Science, Engineering, and Medicine, 2017). For example, at some elementary schools vocabulary and academic language are usually taught as "an end in itself." They rarely connect to the reading that students do that day in their subject areas. Basic reading and reading comprehension skills are taught as a separate curriculum laid out in a textbook series, or students are told to enter a text without attention to the vocabulary needed as a precursor to reading those texts. The sad result is that ELs and other students are not reading very much. Writers workshops take a life of their own, using worksheets to practice grammatical structures instead of techniques for drafting, editing, and revising using a given set of techniques explicitly taught.

THE URGENCY

Elementary schools across the country continue to produce Long-Term ELs, and high schools continue to produce high dropout rates and low graduation rates for ELs. The absence of whole-school (and whole-district) support; the artificial separation of content, language, and literacy; and poor preparation of faculty, instructional coaches, and leaders have resulted in a *crisis* for ELs and other underserved students.

We have failed generations of ELs

- By not keeping pace with the ever-changing, ever-growing population of ELs (e.g., the more recent children separated from their parents/ guardians and escalating fears of deportation).

- By adopting unsound approaches/methodologies/curricula with little or no evidence.

- By not offering comprehensive professional development for the whole school on evidence-based approaches.

- By not sustaining and monitoring implementation of that professional development.

The problem in schools such as the one that Ivan and Ms. Anderson belong to is their failure to address the needs of English learners, Long-Term ELs, newcomers with interrupted formal education, ELs in special education, and the rest of the student population in a systematic whole-school approach. These schools are marked by lack of involvement of the whole school and district in focusing on the EL needs. Without a whole-school approach, the consequences have been low achievement levels, high dropout rates, and the school being labeled as a low-performing school, which in turn have resulted in a *crisis f*or ELs and other underserved students.

The Future Is Here; Time to Move On

Other chapters in this book eloquently elaborate on the many programmatic and infrastructure issues facing ELs today. Federal guidelines and possible ramifications for failing to meet those recommendations are outlined in a previous chapter. In this chapter we will focus on the moral imperative we have to design and develop common, evidence-based instructional features that not only help promote EL achievement but also promote success across the entire student body. This chapter describes instruction for ELs in mainstream/general education core content classrooms that also benefit all learners, thus leveling the field in all schools. It describes instructional strategies that content and ESOL/ELD teachers can use to effectively and jointly develop language, literacy, and content for any learner. (For strategies on team teaching, see Chapter 4.) We also cover the type of professional development that yields such quality instruction, and we share examples of how teachers, instructional coaches, and administrators are systematically moving into a whole-school instruction focused on EL success.

Why the Need to Move On?

For decades, many second language instructional approaches and curricula have been introduced and have become commonplace. They have been popularized by word of mouth but have scant or no evidence of effectiveness with ELs. More significantly, they are not working for ESOL/ELD teachers who pull out students for 30 minutes or push in to a classroom where they are asked to translate or help the ELs in any way they can. Additionally, in some states, instructional assistants are still the main instructors for ELs.

Historically, certain sheltered English strategies have not worked for math, science, social studies, language arts teachers who primarily teach native English speakers, as evidenced by the high percentages of Long-Term ELs in states that required this instruction. For example, California has 14.7% and Massachusetts 12% (Migration Policy Institute, 2018). Sheltered English instruction sets out to make content comprehensible to ELs. However, most core content teachers are not well prepared to shelter their content, or they shelter too much with low expectations. Even in a class full of ELs, we find that some sheltered instruction strategies can't seem to help ELs pass their language proficiency exams because they lack rigorous systematic instruction. It is time to move away from pedagogy that has yielded 70% to 85% Long-Term ELs nationwide, like Ivan in our opening vignette, who has been in U.S. schools since kindergarten and is still unable to pass English proficiency or core content tests in middle or high school. While secondary schools are the ones where failure is most evident for ELs, we must acknowledge that elementary grades are the "make it or break it" foundation for middle and high school ELs' success. To support and set the stage from the beginning, the instruction and professional development frameworks delineated here also need to be enacted in elementary schools. We cannot emphasize enough that instructional rigor and higher expectations must start from day 1 of a student's education in the early grades. As researchers point out, ELs must learn 3,000 to 5,000 words a year before they get to middle school (Graves, August, & Carlo, 2011). Elementary schools can now have the instructional wherewithal and educator skill and disposition if they wish to ensure that no Long-Term EL goes on to middle school.

As Dual Language programs begin to emerge once again in California and across the country, particularly in elementary schools, the quality of student outcomes must be the ultimate goal (see Chapter 8, "From Monolingualism to Multilingualism"). Teachers need to be prepared to provide rigorous academic language, depth of reading comprehension, and text-based writing skills in all subjects to enable students to be ready for middle and high school success. Unfortunately, disjointed language, literacy and content approaches, lack of rigor, and/or not enough attention to one of the two languages also become particularly detrimental to students in Dual Language programs. Moreover, collaboration between and among teachers and administrators of the two languages is meager due to school structures that have not changed in decades. In English-only or English-mainly classrooms when ESOL/ELD teachers and core content teachers use two different sets of instructional strategies and philosophies, students often become confused, learning is made more difficult, and precious instructional time is wasted. Second language learners or Dual Language Learners benefit from consistency, challenging yet achievable goals, and quality instruction.

Margarita and Shawn beautifully capture the complex challenges that many educators are experiencing. Despite our individual commitment and dedication to the success of English learners, our work must be a collective effort where everyone participates in finding the just-right scientifically proven practices that are successful for our particular ELs.
—Debbie

THE VISION

Meeting the Challenge and Implications for Practice in Culturally and Linguistically Diverse Classrooms

Mr. Martinez—A middle school principal in a different school states: Now that all our middle school teachers and administrators have been trained on how to integrate language, literacy, and content, we are scheduled to meet with our feeder high school counterparts before school starts in August. They were also trained a year ago and are looking forward to building on our efforts to support the ELs we will send their way next September. The high school principal spoke at our eighth-grade graduation to set a welcoming tone, while still setting high expectations. From now on, department chairs from both schools will meet once a quarter to review EL progress trajectories and plan forward by disciplines. We used to say, "ELs are the responsibility of the ESOL teacher." Now, teachers from feeder schools say, "We are all language, literacy, and content teachers. We know this new mindset and our instructional tools are helping our ELs, along with their classmates, our former ELs, and even our advanced placement students! We already saw last year's student gains. This year promises to yield stronger results as our schools share responsibility and collective efficacy toward teaching and reaching all our students." As the principal, I have the responsibility to support the teachers and students.

The Principal's Dedication. Mr. Martinez's determination to have the whole school involved is indicative of a school and district's commitment to serving middle and high school ELs in a way that promotes not only the multilingual student population but also students at large. Martinez, the principal of this Virginia middle school, has attended a series of in-depth professional development sessions with his whole staff on EL instruction and participated in two additional leadership development days on how to design the right infrastructure to serve the students, how to support teachers, and tools to sustain a quality implementation.

The District's Support. The Loudoun County Public Schools' district office has supported Mr. Martinez with messaging and resources for his school and staff as well as the other middle and high schools that educate large numbers of immigrant students from Central America, Mexico, Eastern European countries, Africa, Asia, and the Middle East. The district set the tone for commitment by establishing monthly meetings where Mr. Martinez and his fellow leaders at the other schools exchange plans and review students' learning progressions. Moreover, the district administration added the resources so that all 400+ teachers and administrators from the four schools could receive comprehensive professional development (PD) on integrating academic language, reading comprehension, and writing for ELs into all disciplines. After the comprehensive PD sessions were delivered, lesson development and teacher collegial opportunities were established by the schools for continuous learning and checking progress. Mr. Martinez and his fellow principals and the district staff are wholly committed to a quality implementation.

These Virginia schools are quite a contrast with Ivan's and Ms. Anderson's schools, where their experiences illustrate different levels of inequity, prejudice, neglect—occurrences still prevalent in so many schools across the country. In contrast, the dedication and determination to properly serve ELs as shown by Mr. Martinez and his colleagues' commitment is one of the best exemplary efforts we have seen recently. Their buy-in came from attending extensive professional development along with their teachers and their own follow-up academy on how to support and coach their teachers. If this school district in northern Virginia can do this, any district across the country can.

As discussed in Chapter 2, recent revisions to the accountability provisions of the Elementary and Secondary Education Act, beginning with No Child Left Behind and continuing with ESSA (Every Student Succeeds Act), have been an impetus for taking a closer look at instruction of ELs. Schools/educators must now seek student performance improvement. Such efforts must start with improving all language and content knowledge and skills and reversing the soft bigotry of low expectations that lead to low academic performance of Hispanic and other language-minority students in the middle and high school settings. Middle and high school students must be ready to participate in rigorous academic programs that will lead to college, career, and productive citizenship.

ESSA calls for qualified teachers for ELs and all students. In addition to professional qualifications of teachers, ESSA also calls for teachers to have a profound knowledge of student achievement disaggregated by subgroups; comparisons of students at basic, proficient, and advanced levels of language and literacy development, assessment processes to measure progress, interpretation of data, and implications for instructional improvement; and an ample instructional repertoire that reaches all students—a tall order for all schools because all schools now have ELs. As we work with schools in states where one would not expect to find ELs, we encounter whole faculties and their administrators wanting to know how to create better teaching and learning environments. They just need the right tools.

It is our hope and vision that in the near future, Pre-K–12 schools, regardless of program type (Dual Language programs, the variety of Structured English Immersion/Sheltered English programs, and the required ESOL/ELD blocks), embrace an integrated, systematic instructional approach to teaching vocabulary/academic language, reading comprehension, and writing, integrated with social-emotional skill development and core content mastery.

The evidence-based challenge across all content areas is to include instruction on basic and academic vocabulary/discourse (Carlo, August, & Snow, 2005;

Nagy, 2005; Calderón, 2005; Calderón et al., 2005; Graves, August, & Carlo, 2011; Calderón & Soto, 2017) as a precursor to reading comprehension (August & Shanahan, 2006; Fisher, Frey, & Lapp, 2012; Zwiers & Soto, 2017) that leads to excellent academic writing (Graham & Perin, 2007). Well-designed cooperative learning (Slavin, 1995; Calderón, 1994; Calderón, 1999) and the positive evidence from using bilingual cooperative reading and composition on making the transition from Spanish to English (Calderón, Hertz-Lazarowitz, & Slavin, 1998) fortify this instruction in order to simultaneously develop language, literacy, content, and social emotional skills. This comprehensive instruction is integrated within all subject areas, not just language arts. Math, science, social studies, and electives teachers adopt the same instructional focus for all students to succeed. Instruction is aligned with curricula and integrated with existing requirements from state standards, WIDA or other language assessments, and district trends. Such a challenge can only be met by engaging whole schools in comprehensive, long-term (ideally three to five years, depending upon the size of the district) professional development focused on fidelity, but not rigidity, and quality of implementation connected to and grounded in content and standards.

THE EVIDENCE

The practices that we advocate in the remainder of this chapter are grounded in a rich body of scientific evidence. The latest research panel from the National Academies of Science, Engineering, and Medicine (2017) was convened to examine evidence based on research relevant to the development of Dual Language Learners and ELs from birth to age 21 to inform education and health policies and related policies that can result in better education outcomes (p. S-1). The panel reached several conclusions about instruction in elementary, middle, and high schools.

Their conclusion for **elementary schools** was that

> the following instructional practices are effective in developing elementary school-aged ELs' knowledge of academic subject matter: providing explicit instruction focused on developing key aspects of literacy; developing academic language during content area instruction; providing support to make core content comprehensible; encouraging peer-assisted learning opportunities; capitalizing on students' home language, knowledge, and cultural assets; screening for language and literacy challenges and monitoring progress; and providing small-group academic support for students to learn grade-level core content. The report declared that, "Instruction that fails to address appropriately the linguistic, cultural, socioemotional, and academic needs of ELs when they first enter elementary school leads to their lack of progress and to the growing number of Long-Term ELs in secondary schools which in turn can lead to disengagement in these students. (National Academies of Science, Engineering, and Medicine, 2017)

The fundamental recommendation for **middle schools** was that

> literacy engagement is critical during the middle school grades. During these grades, students are required to read and learn from advanced and complex grade-level texts. For ELs, this problem is acute because instructional support for Long-Term English learners tends to emphasize skills instead of dealing with the barriers to their motivation to learn, engagement in the classroom, and literacy engagement. (pp. 8–27)

For high schools, they assert that while there is little research at the **high school** level,

> some promising practices include a focus on academic language development that embraces all facets of academic language and includes both oral and written language across content areas; structured reading and writing instruction using a cognitive strategies approach and explicit instruction in reading comprehension strategies; opportunities for extended discussion of text and its meaning between teachers and students and in peer groups that may foster motivation and engagement in literacy learning; provision of peer-assisted learning opportunities; and rigorous, focused, and relevant support for Long-Term ELs. (pp. 8–28)

An early report that called attention to EL literacy was the Carnegie Report, *Double the Work: Challenges and Solutions to Acquiring Language and Academic Literacy for Adolescent English Language Learners* (2007). The Advisory Panel states that although many strategies for supporting literacy in native English speakers are applicable to adolescent ELs, there are significant differences in the way that successful literacy interventions for the latter group should be designed and implemented. Since ELs are still developing proficiency in academic English at the same time they are studying core content areas through English, ELs must perform double the work of native English speakers in middle and high schools (Short & Fitzsimmons, 2007, p.1). They broadly list the following eight "potential solutions" with the research supporting each:

1. Integrate all four language skills into instruction from the start.

2. Teach the components and processes of reading and writing.

3. Teach reading comprehension strategies.

4. Focus on vocabulary development.

5. Build and activate background knowledge.

6. Use native language strategically.

7. Pair technology with existing interventions.

8. Motivate ELs through choice.

These conclusions are very similar to those recommended by a second panel convened by the Carnegie Corporation (2010) of New York in the report titled *Time to Act: An Agenda for Advancing Adolescent Literacy for College*

> The National Academies of Science, Engineering, and Medicine findings show us the importance of using an approach that taps into students' individual and collective social, cultural, and linguistic strengths.
> —Debbie

and Career Success. This report adds to the first by describing ways to re-engineer schools for a culture that is organized for learning. For instruction, they highlighted the need for "all content area classes be permeated by a strong literacy focus" (p. 36).

The Carnegie vision is literacy for all. Yet they found that the pace of literacy improvement has not kept up with the pace of growth in the global economy, and literacy gains have not been extended to adolescents in the secondary grades. Hence, the urgency is for districts to provide the leadership and financial support to build principals' and teachers' capacity in schools with large numbers of striving readers, including ELs. For ELs, they recommend that assessments guide the enrollment and placement in an appropriately supportive educational program and monitor students' academic and social development. They highly recommend establishing programs and processes for the students who self-select to transition out of bilingual programs, from one grade level to another, into general education classrooms, into college and careers (Carnegie Council on Advancing Adolescent Literacy, 2010).

Simultaneously, the Carnegie Corporation of New York funded a five-year empirical study for developing and testing a model that integrated language, literacy, and subject areas as outlined in their reports. Their request was to focus on instruction and professional development models that could be used for general education, ESOL/ELD, and Dual Language teachers in sixth to twelfth grades. The model was tested in middle and high schools in New York City and Kauai, Hawaii, in math, science, social studies, electives, and language arts classrooms with small and large numbers of ELs, SPED-ELs, and general education students. Students in experimental schools outperformed students in matched control schools on the Woodcock-Muñoz vocabulary/reading battery and state assessments (Calderón & Miyana-Rowe, 2011; Calderón & Slakk, 2018).

The whole-school model, supported by five years of student and implementation evidence from New York and Kauai, mirrored the recommendations in the National Academies' 2017 publication. More importantly, abundant evidence from the Carnegie studies demonstrated great gains for ELs *and all students* when instruction is organized in a similar way and embraced as a schoolwide initiative. Since then, we have seen the same positive results in many schools in Virginia, Salt Lake City, Memphis, among other areas, where all core content/ESOL/ELD teachers in a school are involved as well as site and central office administrators. The experimental schools that used this language, literacy, content model schoolwide continue to show positive effects over the years. Schools went from low-achieving to exemplary in two years. This framework for instruction and professional development continues to be refined and is now widely implemented as a whole-school approach to ensure success for ELs and all students.

> Margarita and Shawn's research findings show the urgency for a holistic school-district-wide approach to educating ELs.
> —Debbie

As the framework is used across United States and other countries, educators are beginning to see and experience how its all-embracing core turns perspectives 180 degrees as it approaches whole-school student success from a different lens. The lens zooms out from an English learner perspective to encompass all striving readers, reluctant writers, and students in advanced placement classes who need all those pieces they were not offered along the way. Most importantly, it integrates English learners from diverse cultures into a well-cared-for environment where they can practice social emotional strategies (Montenegro, 2017).

This type of comprehensive model adheres to the ESSA focus since (1) both content and process are connected, (2) the approach is evidence-based by empirically testing components in experimental-control schools for five years, (3) the model addresses the need of rigorous instruction for all students in low- and high-diversity schools, (4) it proposes content-focused collaboration opportunities for all teachers and administrators, and (5) contains effectiveness measures to evaluate designs, teacher efficacy through growth-oriented feedback from a valid and reliable observation tool, implementation and evaluation tools, and administrative and structural support systems.

Additionally, state education agencies have begun to recognize this need for highly qualified instruction of content integrated with English instruction when serving ELs. Under a consent decree with the U.S. Department of Justice, the state of Massachusetts implemented new regulations for educators serving ELs. In order to renew, advance or retain their educator license, Massachusetts now requires its teachers and administrators to earn an EL instructional endorsement that integrates language teaching in all subject areas. Newly licensed teachers are likewise required to take courses designed to meet these needs of ELs. The professional development design revamped the traditional ways of teaching sheltered English instruction and instead used evidence-based instruction for academic English, reading, and writing skills development integrated into math, science, social studies, electives, and language arts (Calderón, 2012–2014).

> The MA educator licensure requirement is not and should not be seen as an end unto itself. Rather, the ideals behind it are that every educator continuously develop, innovate, and remain steadfast in supporting the dynamic and ever-changing ELs in our schools.
> —Debbie

WHY THE WHOLE-SCHOOL APPROACH MAKES A DIFFERENCE

The key to the whole-school success is that instead of relying on textbook series, software, disjointed sets of activities, watered-down curriculum, or reading programs that isolate and label students in a school, teachers learn new skills and dispositions while working together. ESOL/ELD and core content teachers (see Chapter 4 on co-teaching and collaboration) and administrators participate in the same continuous professional development to shift to a different mindset, get on the same page, experience the same growing pains, and celebrate small successes all the way. They find that the framework described in the Call to Action in this chapter works for "the type of school population we have today," as one Virginia principal stated.

As schools become more and more cosmopolitan, encountering new languages and cultures, educators need tools to understand their diverse students and ways to ensure all achieve at high levels. Concomitantly, teachers want to design lessons, units, and learning environments that support English learners in language, literacy development, and content learning simultaneously, while also fortifying the other students in their classrooms.

To ensure success for all learners, regardless of primary language or target language, the vision must be to have all core content teachers, counselors, instructional coaches, district, and site administrators profoundly skilled at integrating language, literacy, and content in a way that helps ELs and their peers have equitable access to high-quality curriculum and instruction in all subjects.

INTEGRATING LANGUAGE, LITERACY, AND CONTENT IN ALL SUBJECTS

Implications for Practice

Integration is the key.

- Integration of language/literacy/content instruction

- Integration of vocabulary study, reading comprehension, and text-based writing

- Integration of staff around a common framework and goal

- Integration/alignment not only across schools but also across large systems

Instructional strategies, professional development, curriculum materials, district mandated models, school non-negotiables, and all students' needs must be integrated into everyday tasks. It begins with the integration of instruction in each class. The goal is to connect academic language, key vocabulary from the text students are about to read, a reading comprehension strategy to delve deeply into the text, and text-based writing as the building blocks for all subjects.

COMPONENTS OF AN INTEGRATED LESSON

After the training and on-site coaching in use of the methodologies described in this chapter, core content teachers in middle and high school find that

1. They easily fit preteaching vocabulary for 10 minutes before students read in any lesson so that they can jump into a text and understand it.

2. They can clarify and connect language and content objectives to assessments.

3. When they model a reading comprehension strategy using a couple of complex sentences from the text, their students learn how to use that strategy as they read the rest of the text.

4. When students conduct Partner Reading by alternating sentences and summarizing after each paragraph, ELs automatically use the pretaught words/phrases and more academic language from the text. As they struggle to verbally summarize each paragraph with a partner, they jointly construct meaning to what they read.

5. As new words and phrases pop up during reading, summarizing, or class discussions, even more vocabulary can be identified for further teaching as the teacher walks around monitoring and documenting performance.

6. Instead of answering book questions after reading, the students are shown how to write Bloom's Taxonomy–style questions. In teams of four, students write one or two questions from the text they just read. This generates the development of additional reading, communication, self-monitoring, and higher-order thinking. An additional benefit is that students go back into the text one more time for closer reading and learning more information to strengthen their questions before they share them with other teams.

7. As a follow up, teachers use those team questions in a Numbered Heads Together or other cooperative learning activity to test the students' knowledge. Not surprisingly, students go back into the text to make sure their team answers are going to be correct.

8. Now that students have sufficient information stored in their heads, they can draft a lengthy composition. Their first attempts at drafting turn out better when working in teams of four.

9. When that first draft is completed, a strategy called Ratiocination is used to edit grammar or make the language more academic by finding and fixing common mistakes (e.g., punctuation, capitalization), repetitions of Tier 1 words (e.g., because, but, like), to substitute Tier 1 for Tier 2 connectors and transition words (e.g., hence, nevertheless, subsequently), and add more subject-specific technical (Tier 3) words.

10. A strategy called Cut-n-Grow is used to add more facts, evidence, citations, or other elaborations, even reduce some of those long-winded sentences that do not say anything anyway.

11. A quick modeling of how to write a powerful conclusion, thesis statement, and attention-grabbing titles helps all students.

12. Students are motivated to want to write again when the team compositions are completed, and a student from each team reads the final version, and the whole class celebrates.

Using performance assessments for the 12 main components we just listed helps teachers gauge students' language and content learning progressions much better than traditional tests. This helps them know their students at deeper levels. (See Calderón, Slakk, Carreón, & Payton, 2018, and Calderón & Slakk, 2017 for further descriptions of all these instructional strategies and teacher support systems.)

WHAT WOULD IT LOOK LIKE IN THE CLASSROOM?

Teachers begin collaborative lesson planning by starting to analyze and parse the text students are about to study, looking for vocabulary and standards to highlight and later assess. They select five words or phrases to preteach at the beginning of each lesson. These words are selected with ELs in mind from the text students are about to read in class.

After preteaching vocabulary and before students read, the teacher conducts a think aloud to model comprehension strategies (e.g., how to read the long sentences in social studies, how to find the definition of a word in a science paragraph, how to break apart a succinct written math problem). This simple strategy models for students how to metacognitively process a text. These strategies are then applied during Partner Reading with Summarization. Summarizing after each paragraph with a peer helps ELs and their peers comprehend the content and learn more vocabulary and sentence structure to use in the summaries and later discussions. We call the text "the mentor" or "the anchor" text because it serves as a model for learning to combine discourse and write academic compositions.

We are pleased to find that most science teachers are being more intentional in the selection of readings, using not only textbook readings that might contain obsolete information, but using authentic sources for scientific studies and projects. Authentic web-based cutting-edge science is much more interesting to students than traditional textbook reading. Articles are complemented with sections from a textbook for comparison discussions and writing.

Reading newspaper articles, along with selective portions from history textbooks, brings history, civics, and government to life. Short online biographies, historical and primary source documents, and character education pieces serve to make connections to current events and students' lives. Social-emotional skills are learned when students read about such topics, discuss, and write about the issues. Most schools are also moving toward Project-Based Learning because they can integrate the concept of learning language and content by solving authentic problems and producing results that are meaningful for the students, particularly ELs because they can display their talents. Students also practice specific digital literacy. They use digital tools, videos, photography, and art to collaborate on high quality products that entail both reading and writing. Working on these projects together with non-ELs has other benefits: students learn tenacity, diligence, creativity, empathy, passion, and adaptability through this process.

After reading, students' linguistic skills grow when challenged to self-create questions at the higher-order cognitive levels (e.g., analyzing, evaluating, synthesizing). For this task, they must go back into the text to do closer reading—ensuring that the answers to the questions just created are in what they read. Teachers begin by establishing criteria for the questions. The teacher expects them to use specific words, phrases, grammatical patterns, sentence structures, sentence starters, text features, and text structures that have been pretaught. Teachers need to be sure to provide examples and protocols for peer feedback. After questions have been written, they are submitted to the teacher on cards (with the answer in the back). These cards are used with a Cooperative Learning discourse activity to test those questions with the whole class. More tools for dialogue and argumentative discourse are provided as students from each team build on one another's responses. Writing questions also leads to inquiry for other projects. When ELs are placed in heterogenous teams of four (mixed with ELs and non-ELs, boys and girls, ELs at different proficiency levels), their discourse and comprehension accelerate with peer interaction and peer assistance. They and their peers can process multiple types of documents and practice social-emotional skills (e.g., responsible discourse, self-management, self-awareness, collaboration, responsible decision-making) (CASEL, 2018). The writing also rises to a higher level when students do collaborative writing.

Writing in teams of four the first few months of school generates more synergy—creativity and rich ideas. It helps ELs, reluctant writers, and others by providing support to build confidence and skills. The strategies for drafting, revising, editing, and writing appropriate conclusions and awesome titles prepares students for all their disciplinary writing and all their college writing or employment documentation. Grammar, spelling, punctuation, text-based or discipline-based words, transition words, and connectors are learned from the texts they have read. Through the phases of editing and revising, they master the target grammar and mechanics of the discipline. Writing in teams also helps teachers keep better track of authentic individual learning progressions. Mini-lessons on items students need become easily identifiable. Instead of wasting time on pre-fabricated disconnected mini-lessons that might not apply, the team writing/revising/editing activities are more useful and appreciated by the students.

THE CALL FOR ACTION

Integrating Everyone Into the Professional Development: Administrators, Counselors, Teachers, Coaches, District Specialists/Coaches

As stated previously when individual teachers consistently implement the aforementioned practices, student achievement gains result. However, isolated "pockets of excellence" will not result in the school-wide improvements that will reverse the odds of predictable failure for our multilingual learners. Instead, the entire school community must commit to this powerful change effort.

Whole-school implementation of academic discipline-based language, literacy, and core content lets adults and students alike know that this is not the educational flavor of the year, but rather, a long-term commitment. It shows that using these strategies is a given and an expectation. Continuous professional development to support these teaching practices is here to stay until all the elements are reasonably implemented. It typically takes three years to fully implement a large-scale change of this nature, but schools begin to see growth the first year. The messaging is always clear to everyone. The schools that embrace and sustain a flow of text-based instruction easily show that their focus is on academic language and authentic literacy in all subjects. However, to have success, ESOL/ELD, special education, electives teachers, health/PE, counselors, and all instructional coaches must be in it for the long-haul. As Jim Collins says in "Good to Great" (2001), the whole faculty, administration, and district administration learn to say "no thank you" to any other trend of the month and stay true to their priority.

Integration within the professional development/workshop sessions must be included and stressed for all teachers, coaches, counselors, and administrators as we describe below. It begins with in-depth workshops on

1. How to teach vocabulary/academic language and discourse before, during, and after reading.

2. How to develop reading comprehension.

3. How to develop text-based writing skills, self-editing, and revising.

4. How to effectively use cooperative learning to practice language, reading, and writing and master content knowledge.

5. How to use formative and summative assessment to make instructional decisions.

Continuing with the approach that Loudoun took for their professional development, the following design integrated the professional development, follow-up learning, and annual sustainability of implementation.

The professional development process: Participants spent a day practicing how to select words to teach from the texts students are about to read that day and practicing how to teach key vocabulary before, during, and after reading. The next day is spent learning how to develop depth of comprehension before students read, during student reading, and after reading to anchor vocabulary, discourse, comprehension, and content learning. On the third day, the participants practice strategies for engaging students in a variety of team writing activities for various genres based on the texts and content they have been reading and learning. At the end of each day, participants worked on lessons they aligned to state standards and essential questions. The teachers determined the types of performance assessments and how to collect assessment of learning progressions in each subject area. Administrators and coaches participated in the development and alignment of those lessons so that they could have a firm grasp of the concepts and strategies to be used in each lesson—if not, they would have no basis on which to coach and provide support for implementation.

In addition to attending the three-day preliminary training with the teachers, all those who provide support to teachers attended two additional days for practicing how to observe and recognize quality teaching/learning of vocabulary, reading, and writing, how to collect observational data with a protocol specific to each component, and how to give feedback in order to help the teacher plan next goals. Also included in the two additional days were ways to set up and sustain teachers' learning communities and other support systems such as scheduling common planning times, team content planning, and peer support sessions, stressing that these collaborative activities happen regularly and throughout the semester, protected from unnecessary interruptions or cancellations.

Cooperative Learning and Social Emotional Learning strategies were modeled at the workshops the way they should be integrated during vocabulary, reading, and writing in a lesson.

The core content and ESOL/ELD teachers found these strategies particularly helpful for their newcomers, particularly newcomers with interrupted formal education as they arrive at different times of the year.

GETTING STARTED: HOW THE DISTRICT IS MOVING FORWARD

As the four schools enter their second year of implementation, half of the teachers (177) are now applying the practices described in this chapter, and the other half were trained the summer of 2018. The remaining few were trained in August by a cadre of Rock Stars. They are called Rock Stars because in one year they were able to implement with fidelity and quality all 12 components. The criteria for their selection included (a) three observations by their administrators using the Walk-through with Instructional Strategies for ExC-ELL (WISEcard) Observation protocol, (b) three observations by the expert professional development providers, and (c) their students' progress on the English proficiency test and Virginia Standards of Learning. These Rock Stars continued to be observed by the coaches and site administrators several times and received additional training to become District Support Cadre (DSCs) sanctioned to provide additional workshops as necessary. All administrators, coordinators, and counselors, except a new principal, had been trained the first summer. Nevertheless, they all returned to the training with the other half of the teachers the following summer. In a recent interview of all administrators, randomly selected teachers, and newcomers/ELs, they concurred that having all the teachers (not just the ESOL) become well equipped with cooperative learning, vocabulary/discourse, reading, and writing strategies makes a huge difference for all students. Advanced Placement students scored higher than any year on their A.P. tests and state tests.

A WAY TO RESPOND TO THE CHALLENGES FACING ALL SCHOOLS

Fortunately, there is a growing consensus that ELs and other striving readers and writers must engage in grade-level academic learning and develop language throughout a school day to stay on pace with long-term expectations and content standards. The field is finally recognizing that language in all learning throughout the school day is critical for everyone. Schools that have bilingual programs find that teaching in two languages throughout the day across the grade levels and subject areas improves the quality of teaching as well as learning. High schools have discovered that this holistic and inclusive approach is a much better (and enjoyable) way to reach all students. This inclusive and holistic approach to instructional design applies in every educational setting, in recognition of the pertinence of language in all learning and the need to focus on its development throughout the school day and beyond.

The features for sustaining a quality implementation and the instructional components in this chapter can help a school attain desired goals for ELs and their classmates—when a whole school works together with an EL focus. To accomplish great results, we pose the following challenges:

- All core content teachers in middle and high schools
   - Preteach five key words/phrases that will help students enter the text with some familiarity.
   - Know how to select and teach vocabulary before, during, and after reading.
   - Know a variety of strategies for teaching reading integrated into their content-area lessons.
   - Know how to teach text-based formal writing.
   - Use interaction strategies and cooperative learning strategies that enable ample interaction and development of social emotional skills.
   - Integrate the 12 proven components into existing mandated programs.
   - Participate in intensive, sustained, EL-focused professional development such as the framework with 12 components, followed by extensive coaching, and follow up PLC/TLC training and implementation.
   - Meet with ESOL/ELD teachers to plan co-teaching for the week.
- ESOL/ELD teachers are prepared for
   - Teaching basic English: Vocabulary Tiers 1, 2 and 3 as relevant to ESOL classroom discourse, schooling, and the content areas the students might be encountering beyond the ESOL block.
   - Planning lessons and team teaching with core content teachers.

- Administrators are committed to
  - Demonstrating deep knowledge about language, literacy, and content by attending all professional development sessions on ELs with their teachers.
  - Establishing support structures for teachers to sustain quality instruction for ELs in all core content classrooms (e.g., ESOL-core content teachers' planning schedules, interdisciplinary Teacher Learning Communities, financial resources, saying "no" to competing initiatives, coaching as a natural part of learning).
  - Cultivating positive relationships among teachers, students, and all school staff.
  - Cultivating positive relationships between school personnel and newcomer/ELs' parents.
- The school district
  - Provides necessary funding for implementing evidence-based practices as a whole school endeavor.
  - Safeguards the efforts for a long-term implementation until quality is attained by protecting schools from other trends.
  - Supports specialists who provide the school(s) with coaching, supplies, implementation checks, and positive messaging.
- The state department of education
  - Yearly sponsors six institutes for 600 teachers and administrators, teaching vocabulary, reading comprehension, and text-based writing as described above for school divisions/districts throughout the state.
  - Offers institutes for five audiences: Pre-K through second grade, elementary, secondary, newcomers' focus, and School Support Cadres in order to make them more relevant to the participants.
  - Provides grants to school districts that want to do extensive follow-up coaching and refresher workshops after they have completed the institutes.

Summary and Conclusions

The Challenge. We have strong evidence of what works. We also know what doesn't because when we do that year after year, we still have huge numbers of Long-Term ELs. We can show that our ELs are progressing, but not enough to prevent them going into middle and high schools still identified as Long-Term ELs with only 60% of them graduating. We still wonder about how to accelerate language, literacy, and knowledge for newcomers. Nevertheless, we continue to espouse beliefs and theories that have no evidence as effective for newcomers. Hence, our challenge is to begin to build a knowledge base and systematic implementation plan where everyone moves forward systematically. For this plan to succeed, the whole faculty in a school needs to be retooled to forego the methods that are not supported by research and to change their mindsets on how to work with newcomers, ELs, and their classmates. This book offers many potential solutions. This chapter details how to move toward an evidence-based comprehensive instructional and professional development approach. Instead of isolated activities or watered-down curriculum or texts that are way below grade level, teachers can now move easily from preteaching vocabulary to reading challenging texts with critical thinking strategies through additional peer learning activities and strategies to anchor knowledge, language, and literacy before students write.

Potential Solutions. At Loudoun County Public Schools, district and site administrators share the goals for ELs with their teachers on a constant basis. They set up whole-school professional development in the summer and follow-up refresher days and extensive coaching by their own district and school-based coaches and by expert trainers/coaches of the model described above. They establish collegial activities for teachers to delve deeper into EL learning progressions and joint lesson adaptation/integration. The administrators meet on a monthly basis to exchange successes and seek potential responses to challenges. The district specialists are constantly at the schools to help with coaching or see what else is needed. It takes hard work and renewed commitment, but it works.

> The work that Margarita and Shawn are doing in Loudon County and elsewhere speaks strongly about what is possible and we are advocating in our book. When we intentionally see our work with English learners as a collective effort and use practices that are scientifically grounded and proven to work, then we have a much better chance to make the essential shifts that are needed so that all English learners are successful.
>
> —Debbie

Moving From Language to Language, Literacy, and Content

FIGURE 6.1   **Checklist for Further Reflection and Conversations**

To make these changes today:

☐ In my vocabulary instruction, I need to . . .

☐ In my reading instruction, I need to . . .

☐ In my writing instruction, I need to . . .

☐ As a complete lesson involving vocabulary, reading, writing, curriculum, and assessment, I need to . . .

☐ I can incorporate these social-emotional strategies and language for each through these Cooperative Learning activities . . .

To collaborate with my colleagues to make these changes, I need to . . .

☐ Attend and actively share, help, and continuously learn to . . .

☐ Ask for feedback and coaching from . . .

☐ Invite colleagues and school and district leaders to observe how my students are learning . . .

As principal/assistant principal/instructional coach, to make these changes, we need to . . .

☐ Attend all the professional development sessions with our teachers in order to establish these support systems for the teachers . . .

☐ Ask teachers what they need to implement . . .

☐ Participate in classroom walkthroughs and coach/provide feedback to teachers every . . .

☐ Here's the evidence that we have accomplished that . . .

As school district leaders, we will support our schools with ELs by . . .

☐ Participating in their classroom walkthroughs and coaching/feedback to teachers to . . .

☐ Conducting frequent meetings to share implementation progress, do problem solving, and celebrate with administration

☐ Providing appropriate funding for new activities

As the state education agency, we will support our local education agencies by . . .

☐ Providing on-going evidence-based professional development

☐ Providing additional funding to schools ready to implement follow-up from our professional development academies

References

August, D., & Shanahan, T. (Eds.) (2006). *Developing literacy in second language learners. Report of the National Literacy Panel on language minority children and youth.* Mahwah, NJ: Lawrence Erlbaum Associates, Inc.

August, D., Beck, I. L., Calderón, M., Francis, D. J., Lesaux, N. K., & Shanahan, T. (2008). Instruction and professional development. In D. August & T. Shanahan (Eds.), *Developing reading and writing in second language learners. Lessons from the Report of the National Literacy Panel on Language-Minority Children and Youth.* Mahwah, NJ: Lawrence Erlbaum Associates, Inc.

Calderón, M. (1994). Mentoring, peer support, and support systems for first-year minority/bilingual teachers. In R. Rodriguez, N. Ramos, & J. Ruiz-Escalante, *Compendium of readings in bilingual education: Issues and practices.* San Antonio, TX: Texas Association for Bilingual Education.

Calderón, M. (1999). Teachers learning communities for cooperation in diverse settings. In M. Calderón & R. E. Slavin (Eds.), *Building community through cooperative learning.* [Special issue] *Theory Into Practice Journal, 38*(2), 94–99.

Calderón, M. (2005). Training teachers on effective literacy instruction for English language learners. In K. Telles & W. Hersh, *Training teachers of language minority students.* Mahwah, NJ: Lawrence Erlbaum Associates, Inc.

Calderón, M. E. (2012–2014). *Recommendations for the Massachusetts Department of Elementary and Secondary Education on the delivery and materials for preparing teachers and administrators on effective instruction for ELLs: Reports to the United States Department of Justice.* Washington, DC: USDOJ.

Calderón, M., August, D., Slavin, R., Duran, D., Madden, N., & Cheung, A. (2005). Bringing words to life in classrooms with English language learners. In E. H. Hiebert & M. L. Kamil, *Teaching and learning vocabulary: Bringing research to practice* (pp. 117–139). Mahwah, NJ: Lawrence Erlbaum Associates, Inc.

Calderón, M., & Carreón, A. (2001). A two-way bilingual program: Promise, practice and precautions. In R. E. Slavin & M. Calderón (Eds.), *Effective programs for Latino children*. Mahwah, NJ: Lawrence Erlbaum Associates, Inc.

Calderón, M. E., Hertz-Lazarowitz, R., & Slavin, R. E. (1998). Effects of bilingual cooperative integrated reading and composition on students making the transition from Spanish to English reading. *Elementary School Journal, 99*(2), 153–165.

Calderón, M. E., & Miyana-Rowe, L. (2011). *Preventing long-term English language learners: Transforming schools to meet core standards*. Thousand Oaks, CA: Corwin.

Calderón, M. E., & Slakk, S. (2017). *Promises fulfilled: A leader's guide for supporting English learners*. Bloomington, IN: Solution Tree.

Calderón, M., & Slakk, S. (2018). *Teaching reading to English Learners, grades 6-12: A framework for improving achievement in content areas* (2nd ed.). Thousand Oaks, CA: Corwin.

Calderón, M. E., Slakk, S., Carreón, A., & Payton, J. (2018). *ExC-ELL: Expediting comprehension for English language learners* (3rd ed.). Washington, DC: Margarita Calderón & Associates.

Calderón, M., & Soto, I. (2017). *Academic language mastery: Vocabulary in context* (I. Soto, Ed.). Thousand Oaks, CA: Corwin.

Carlo, M. S., August, D., & Snow, C. E. (2005). Sustained vocabulary-learning strategy instruction for English language learners. In E. H. Hiebert & M. L. Kamil, *Teaching and learning vocabulary: Bringing research to practice* (pp. 137–154). Mahwah, NJ: Lawrence Erlbaum Associates, Inc.

Carnegie Council on Advancing Adolescent Literacy. (2010). *Time to act: An agenda for advancing adolescent literacy for college and career success*. New York: Carnegie Corporation of New York.

CASEL. (2018). *What is SEL?* Retrieved from https://casel.org/what-is-sel/

Cheung, A., & Slavin, R. E. (2012). Effective reading programs for Spanish-dominant English language learners (ELLs) in elementary grades: A synthesis of research. *Review of Educational Research, 82*(4), 351–395.

Collins, J. (2001). *Good to great*. New York: Harper Business.

Fisher, D., Frey, N., & Lapp, D. (2012). *Text complexity: Raising rigor in reading*. Newark, DE: International Reading Association.

Fullan, M. (2010). *The skinny on becoming change savvy*. Thousand Oaks, CA: Corwin.

Goldenberg, C. N. (2010). Improving achievement for English learners: Conclusions from recent reviews and emerging research. In G. Li & P. A. Edwards (Eds.), *Best practices in ELL instruction*. New York: Guilford.

Graham, S., & Perin, D. (2007). *Writing next: Effective strategies to improve writing of adolescents in middle and high schools. A report to Carnegie Corporation of New York*. New York, NY: Carnegie Corporation of New York.

Graves, M., August, D., & Carlo, M. (2011). Teaching 50,000 words. *Better: Evidenced-Based Education, 3*(2), 6–7. Baltimore, MD: Johns Hopkins University.

Montenegro, H. (2017). English language development and social emotional skills. In M. Calderón & S. Slakk, *Promises fulfilled: A leader's guide for supporting English learners* (pp. 13–28). Bloomington, IN: Solution Tree.

Nagy, W. (2005). Why vocabulary instruction needs to be long-term and comprehensive. In E. H. Hiebert & M. L. Kamil, *Teaching and learning vocabulary. Bringing research to practice* (pp. 217–244). Mahwah, NJ: Lawrence Erlbaum Associates, Inc.

National Academies of Sciences, Engineering, and Medicine. (2017). *Promoting the educational success of children and youth learning English: Promising futures.* Washington, DC: The National Academies Press. doi:10.17226/24677

Short, D., & Fitzsimmons, S. (2007). *Double the work: Challenges and solutions to acquiring language and academic literacy for adolescent English language learners. Report to the Carnegie Corporation of New York.* New York, NY: Alliance for Excellent Education.

Slavin, R. E. (1995). *Co-operative learning: Theory, research, and practice.* Boston, MA: Allyn and Bacon.

Slavin, R., & Cheung, A. (2005, Summer). A synthesis of research on language of reading instruction for English language learners. *Review of Educational Research, 75*(2), 247–284 . Retrieved from https://doi.org/10.3102/00346543075002247

Sugarman, J. & G. Geary (2018). *English learners in California: Demographics, outcomes and state accountability policies.* Washington, DC: Migration Policy Institute.

Sugarman, J. & G. Geary (2018). *English learners in Massachusetts: Demographics, outcomes and state accountability policies.* Washington, DC: Migration Policy Institute.

Wexler, N. (2018, April 13). Why American students haven't gotten better at reading in 20 years. *The Atlantic.* Retrieved from https://www.theatlantic.com/education/archive/2018/04/-american-students-reading/557915/

Zwiers, J., & Soto, I. (2017). *Academic language mastery: Conversational discourse in context* (I. Soto, Ed.). Thousand Oaks, CA: Corwin.

chapter seven

From Assessment *of* Learning to Assessment *for* and *as* Learning

MARGO GOTTLIEB
AND ANDREA HONIGSFELD

PREMISE

Linguistically and culturally sustainable classroom assessment, where teachers and students co-plan and co-construct performance tasks, use mutually agreed-upon criteria for success, and provide evidence *for* and *as* learning, represents equitable practices for multilingual learners.*

VIGNETTE

Patchogue-Medford Union Free School District is one of the largest, most diverse districts on Long Island, NY, with a unique focus on four key aspects of education: physical, emotional, academic, and social (PEAS). Serving about 7,500 students (50% white, 41% Hispanic, 4% African American, 3% Asian, and 2% multiracial), 55% of the students are economically disadvantaged, 12% are students with disabilities, and 13% are English learners, the majority of whom are Spanish speakers (NYSED, 2017). The district is deeply committed to bringing together its stakeholders with the goal of maximizing the potential of each.

In PatMed, as the community endearingly refers to the district, a huge priority is placed on allowing children to engage in divergent thinking opportunities, hands-on discovery, and inquiry-based learning, as well as unstructured play, mindfulness, and yoga. The district is also committed to linguistic diversity and cultural sustainability. PatMed is an educational system that has purposefully and persistently moved away from a culture dominated by top-down testing and high-stakes decisions to one where an engaging, child-centered learning environment prevails with all stakeholders having a voice in decision-making. How did this shift happen? We interviewed the district superintendent to find out.

Under the leadership of Dr. Michael Hynes, the district has undergone a paradigm shift in pedagogy and culture to ensure the full support of all its students. Dr. Hynes recognizes that "in an era where childhood anxiety is at an all-time high, and teacher morale on the decline, it is essential that we redefine the purpose of education" and notes that "by looking to prominent child development psychologists, we are reminded of the practices that support child development, where developing children's social competencies and emotional well-being must come before they can achieve in their academics." Implemented for the past six years, he has made it a top priority to create a safe learning environment for all children to maximize their potential, feel comfortable taking risks, and have opportunities during the school day to grow their individual talents and passions.

When it comes to assessment practices, Dr. Hynes emphasizes that "through extensive, focused feedback, teachers are expected to instruct children in the way they know children learn best. Teachers assess students using multiple measures- with diagnostic, formative, summative, portfolio, and performance-based assessment- to determine the next steps in instruction based on each individual's needs." Multilingual learners benefit from this approach since it affords them time to interact with their peers and to engage in real-world, authentic experiences of project-based learning. Dr. Hynes concludes that "with a child-centered approach to learning, children understand that it's okay to make mistakes, and therefore, they take more risks. This builds self-esteem and self-confidence, which translates into maximized individual academic potential."

Just like PatMed, this chapter addresses how schools and districts can transition from a testing-oriented culture to one that centers on their stakeholders—in particular, students, teachers, and school leaders—and how each can benefit from information gleaned from different types of assessment. We illustrate this movement from a high-stakes testing environment to more equitable and balanced assessment practices by providing a rationale for the change, offering evidence in support of this paradigm shift, sharing our vision of assessment *as* and *for* learning, enlisting a call for action, and envisioning the future role of assessment in K–12 education. It is our belief that unless our educational system abandons its focus on test scores and assumes an advocacy stance for its students, families, and educators, the academic advancement of our country will be in jeopardy.

In an assets-based model, we must find all of the ways that multilingual learners can demonstrate what they do know! Some of the many benefits of project-based learning are that multilingual students can have more language practice and be more engaged. Additionally, they will comprehend more when intentionally working with linguistic models on projects. Multilingual students will also have more access and connectedness to the learning process, as well as to each other, via project-based learning.
—Ivannia

THE URGENCY

What were your feelings when you took a test in a language other than English or one to enter a university or to join the teaching profession? Now, imagine you are a teacher of second-grade multilingual learners whose literacy is stronger in their home language than in English and their ticket to third grade is passing an English reading test. How do you think your multilingual learners feel? What if you are a high-school teacher who wishes that your multilingual learners take Advanced Placement classes or participate in the International Baccalaureate Program, but they are denied from doing so due to their English language proficiency status—what would be your reaction to that situation?

Educators have been reliant on testing to make high-stakes decisions for decades. However, most standardized achievement tests have not been designed for nor developed with multilingual learners in mind. As a result, these measures are linguistically complex, mask multilingual learners' access to the content, refer to experiences that are outside the socioeconomic realm of the students, and lack consideration of multicultural perspectives. Additionally, few multilingual learners participate in the development process that includes cognitive labs, piloting, and field-testing of test items. Their low participation numbers are compounded by invalid inferences from testing results, which, more often than not, are seen through an anglocentric lens. In essence, assessment policies and practices in the United States are based on monolingual constructs whereby multilingual learners are required to demonstrate their language proficiency in one language—English—without acknowledgment of their full linguistic potential (Escamilla et al., 2013; Shohamy, 2011; Menken, 2008).

Some educators are of the belief that the disparities of standardized testing practices for multilingual learners can be ameliorated through "accommodations." That is, if tests can be retrofitted linguistically (as in allowing the use of dictionaries or reading instructions in the students' home language) and logistically (as in special seating arrangements or extra time), then we will have equalized the playing field in regards to eradicating the inherent inequities of testing. A meta-analysis on effectiveness of accommodations for English learners, however, reveals little impact on their performance (Kieffer, Lesaux, Rivera, & Francis, 2009). Accommodations are indeed legitimate for multilingual learners with Individual Education Programs (IEPs), but in general, their appropriateness for measuring academic achievement in English is questionable. Rather, from the onset, achievement tests should be crafted from Universal Design for Learning rather than being back mapped for specific student populations.

Results from measures in English tend to reinforce the vulnerability and marginalization of multilingual learners. Think about it! What typically happens in your school or district when Anita walks in without a word in English yet is highly literate in her home language? How equitable are your initial identification and placement practices? What procedures are in place for Ivan and Ilsa who were born and raised in the United States. but who have been minimally introduced to English before enrolling in school? Are there any policies for collecting baseline data in the students' home languages?

Test scores in English problematize references to students who are subsequently categorized as "Long-Term English learners," "struggling readers," "students at-risk," or "students with limited or interrupted education" (Kibler & Valdés, 2016), all of which reinforce what multilingual learners lack. Assumptions about these students' potential are being made with limited data that preclude multilingual learners from demonstrating their true abilities and performance. Perhaps content and language teachers could collaborate to devise their own language use survey to ascertain multilingual learners' language patterns inside and outside of school to better co-plan instruction. Questions could explore the students' literacy and oral language practices that could then be charted, such as

- With whom do you speak your home language? With whom do you speak English? With whom do you speak both languages?

- Where do you speak your home language? Where do you speak English? Where do you speak both languages?

When interim or annual achievement testing, a form of assessment *of* learning, is externally imposed upon the educational community, it has potential deleterious effects on multilingual learners and their teachers. Yet large-scale testing has dominated our educational landscape and has driven curriculum, instruction, and classroom assessment for the last several decades. In doing so, unfortunately, it has failed to capture the full linguistic repertoires of our multilingual learners. For multilingual learners, it is classroom assessment that specifically supports language development (Davison & Leung, 2009); specifically, it focuses on the interaction and collaboration between teachers and students, or assessment *for* learning, and is interwoven into instruction As an extension, assessment *as* language learning is student-driven and legitimizes multilingual learners' funds of identity (Esteban-Guitart & Moll, 2014) along with their funds of knowledge (González, Moll, & Amanti, 2005) as part of teaching and learning.

There is an overwhelming urgency for educators to overcome their over-reliance on data that exemplifies assessment *of* learning generated from large-scale achievement testing. In this chapter, we present a case for offsetting assessment *of* learning at the national, state, and district levels with assessment *for* and *as* learning at the school, classroom, and individual student levels. In doing so, we advocate for moving assessment practices to a more learner-oriented stance (Jones & Saville, 2016; Turner & Purpura, 2016) and encourage teachers to collaborate in co-planning, co-implementing, recording, and interpreting assessment information. With acceptance of this more balanced approach to assessment and learning, we expand the net of inclusion so that more stakeholders, starting with multilingual learners, can gain a sense of ownership, agency, and advocacy.

THE EVIDENCE

Summative achievement testing that is administered under sterile uniform conditions to maximize standardization has become the modus operandi in the United States. In particular, the Elementary and Secondary Education Act, starting with the Improving America's School Act of 1994, has perpetuated this state of heightened anxiety for educators by mandating such testing, minimally in English language arts and mathematics in Grades 3 through 12. Greater accountability for schooling has placed enormous pressure on stakeholders, as oftentimes, these high-stakes measures carry negative consequences for students, especially for multilingual learners, teachers, and schools. With all this attention to numbers and scores, there has been little interest in the linguistic, cultural, and experiential relevance of these tests for the ever-growing, super diverse, multilingual student population. Although the linguistic and cultural validity of the inferences drawn from these measures has been challenged, there has been little acknowledgment of the worth of these claims (Basterra, Trumbull, & Solano-Flores, 2011; Abedi, 2010; Menken, 2008).

In the name of federal funding, testing at the national level and its accompanying accountability policies have reverberated across states, districts, and schools. multilingual learners who are in the midst of developing English are being unfairly punished for not having reached academic parity with their proficient English peers when testing is only in English, but when instruction is increasingly becoming more prevalent in two languages. Deficit thinking is constantly being perpetuated by the press and in the literature by reminding the public and educators of an ever-present achievement "gap" that exists between English learners (ELs) and other student groups.

Admittedly standardized tests play a role in education, primarily for accountability purposes; inspiring passion in learning, however, is not among these roles (Siddall, 2018). As mentioned previously, mandated testing falls under the scheme of assessment *of* learning; it is a snapshot of student performance at one point in time. In this same vein, district and classroom testing in the traditional psychometric view of assessment *of* learning is a discrete activity that occurs at the culmination of a predetermined period of learning where students are acting alone (Moss, 2008). We cannot continue the gamesmanship so pervasive in testing, as it is destructive for our multilingual learners and demoralizing for our teachers.

EMBRACING ASSESSMENT *FOR* LEARNING

Understanding that testing can take on different formats and purposes, we view its summative nature as one data source for decision-making. Testing results are most meaningful when they are folded into assessment that is inclusive of multiple data sources and contextualized according to the characteristics of its test takers, in this case, multilingual learners. Rather than aimed at generating and reporting scores, we take a sociocultural stance of assessment that is descriptive of what teachers and students do on an ongoing basis to gather and share information to improve teaching and learning. As a series of socially constructed activities, assessment *for* learning is considered a process that is integral to and embedded in the instructional cycle, not divorced from it (Gottlieb & Katz, 2020).

In the assessment culture of the 21st century, the connection between learning and assessment is much closer than ever before as teachers are challenged to take on a more active role and pay closer attention to multilingual learners' language development within content learning. The stage has been set for assessment *for* learning that embraces increased decision-making power of teachers working together and a more collaborative spirit between teachers and students. Teachers are keenly aware of where the students are in their learning and where they are to go next. Fairness and equity in assessment occur within each student's zone of proximal development (Swain, Kinnear, & Steinman, 2011), and there are provisions to ensure that multilingual learners' experiences are scaffolded so that they have access to content through language.

Students as partners and co-collaborators in classroom assessment epitomizes assessment *for* learning. Similarly, we accept the tenets of the definition of formative assessment posed by the FAST SCASS as foundational for assessment *for* learning: "Formative assessment is a planned, ongoing process used by all students and teachers during learning and teaching to elicit and use evidence of student learning to improve student understanding of intended disciplinary learning outcomes, and support students to become self-directed learners" (CCSSO, 2018). In addition, we offer another feature of assessment *for* learning—ensuring that students have choice and voice throughout the assessment process. Increased student motivation and engagement stem from teachers who give multilingual learners opportunities to use their preferred language when interacting with students from the same language group to co-construct learning, selecting topics of interest they wish to personally pursue for learning, and using multimodalities to express their learning.

There is solid research worldwide that supports assessment *for* learning. Black and Wiliam's 1998 seminal article, supported by the work of Hattie and Temperley (2007), sets an empirical and theoretical foundation for the effectiveness of "for"mative assessment. In particular, their research chronicles the positive effect of timely, concrete, realistic, and actionable feedback to students during instruction as the mainstay of classroom assessment and for advancing learning, especially for multilingual learners and other minoritized groups. Figure 7.1 summarizes the contribution of the literature that advocates for assessment *for* learning. These influencers in the field of classroom assessment have been our thought leaders who have provided the theoretical base that undergirds our work. Although the majority of these scholars have not dabbled in the field of language education, the principles they propose are readily applicable to multilingual learners and their teachers.

FIGURE 7.1 Expert Evidence of the Effectiveness of Assessment *for* Learning

Assessment Expert	Stance on Assessment *for* Learning
Moss & Brookhart (2009)	"The primary purpose of formative assessment is to improve learning, not merely to audit it. It is assessment *for* learning rather than assessment *of* learning." (p. 6)
Earl (2013)	"Assessment *for* learning (has) feedback loops to ensure students are given cues to review their learning and move forward. Assessment *as* learning goes even deeper and draws on the role of personal monitoring and challenging of ideas that are embedded in the learning process and the role of both students and teachers in fostering this self-regulation process." (p. 4)
Fisher & Frey (2014)	Checking for understanding is a systematic approach to formative assessment that consists of four phases: "1. Feed-up: Clarifying the purpose, 2. Feedback: 3. Responding to student work, and 4. Feed-forward: modifying instruction." (pp. 2–3)
Heritage (2010)	"Formative assessment is a process that takes place continuously during the course of teaching and learning to provide teachers and students with feedback to close the gap between current learning and desired goals." (p. 10)
Murawski & Lochner (2011)	"Co-teachers should be able to describe or demonstrate ways in which they accommodate, provide alternative assessments, and otherwise treat students as individuals in determining their mastery of content standards and curriculum." (p. 3)
Shephard, Penuel, & Davidson (2017)	"Under ESSA . . . . formative assessments (can be) codeveloped and integrated with local curricula, instruction, and professional learning—all of which are grounded in a research-based model of learning."
Chappuis, Stiggins, Chappuis, & Arter (2012)	"The keys to quality classroom assessment (or assessment *for* learning) are: 1. Clear purpose, 2. Clear targets, 3. Sound design, 4. Effective communication, and 5. Student involvement." (p. 5)
Wiggins (2012)	Helpful feedback is goal-referenced, tangible and transparent, actionable, user-friendly (specific and personalized), timely, ongoing, and consistent.
Black, Harrison, Lee, Marshall, & Wiliam (2004)	"Assessment *for* learning is any assessment for which the first priority in its design and practice is to serve the purpose of promoting students' learning." (p. 10)

EXPANDING ASSESSMENT *FOR* LEARNING TO ENCOMPASS ASSESSMENT *AS* LEARNING

As a complement to assessment *for* learning, assessment *as* learning is a social and cultural activity where performance is co-constructed among students or students under the guidance of teachers. Multilingual learners, attend to their academic language use within content as students engage in hands-on performance tasks, interact and negotiate with peers, and discuss issues with each other and their teachers. Students are valued as educational partners and are ongoing contributors to teaching and learning.

Assessment *as* learning gives students their much-needed space, recognition, and stature within the educational system. It leverages and builds upon multilingual learners' languages, cultures, backgrounds, and experiences. Having independence in thinking leads multilingual learners to become more autonomous, self-regulated students. It is the development of student agency and self-advocacy that drives assessment *as* learning. Respect for multilingual learners within linguistically and culturally sustainable classrooms and schools adds value, engenders appreciation, and projects a positive image that helps shapes the students' identities (Miramontes, Nadeau, & Commins, 2011; Zacarian, 2011).

The standards-driven movement of 21st-century classrooms, sparked by challenging college and career readiness standards, recognizes that active and intentional interaction of students with each other leads to learning. Students of all ages are expected to be able to collaborate in small groups, use technology to mediate multimodal learning, and engage in a range of discussions (CCSSI, 2010). Classroom-generated data that are personalized and authentic for multilingual learners have the greatest face validity and are closest to the student learning experience. Yet, by not acknowledging information that is reflective of multilingual learners' entire linguistic expertise as an important facet of the whole child, educational equity remains elusive.

> We must apprentice students into becoming effective collaborators where they can demonstrate what they know via multiple forms of discourse. Academic discourse is a scaffold for the writing process as speaking is a mental outline for writing.
> —Ivannia

Assessment *for* and *as* learning must join the dominant paradigm of assessment *of* learning to create a viable and balanced representation of sources of information for educational decision-making (Gottlieb, 2016; 2017). It is the strength of teachers working together in co-planning and then revisiting how to co-assess learning, how to record the information, and how to provide relevant feedback that yields results to help improve their craft. At the same time, to enact equitable assessment practices, students, inclusive of multilingual learners, must be integral to the process.

THE VISION

Research-informed evidence as well as practitioner understanding about equitable assessment practices for multilingual learners is growing across the nation. Based on this expanding knowledge base, we present a vision for an educational environment in which multilingual learners fully benefit from all three approaches—assessment *as, for,* and *of* learning—while their teachers and school administrators also develop agency and advocacy for their students and their families.

Our vision highlights the complementary nature of the different forms or approaches of assessment and their contributions to the creation of a fluid system internal to a school or district where stakeholders have individual and collective voice in decision making. As shown in Figure 7.2, these assessment approaches are envisioned as three nested circles to represent the roles of the major stakeholders. Assessment *as* learning is the heart and anchor of the other approaches where multilingual learners and other students have opportunities to engage in challenging activities, often with their peers, to demonstrate their language development and learning in multiple multimodal ways. In the center circle, assessment *for* learning touches on both students working in tandem with teachers and teachers co-planning and collaborating with school leaders in enacting assessment. The outer circle represents school and district leaders, including coaches, directors of programs, and principals, who understand and apply the broadest and most far reaching of assessment purposes and uses.

The approaches to assessment are relationship driven, primarily among students (in assessment *as* learning), teachers (in assessment *for* learning), and school leaders (in assessment *of* learning). The essential features of stakeholder engagement and examples of applicable tools for each approach are elaborated in Figure 7.3.

FIGURE 7.2 **A Nested View of Assessment *as, for,* and *of* Learning**

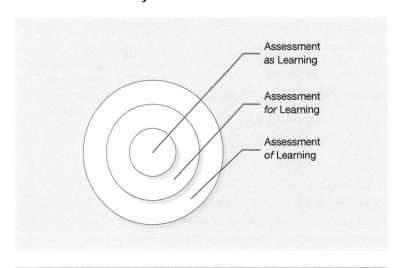

Assessment
as Learning

Assessment
for Learning

Assessment
of Learning

FIGURE 7.3 Approaches of Assessment Along With Associated Features for Stakeholder Engagement and Examples of Tools

Approaches of Assessment	Features of Stakeholder Engagement	Examples of Tools
Assessment *as* Learning	Student-centered: Student agency and advocacy • Students are trusted to take responsibility for their own learning. • Students are supported to monitor their own learning. • Students learn to document and show evidence of growth. • Students self- and peer reflect. • Students advocate for their own learning needs.	Students contribute to and/or use. • Self- and peer assessment. • Peer-editing checklists. • Learning logs. • Interactive journals. • Reflection tools.
Assessment *for* Learning	Teacher-guided: Teacher agency and advocacy • Teachers co-construct success criteria with students. • Teachers co-create a menu of assessment tasks to encourage student choice. • Teachers integrate students' ideas on how to show growth.	Teachers, often with students, craft and use. • Graphic organizers. • Checklists. • Rubrics or project descriptors. • Templates of criteria for success. • Action research, along with reflection tools.
Assessment *of* Learning	School leader-supported: Leader agency and advocacy • School leaders serve as assessment liaisons to help determine and disseminate school- and district-wide trends. • School leaders mentor coaches and teachers on assessment literacy. • School leaders form networks to discuss assessment issues with implications for curriculum and instruction.	Administrators and school leaders, often with teachers, interpret and use. • Score reports from tests. • Data from student portraits. • School or district rubrics. • Templates for determining/maintaining inter-rater reliability of oral and written student samples. • School or district portfolios.

Since students are the center of our universe and the reason for our professional being, it is of utmost importance that we focus on moving students' learning forward and documenting their learning in equitable ways. Student-centered approaches to assessment practices privilege assessment *as* learning and recognize the power of self- and peer assessment. We envision providing multilingual learners ample opportunities for goal setting (see examples on pages 145 and 146 of this chapter) and for monitoring their own language and literacy development across the content areas and specialized subjects, such as technology and STEAM. As a result, students gain self-confidence and assert their agency as they assume multilingual identities, engage successfully in grade-level learning opportunities that are appropriately scaffolded for them (see Chapters 3, 5, and 6), and move towards becoming autonomous, self-regulated learners who take pride in their growing skills and reflect on challenges they face.

ASSESSMENT *AS* LEARNING

Let's visit some classrooms in which students have opportunities to set short-term and long-term goals, determine their position on a continuum of language and literacy development, and reflect on their own progress with guidance and support from their peers and teachers. In this whirlwind tour, we see how teachers engage their multilingual learners in converting language proficiency levels derived from test scores into realistic goal setting. We begin with assessment *as* learning to reinforce the importance of our multilingual learners as stakeholders.

IDEAS FOR STUDENT GOAL SETTING

Goal setting is one area where student voice is most effective. The following synopses are different ways of having students actively involved in their own learning. Each vignette illustrates how students have opportunities to reflect on and consciously think of planning for language and learning

Emily Francis, a high school English language development (ELD) teacher in North Carolina, welcomes her multilingual learners back to school with an activity that helps them understand and analyze their language proficiency. To maximize the meaningfulness of this activity, students select WIDA Can Do Descriptors, Key Uses (see https://wida.wisc.edu) for a specific key language use (discuss, argue, recount, or explain), language domain (listening, speaking, reading, or writing), and grade level to place in the first column of a three-column chart as a language goal they wish to pursue. Next, the multilingual learners generate *I can* statements to share what they are confident in doing and *I will* statements that exemplify ambitious but attainable goals for themselves. Figure 7.4 is a possible template inspired by Emily's work to initiate this kind of work.

Shelley Sanchez Terrel, a Texas educator, encourages her students in making multimodal and multilingual vision boards for goal-setting purposes—in both traditional and digital formats. As a highly motivating tool, vision boards capture students' dreams and aspirations in the form of a collage consisting of images, photographs, quotes, and drawings with a possible focus on personal, academic, and linguistic development.

We must empower students to know themselves academically by sharing with them their achievement progress and teaching them how to set measurable goals. Your goal-setting process reminds me of the "Road to Reclassification" process that I have worked on with districts, whereby multilingual students learn why they are English learners and how to monitor their own academic progress.

—Ivannia

FIGURE 7.4 An Example of a Tool for Student Goal Setting

Can Do, Key Use Descriptor for Argue	I can	I will
Listening:	_____ _____ _____	_____ _____ _____
Speaking:	_____ _____ _____	_____ _____ _____
Reading:	_____ _____ _____	_____ _____ _____
Writing arguments for Level 5: *"Integrating multiple perspectives and evidence from a variety of sources"*	Persuade others with evidence collected from interviews, videos, and articles.	Use citations from websites to convince others of my position.

Our last example of student goal setting is for a group project. Patti Aube, an English as a New Language instructional coach in Massachusetts, relates how multilingual learners in her district expressed feelings of anxiety when they discussed memories of their arrival, in particular, their difficulties in being in a new city surrounded by unfamiliar people and unable to communicate in English. These students, having empathy for incoming peers facing the same situation, decided, along with their teachers, to design a video production to introduce newcomers to their school and community.

As this project was motivated by students and they had input in every phase of the design and execution, it can be considered an example of assessment *as* learning. The students reflected on their personal experiences and determined the extent to which their goals had been met by providing multimodal (using images, technology, and written labels) feedback to their teacher. Using a full-sized paper body, the students worked in groups to fill the head and the heart with words, adhered QR codes for video clips, pasted pictures, and shared representative realia of what they learned and how they felt during the video production unit. On the feet of the body, the students proudly showed how their new language and technology skills applied to their learning.

ASSESSMENT *FOR* LEARNING

As part of our bold vision for reframing assessment, we anticipate teachers partnering with their students in co-constructing criteria for success, sharing evidence for learning, and providing feedback to one another. In the following cases, assessment *for* learning goes beyond formative assessment that informs instruction; rather, it illustrates assessment as a dynamic, interactive, ever-evolving process between teachers and students with the goal of continuously defining and redefining what the students need and what they and their teachers can do to achieve it.

Let's see some examples of these practices where assessment *for* learning between teachers and students is in action.

In Illinois, Mara Barry and her co-teachers collaborate with their kindergarten multilingual learners to select the most appropriate Thinking Maps™ for various topic explorations along with student assessment of their prior knowledge of those topics. (The district uses the term "culturally and linguistically diverse students" to describe multilingual learners who could benefit from culturally responsive/sustaining pedagogy and ongoing language and literacy support). All teachers have participated in professional learning in Thinking Maps™ and Kagan cooperative learning structures, two strategies that are infused into instructional and assessment practices every lesson, every day!

The continuity and consistency with which teachers in Mara's school (and the entire district) use these tools lead to a shared frame of reference for teachers and students for concept development, and language and literacy skill building. In one lesson we observed, Mara asked the kindergarteners which Thinking Map™ would best capture their ideas. For this task, students demonstrated their familiarity and the applicability of other Thinking Maps™ as well as jointly decided which items shared by their peers were to be placed and where they were to be placed on the graphic organizer.

Katie Toppel, an elementary ELD teacher in Oregon, takes a holistic approach when she invites her students to answer the following four questions for individual goal setting. The students explore the concepts of "glow" (referring to already-existing accomplishments) and "grow" (meaning areas of need).

My language "glow" is _____

My language "grow" is _____

One goal I have at school this year is _____

One goal I have outside of school this year is _____

In addition to beginning of year or unit goal setting, student self-assessment and progress monitoring also contribute to nurturing students' independence and growing their metacognitive and metalinguistic awareness. Claudia Leon, a middle school English as a New Language (ENL) teacher from New York, uses a simple checklist (inspired by resources published on www.engageny.org) that ensures that quick writes (shown below) are guided by rigor and relevance to the grade-level English Language Arts standards for her students:

Have I answered the questions completely?

Is the evidence I provided relevant and complete?

Does my paragraph include the following?

___ A topic sentence

___ At least three pieces of specific information from the text

___ An explanation of what each piece of evidence means

___ A closing sentence

ASSESSMENT *OF* LEARNING

School leaders can support teachers in the design of linguistically and culturally sustainable assessment that provides useful information for improving teaching and learning. These common assessment tools, internal to the functioning of classrooms and schools rather than external to it, can positively impact student performance. When teachers have agency in making decisions regarding information from measures that they have crafted, then we see how classroom assessment *of* learning, as part of the teaching-learning cycle, can be most effective. The example in Figure 7.5, the SWELL tool, illustrates how a grade, department, or school can come together in reaching consensus on how to celebrate the work of their multilingual learners.

FIGURE 7.5 *Sampling Work by English Language Learners* (SWELL): An Assessment Protocol

Instructions: As you examine oral, written, or multimodal samples produced by your multilingual learners with your colleagues, complete the identifying information and then use the open-ended checklist to interpret and document different aspects of the students' learning and language development.

Identifying Information for the Student Sample:

Oral sample _____ Written sample _____ Multimodal sample _____

Language(s) of the sample _____

Topic of sample: _____ Content area: _____

Student: _____ Grade: _____ Date: _____

Multilingual Learner's Development:

1. **Language Development**

    1a. _____ The sample consistently uses some linguistic features. If so, which ones?

    1b. _____ The sample shows specific linguistic challenges. If so, which ones?

    1c. _____ The sample demonstrates that the student can meaningfully communicate ideas. If so, which ones?

    Additional Comments:

2. **Conceptual Development**

    2a. _____ The sample illustrates content-based knowledge and/or skills. If so, which ones?

    2b. _____ The sample illustrates conceptual challenges. If so, which ones?

    2c. _____ The sample shows that the multilingual learner has reached the content goals for the project. If not, what do you suggest?

    Additional Comments:

3. **Cultural Influences**

    3a. _____ The sample reflects the student's cultural experiences. If so, which ones?

    3b. _____ The sample reflects the student's experiential base. If so, how?

    3c. _____ The sample exhibits cultural misunderstandings or misconceptions. If so, how?

    Additional Comments:

4. **Social-Emotional Influences**

    4a. _____ The sample shows evidence of motivated, self-directed learning. What evidence do you see or how does the student tell you?

    4b. _____ The sample shows student engagement in the task or project. How?

    4c. _____ The sample shows evidence of task persistence. How?

    Additional Comments:

Source: Honigsfeld & Dove (2010); adapted by Gottlieb & Honigsfeld (2019).

Having shared some concrete examples and tools for assessment—*as, for*, and *of* learning from a variety of schools and districts around the country—we now turn to how these assessment approaches might collectively make a difference.

THE CALL FOR ACTION

How do we as an educational community stimulate change in classroom practices to place more emphasis on assessment *as* and *for* learning? That is, how do we ensure that teachers have opportunities to collaborate in formulating goals for learning, co-constructing the design of or strategies for assessment and crafting criteria of success? Equally important, how are multilingual learners' interests and identities being tapped during instruction and assessment and how do they assume ownership in the process? This section offers concrete suggestions as to how stakeholders might consider assessment *as* and *for* learning as an advocacy tool for students and teachers.

Provide Opportunities for Ongoing Professional Learning for Multiple Stakeholders

One of the first steps in altering the perception and raising the status of classroom assessment *as* and *for* learning is to engage students, family members, teachers, and school leaders in ongoing professional learning. Professional learning encompasses a broad range of activities and certainly is not limited to typical workshop-style events. Professional learning should be designed for the interests of stakeholders and shaped by their input, such as a hybrid course for school leaders or coaches, an action research project for teachers and students, or an ongoing discussion forum (in English and other languages) for family members. Here are some more specific ways for expanding the scope of professional learning to embrace assessment *as* and *for* learning.

Exploring assessment literacy. Professional learning geared to evoke change in classroom assessment practices should build assessment literacy across the educational community. Teachers, in particular co-teachers, need to have a shared understanding of assessment (Dove & Honigsfeld, 2019). *Assessment literacy* refers to the knowledge about the basic principles of assessment practices, including the design and development of measures, the interpretation of results, and subsequent data-derived decisions. As an extension, language assessment literacy, understanding of multilingual learners' performance, involves teachers' familiarity with testing constructs and the application of this knowledge to classroom practices with specific attention to issues related to language assessment (Malone, 2013).

The tensions of teachers in dealing with assessment are palpable; they must be able to differentiate the different roles, purposes, and audiences of classroom assessment aimed at improving teaching and learning while simultaneously abiding by large-scale accountability requirements of their school, district, and state. The more that stakeholders are well-versed in fair and equitable assessment practices, where students and teachers are recognized partners, the greater the likelihood that assessment *as* and *for* learning will take root and become a stronghold in the educational community.

As co-planning, co-instructing, and co-assessing intersect with assessment *as, for*, and *of* learning, what might serve as a roadmap to professional learning throughout a school year?

We offer Figure 7.6, with an emphasis on language assessment literacy for multilingual learners, as a starting point for students, teachers, and school leaders to identify agreed-upon topics for exploring assessment literacy, such as applying the examples in each cell. With multiple stakeholders participating and sharing in the process, there is greater transparency of meaningful information gleaned from assessment approaches. We suggest that mixed stakeholder teams (inclusive of students, families, teachers, and administrators) collaborate in using this framework as an entrée to assessment literacy and for presenting and solving pressing assessment-related issues throughout the school year.

FIGURE 7.6 Framework for Assessment Literacy: Assessment *as*, *for*, and *of* Learning Across Phases of Collaboration

	Assessment as Learning . . . Students share:	Assessment for Learning . . . Students and teachers work on:	Assessment of Learning . . . Teachers and school leaders interact to:
Co-planning	• Strategies for problem-solving with each other • Contributions to personal and group decision-making	• Setting goals for learning in one or more languages • Brainstorming projects of student interest	• Interpret score reports from high-stakes tests • Contemplate placement of grouping of students
Co-instructing	• Insights from academic conversations • Original ideas, including multimodal representations of concepts	• Researching student-initiated projects • Providing reciprocal feedback	• Apply assessment results to design school-wide programs • Become assessment literate
Co-assessing	• Personal reflections of their work • Evidence of approaching or meeting learning goals	• Crafting checklists and rubrics for performance tasks • Applying agreed-upon criteria for success to different samples	• Engage in professional learning regarding administration and interpretation of state tests • Share feedback on the testing experience

ENACTING THE COLLABORATIVE INSTRUCTIONAL CYCLE

While co-planning, co-teaching, and co-assessing are intertwined, we also believe that the collaborative instructional cycle includes a fourth practice, reflecting. Schon (1990) suggests that educators engage both in *reflection in action* (while being engaged in a classroom experience with students as well as varied interactions with leaders, parents, and community members) and *reflection on action* (through action research and lifelong learning). Both types of reflective practice—reflection in action and on action—provide educators (teachers and leaders alike) opportunities for professional learning. More recently, Brookfield (2017) claims that educators use four different lenses, presented in Figure 7.7, to reflect on what they do and how they make decisions about the teaching-learning process.

FIGURE 7.7 **Different Perspectives for Reflecting on Learning**

The Lens	The Key Question	Connections to the Collaborative Instructional Cycle
The students' eyes	What are the students seeing and experiencing?	Students see that they have two or more teachers who care about them.
Colleagues' perceptions	What are colleagues seeing and experiencing?	Teachers recognize that they are more impactful when two or more educators collaborate for the sake of student learning.
Own personal experiences	What have we experienced in the past that is similar or different?	Individuals make connections to their own prior teaching and their impact on student learning.
Relevant theory and research	What do related educational theory and research have to say about these experiences?	Educators review emerging research about collaboration and co-teaching for the sake of teachers' experiences.

Since reflection is a multi-dimensional process, Brookfield (2017) cautions that it cannot be a single event or irregular occurrence. Instead, a more pedagogically sound approach is to engage in regular, disciplined, and critical reflection. One unique form of engaging in regular and systematic reflection is to design action research. Action research, a disciplined process of inquiry conducted by and for those taking the action, affords teachers to take control over their professional destiny through assessment *for* learning while students contribute to their personal growth through assessment *as* learning. Try the following steps in the suggested outline for designing, implementing, and analyzing action research:

Action Research Outline

Background

Give a brief description of a pressing educational issue of personal interest.

Research Questions

Generate questions that are researchable, answerable, and relevant to the students' needs.

Participants

Describe the context: the community, school, and classroom in which the study will take place.

Describe the students (abilities, language and cultural backgrounds).

Data Sources

Identify the purpose of each data source (the tools for data collection and analysis) and how it will help answer one or more of the research questions.

Data Collection Procedures

Describe week-by-week (if applicable, day-by-day) sequential steps of the activities associated with data collection.

Data Analysis

Plan how analysis and interpretation of data will answer each research question.

Anticipated Outcomes

Identify some desired or anticipated outcomes.

Action Plan

Outline a possible action plan as a follow up to the study.

Source: Adapted from Honigsfeld & Dove (2019).

EXAMINING COLLABORATIVE INQUIRY FOR TEACHERS

Collaborative inquiry exemplifies high-quality professional learning that respects the role of educators in increasing student learning (Donohoo & Velasco, 2016). It is driven by a central perplexing question formulated by teachers, such as "How can we elevate the status of classroom assessment in multiple languages for multilingual learners when accountability seems to only honor data in English from high-stakes measures?" Teachers have control of each phase of an iterative professional learning cycle that involves: (1) identifying features of student success, (2) exploring promising practices that address those features, (3) trying out the practices in their classrooms, (4) collecting evidence of their effectiveness, and (5) reflecting on their impact. The collaborative inquiry cycle is a means for teachers to accrue agency as they collectively work toward improving their craft.

FOSTER STUDENT ENGAGEMENT IN ASSESSMENT

One way to build enduring student trust that, in turn, will facilitate student engagement in learning, is to convert your classroom into a community of practice (Lave & Wenger, 1991). Communities of practice are grounded in the premise that learning occurs in interactive social contexts that emerge and evolve from the setting of common goals. In classrooms with multilingual learners, these classrooms need to be safe spaces for honoring students' identities, cultures, and languages as their bases for learning. Figure 7.8, a checklist of strategies, is a starting point for having teachers encourage students to become more active participants in their own learning through their ongoing participation in assessment activities as part of the classroom routine.

FIGURE 7.8 **A Checklist of Strategies for Teachers of Multilingual Learners to Promote Student Agency**

My multilingual learners demonstrate agency by engaging in classroom assessment involving:
1. Setting goals for content and language learning.
☐ They negotiate attainable goals or outcomes with their teachers.
☐ They periodically review and evaluate their goals based on models or exemplars.
☐ They revise their goals based on concrete descriptive feedback and evidence.
2. Heightening awareness through self-assessment and reflection.
☐ They communicate *what* they are thinking (metacognitive awareness).
☐ They communicate *how* they use language (metalinguistic awareness).
☐ They communicate *what* they know about different cultures and how that affects their message (metacultural awareness).
3. Teaching others.
☐ They participate in content-related activities, becoming experts in some aspect, and share their learning with others (e.g., small group jigsaws).
☐ They tutor or mentor younger students or peers and purposely interact with them in their language(s) of choice.
☐ They form partnerships and collaborate with their peers.

Adapted from Gottlieb & Castro, 2017, p. 155.

Students who set high expectations for themselves generally see a positive impact on their learning (Dewitt, 2017). In addition, increased learner responsibility and self-regulation contribute to improving learning outcomes (Andrade & Cizek, 2010). Students who collaborate with each other in co-planning, co-instructing, and co-assessing strengthen their bond and relationships. Suggestions for this tri-part collaboration among multilingual learners, shown in Figure 7.9, underscore how multilingual learners can engage in classroom assessment practices.

FIGURE 7.9 **A Checklist for Co-Planning, Co-Instructing, and Co-Assessing With Multilingual Learners**

1. Co-planning for learning: Multilingual learners . . .

   ☐ Can pair with peers of the same home language to maximize opportunities to dive into deep learning in their language(s) of choice.

   ☐ Generate questions to explore topics of mutual interest that meet teacher approval.

   ☐ Share ideas for identifying sources for seeking answers, including pursuing online resources, with peers.

   ☐ Challenge their peers' questions and brainstorm solutions together.

   ☐ Coproduce graphic organizers, such as semantic webs, of ideas from their chosen topic.

2. Co-instructing, or when engaging in learning: Multilingual learners . . .

   ☐ Revisit questions to explore, along with those of their peers, and decide on a thesis statement to explore, an opinion or claim to investigate, or a perspective to take.

   ☐ Create criteria for success with peers for their project based on questions, evidence, and organization of ideas and information.

   ☐ Participate in academic conversations, discussions, or Socratic seminars.

   ☐ Collect evidence related to their investigation, assist peers with multimodal supports, and analyze the same text or resources to confirm or deny their reasoning.

3. Co-assessing learning: Multilingual learners . . .

   ☐ Apply criteria for success to their project.

   ☐ Self- and peer assess drafts, such as writing pieces, oral language samples, or visual displays.

   ☐ Provide concrete feedback to peers based on the criteria for success.

   ☐ Revise drafts based on self-, peer, and teacher feedback.

   ☐ Prepare for and participate in student-led conferences with teachers and family members.

Summary and Conclusions

Collaboration among stakeholders, from students to school leaders, is critical for creating transparency, building trust, and moving a school or district's educational agenda forward. In this chapter, we have argued for changing assessment practices and offered some tools for helping students, teachers, school leaders, teacher educators, and policy makers shift from assessment *of* to assessment *as* and *for* learning. In doing so, we have exemplified the power of multilingual learners' voices and choices in assessment practices day to day and over time.

Accepting and promoting student and teacher agency helps educators, in particular school and district leaders, realize that information from multiple assessment approaches provides a more comprehensive picture of teaching and learning. Ultimately, a balanced and comprehensive assessment system consists of multiple perspectives and data sources, representing information from students, teachers, and school leaders (Gottlieb & Nguyen, 2007). Figure 7.10 offers potential contributions of each of these important stakeholders to assessment *as, for*, and *of* learning.

FIGURE 7.10 **A Checklist for Enacting a Balanced Assessment System for Classrooms, Schools, or Districts**

In my classroom, school, or district . . .

Multilingual learners, in enacting assessment *as* learning

- ☐ Have voice throughout the assessment process—from planning to using information for making decisions.
- ☐ Have ongoing opportunities to interact with each other in their preferred languages.
- ☐ Share their linguistic, cultural, and experiential resources with classmates and teachers.
- ☐ Engage in self- and peer assessment on a routine basis.
- ☐ Reflect on their growth and accomplishments throughout the year.
- ☐ Contribute to determining their goals for learning.
- ☐ Have input in co-crafting criteria for success for different projects.
- ☐ Are knowledgeable of their learning expectations (i.e., student-friendly standards) and have a plan for meeting them.
- ☐ Co-plan for and participate in student-led conferences.

Teachers, in enacting assessment *for* learning

- ☐ Interact with each other in co-planning, co-implementing, and co-evaluating activities.

☐ Collaborate with each other, collecting and exchanging information during co-teaching and co-assessing.

☐ Have agency in determining types of, content for, and schedules for common (grade and school-level) assessment.

☐ Guide students in designing project-based descriptors or rubrics.

☐ Form, with school leader support, communities of practice and professional learning communities with dedicated time to discuss assessment-related issues.

☐ Agree upon, along with students, contributions to individual, classroom, and school-wide portfolios.

School leaders, in enacting assessment *of* learning

☐ Participate in assessment networks within and across schools and districts.

☐ Determine and analyze, with input from teachers, and act on school-level data for accountability purposes.

☐ Involve multiple stakeholders in (re)formulating a school's or district's mission, vision, and core values around linguistic and cultural sustainability.

☐ Elicit the help of multiple stakeholders in revisiting policies related to assessment and multilingual learners' academic language use in the content areas.

☐ Work with teachers to craft short- and long-term school goals with related action plans.

☐ Plan, along with teacher committees, professional learning opportunities around assessment literacy.

☐ Evaluate with multi-stakeholder teams the effectiveness of school and district initiatives through the lens of equity.

Collaboration between teachers and school leaders in linguistically and culturally sustainable environments where co-planning, co-instruction, and co-assessment practices co-exist is bound to lead to changing the mindset of schools and all their stakeholders from disenfranchisement to empowerment. Often neglected, we also propose that multilingual learners be part of this systemic and seismic shift. With student-oriented assessment practices as the heart of assessment *as* and *for* learning, multilingual learners can become agents of and advocates for their own learning while classrooms, schools, and districts can become more equitable places to learn.

References

Abedi, J. (2010). Research and recommendations for formative asssessment with English language learners. In H. L. Andrade & G. J. Cizek (Eds.), *Handbook of formative assessment* (pp. 181–197). New York, NY: Routledge.

Aiken, E. N. (2011). Student voice in fair assessment practice. In C. F. Webber & J. L. Lupart (Eds.), *Studies in educational leadership: Leading student assessment* (pp. 175–200). New York, NY: Springer.

Andrade, H. L., & Cizek, G. J. (Eds.). (2010). *Handbook of formative assessment.* New York: Routledge.

Basterra, M., Trumbull, E., & Solano-Flores, G. (Eds.). (2011). *Cultural validity in assessment: Addressing linguistic and cultural diversity.* New York, NY: Routledge.

Black, P., Harrison, C., Lee, C., Marshall, B., & Wiliam, D. (2004). Working inside the black box: Assessment for learning in the classroom. *Phi Delta Kappan, 86*(1), 8–21.

Black, P., & Wiliam, D. (1998). *Assessment for learning: Beyond the black box.* Cambridge, UK: University of Cambridge.

Brookfield, S. (2017). *Becoming a critically reflective teacher* (2nd ed.). San Francisco, CA: Jossey Bass.

Chappuis, J., Stiggins, R., Chappuis, S., & Arter, J. (2012) *Classroom assessment for student learning: Doing it right—doing it well.* Boston, MA: Pearson.

Common Core State Standards Initiative (CCSSI). (2010). *Common Core State Standards for English language arts & literacy in history/social studies, science, and technical subjects.* Retrieved from http://www.corestandards.org/ELA-Literacy

Common Core State Standards en español. (2012). Retrieved from http://commoncore-espanol.com/common-core-state-standards-spanish-language-version

Council of Chief State School Officers FAST SCASS. (2018). *Revising the definition of formative assessment.* Retrieved from https://ccsso.org/sites/default/files/2018-06/RevisingtheDefinitionofFormativeAssessment.pdf

Davison, C., & Leung, C. (2009). Current issues in English language teacher-based assessment. *TESOL Quarterly, 43*, 393–415.

Dewitt, P. M. (2017). *Collaborative leadership: Six influences that matter most.* Thousand Oaks, CA: Corwin.

Donohoo, J., & Velasco, M. (2016). *The transformative power of collaborative inquiry: Realizing change in schools and classrooms.* Thousand Oaks, CA: Corwin.

Dove, M. G., & Honigsfeld, A. (2018). *Co-teaching for English learners: A guide to collaborative planning, instruction, assessment, and reflection.* Thousand Oaks, CA: Corwin.

Earl, L. M. (2013). *Assessment as learning: Using classroom assessment to maximize student learning* (2nd Ed.). Thousand Oaks, CA: Corwin.

Escamilla, K., Hopewell, S., Butvilofsky, S., Sparrow, W., Soltero-González, L., Ruiz-Figueroa, O., & Escamilla, M. (2013). *Biliteracy from the start: Literacy squared in action.* Philadelphia, PA: Caslon.

Esteban-Guitart, M., & Moll, L. C. (2014). Funds of Identity: A new concept based on the Funds of Knowledge approach. *Culture & Psychology, 20*(1), 31–48.

Fisher, D., & Frey, N. (2014). *Checking for understanding: Formative assessment techniques for your classroom* (2nd ed.). Alexandria, VA: ASCD.

González, N., Moll, L. C., & Amanti, K. (2005). *Funds of Knowledge: Theorizing practices in households, communities, and classrooms.* Mahwah, NJ: Lawrence Erlbaum.

Gottlieb, M. (2016). *Assessing English language learners: Bridges to educational equity* (2nd ed.). Thousand Oaks, CA: Corwin.

Gottlieb, M. (2017). *Assessing multilingual learners: A month-by-month guide.* Alexandria, VA: ASCD.

Gottlieb, M., & Castro, M. (2017). *Language power: Key uses for accessing content.* Thousand Oaks, CA: Corwin.

Gottlieb, M., & Katz, A. (2020). Assessment in the classroom. In C. Chapelle (Ed.), *The concise encyclopedia of applied linguistics.* Hoboken, NJ: John Wiley & Sons.

Gottlieb, M., & Nguyen, D. (2007). *Assessment & accountability in language education programs: A guide for administrators and teachers.* Philadelphia, PA: Caslon Publishing.

Hattie, J., & Temperley, H. (2007). The power of feedback. *Review of Educational Research, 77,* 81–112.

Heritage, M. (2010). *Formative assessment: Making it happen in the classroom.* Thousand Oaks, CA: Corwin.

Honigsfeld, A., & Dove, M. G. (2010a). *Collaboration and co-teaching: Strategies for English learners.* Thousand Oaks, CA: Corwin.

Honigsfeld, A., & Dove, M. G. (2019). *Collaborating for English learners: A foundational guide to integrated practices.* Thousand Oaks, CA: Corwin.

Honigsfeld, A., & Dove, M. G. (In press). *Collaboration and co-teaching* (2nd ed.). Thousand Oaks, CA: Corwin.

Jones, N., & Saville, N. (2016). *Learner oriented assessment: A systemic approach.* Cambridge, UK: Cambridge University Press.

Kibler, A. K., & Valdés, G. (2016). Conceptualizing language learners: Socioinstitutional mechanisms and their consequences. *Modern Language Journal, 100*(1), 96–116.

Kieffer, M. J., Lesaux, N. K., Rivera, M., & Francis, D. J. (2009). Accommodations for English language learners taking large-scale assessments: A meta-analysis on effectiveness and validity. *Review of Educational Research, 79,* 1168–1201.

Lave, J., & Wenger, E. (1991). *Situated learning: Legitimate peripheral participation (Learning in doing: Social, cognitive and computational perspectives).* Cambridge, UK: Cambridge University Press.

Malone, M. E. (2013). The essentials of assessment literacy: Contrasts between testers and users. *Language Testing, 30,* 329–344.

Menken, K. (2008). *English learners left behind: Standardized testing as language policy.* Tonawanda, NY: Multilingual Matters.

Miramontes, O. B., Nadeau, A., & Commins, N. L. (2011). *Restructuring schools for linguistic diversity: Linking decision making to effective programs* (2nd ed.). New York, NY: Teachers College Press.

Moss, P. (2008). Sociocultural implications for assessment I: Classroom assessment. In P. Moss, D. C. Pullin, J. P. Gee, E. H. Haertel, & L. J. Young (Eds.), *Assessment, equity, and opportunity to learn* (pp. 222–258). Cambridge, England: Cambridge University Press.

Moss, C. M., & Brookhart, S. M. (2009). Advancing formative assessment in every classroom: *A guide for instructional leaders.* Alexandria, VA: ASCD.

Murawski, W. W., & Lochner, W. W. (2011). Observing co-teaching: What to ask for, look for, and listen for. *Intervention in School and Clinic, 20*(10), 1–10.

NYSED. (2017). *Patchogue-Medford Report Card.* Retrieved from https://data.nysed .gov/reportcard.php?year=2017&instid=800000037538

Schon, D. E. (1990). *Educating the reflective practitioner: Toward a new design for teaching and learning in the professions.* San Francisco, CA: Jossey-Bass.

Shepard, L. A., Penuel, W. R., & Davidson, K. L. (2017). Design principles for new systems of assessment. *Phi Delta Kappan, 98*(6), 47–52. Retrieved from http://www.kappanonline.org/design-principles-new-systems-assessment/

Shohamy, E. (2011). Assessing multilingual competencies: Adopting construct valid assessment policies. *The Modern Language Journal, 95*, 418–429.

Siddall, T. (2018, May 11). *Listening to student voices: The sound of assessment for learning.* Retrieved from http://blogs.edweek.org/edweek/next_gen_learning/2018/05/_by_tony_siddall_program.html?cmp=eml-enl-eu-news3&M=58484779&U=1907940

Swain, M., Kinnear, P., & Steinman, L. (2011). *Sociocultural theory in second language education: An introduction through narratives.* Bristol, UK: Multilingual Matters.

Turner, C. E., & Purpura, J. E. (2016). Learning-oriented assessment in second and foreign language classrooms. In D. Tsagari & J. Baneerjee (Eds.), *Handbook of second language assessment* (pp. 255–272). Boston, MA: De Gruyter.

Wiggins, G. (2012, September). Seven keys to effective feedback. *Educational Leadership, 7*(1), 10–16.

Zacarian, D. (2011). *Transforming schools for English learners: A comprehensive framework for school leaders.* Thousand Oaks, CA: Corwin.

Note

* In this chapter, we use the term *multilingual learners* as we believe it is more inclusive and more descriptive of the wide range of students who are exposed to and interact in multiple languages and cultures; we reserve the term *English learners* for legal reference.

chapter eight

From Monolingualism to Multilingualism

IVANNIA SOTO AND MARGO GOTTLIEB

PREMISE

Multilingualism and multiculturalism are central to students' identities and should be a national priority. The cognitive and social/emotional benefits of multilingualism have long been supported by significant bodies of research. Moreover, as we prepare our citizenry for participation in a global economy, the ability to function in multiple languages and cultures has become increasingly urgent.

VIGNETTE

Julian is an EL and senior in high school who will receive the Seal of Biliteracy, which means that he has achieved an Early Advanced proficiency level (4 overall) on the California English Language Development Test (CELDT); completed all of his English-language arts requirements for graduation with an overall grade point average of at least 2.0 or above in those classes; and passed the Spanish Advanced Placement (AP) exam with a score of 3 or higher. In his freshman year, he connected well with his Spanish teacher, Mrs. Fox, who encouraged him to continue with his Spanish for Heritage Speakers classes for the next three years. Mrs. Fox noticed that Julian's Spanish was a strongpoint and she told him about the Seal of Biliteracy, which was a way for Julian to be acknowledged for his strong primary language skills. Julian liked the idea of being acknowledged at graduation for his bilingualism and biliteracy, so he met with his high school counselor and told her that he was interested in meeting this goal, which she assisted him with pursuing. Julian says, "It gives you a motive to finish. Before, I was like, my Spanish is used at home and in the community, but now I see how I can use it to benefit my career goals, as well as my community."

Julian's story is one where several educators—both his Spanish teacher and academic counselor—viewed his multilingualism as an asset and assisted him with his goal of obtaining the Seal of Biliteracy. In this way, multilingual learners' linguistic and cultural assets are to be accentuated, not eradicated, both in school and in life. As was suggested by his student interview, his goal is now to use his multilingualism in his career and to give back to his community. Shifting our philosophies from one of monolingualism to multilingualism allows us to springboard students' experiential base to further their development and honor their multilingualism.

THE URGENCY

To underscore the urgency for supporting multilingualism, former CIA director and secretary of defense Leon Panetta (2018) lashed out at the deplorable state of complacency that prevails in our country for accepting (and at times promoting) a monolingual mindset. In his scathing editorial, "Americans Are Losing out Because So Few Speak a Second Language," Panetta argues that

> we are constrained by our inadequate understanding of other nations and peoples, and by our inability to communicate effectively with them. It is therefore disturbing, and evidence of a dangerous myopia, that we continue to neglect training and education in languages other than English. . . . English alone—(that is) an education in English to the exclusion of other languages—remains insufficient to meeting our needs in a global world. America's leadership in a global world depends on our ability to understand that world. And there is no better way to understand others than to speak their language.

It's time—time for our nation to open its mind, its heart, and its soul to welcome and learn from persons who are have the fortune of being multilingual. For in today's interconnected interdependent world, humankind must coexist in an international network in which immigration, transnational relationships, and technological advancements constantly create new spaces for interaction and the exchange of ideas and ideologies. This chapter focuses on casting away monolingual, English language learning environments and highlighting, advancing, and enhancing multilingualism for pre-K–12 students in school.

Multilingual Education and National Language Policy

The United States has historically been and continues to be a multilingual/multicultural mosaic in its demography. It has had a long precedent of schooling in languages in addition to English, starting in colonial times. Fast forward to the second half of the 19th century when a number of states passed laws that authorized bilingual education. Over 10 languages during this time, in addition to English, were represented in educational systems: German in nine states; Swedish, Norwegian, and Danish in eight states; Dutch in one; Polish and Italian in one; Czech in one; French in one; and Spanish throughout the Southwest (Kloss, 1977/1998, as reported in Ovando, 2003). Support for instruction in languages other than English was also present during the second half of the 20th-century. There was undeniable federal backing of multilingual education during this time, as evidenced by the Bilingual Education Act of 1968, the 1974 *Lau v. Nichols* Supreme Court decision, and the *Castañeda v. Pickard* ruling of 1981.

Despite a growing body of research on the benefits of bilingualism, multilingual language education (and practice) that had prevailed was contested (and almost eradicated) by the end of the 20th century. In 1998, California Proposition 227, the English Language in Public Schools Statute, curtailed the use of languages other than English for instruction; its passage was followed by similar initiatives in Arizona in 2000 with Proposition 203, English for the Children, and in Massachusetts in 2002. However, it was the passage of the reauthorized Elementary and Secondary School Act (ESEA) of 2001, more commonly known as the No Child Left Behind Act, that demolished any semblance of bilingual education for K–12 multilingual learners (then known pejoratively as Limited English Proficient students). Not only was every reference to "bilingual education" stripped away, but also with the institutionalization of high-stakes testing in English for accountability purposes, "English only" became the de facto national language policy (Menken, 2008).

With time comes hope and a glimpse into a brighter multilingual future. We witness it with the passage of the subsequent iteration of ESEA, the Every Student Succeeds Act of 2015, coupled with the rescinding of restrictions on bilingual education in 2016 with the passage of proposition 58 by a wide margin in California and the unanimous passage of the Language Opportunity for Our Kids (LOOK) bill in Massachusetts. Yet with xenophobia in the air and prevailing anti-immigration sentiment, the urgency to have our country and its educational system realize the strength of its multilingualism is greater than ever.

THE EVIDENCE

Multilingual learners have clear advantages over their monolingual counterparts (Genesee, 2016; Rodríguez, Carrasqillo, & Lee, 2014; Goldenberg & Coleman, 2010). The research base on multilingualism has unequivocally demonstrated that multilingual proficiency strengthens how the brain functions. In addition, it is associated with more cognitive flexibility, better problem-solving abilities, a superior working memory, a stronger grasp of abstract concepts, greater social/cultural resources, increased awareness of and self-regulation over language, and yes, academic success (Californians Together, 2017; Umansky, Valentino, & Reardon, 2015; González, Moll, & Amanti, 2013; Barac & Bialystok, 2011; Westly, 2011; Bialystok, 2009).

Moreover, multilingual students are able to simultaneously participate in multiple cultural and language worlds and excel academically. Recent evidence from an analysis of results from the National Assessment of Education Progress (NAEP) suggests that between the years 2003 to 2015, multilingual students showed two to three times more progress in reading and math than students who only speak English. This implies that multilingual students and their peers are now performing significantly better than in the past (Kieffer & Thompson, 2018). The reason for the improvements in these scores has not yet emerged, but we do know that increased emphasis on state accountability for multilingual learners may be related to these outcomes. We also know that, despite the regressive policies of California and other states, multilingual programs expanded significantly during this time period, which might have also impacted these results (Kieffer & Thompson, 2018). The evidence is clear that there are cultural, cognitive, and academic benefits to multilingualism, which we will unpack in this section.

Academic Achievement Benefits to Multilingualism

We know that teaching and learning in two languages offers numerous academic benefits, including that children who are bilingual tend to perform better. It not only prepares students to communicate in both languages, but also increases academic performance in other subjects (Californians Together, 2017). Higher levels of proficiency in two languages are associated with higher levels of performance on achievement tests—particularly those areas related to language and literacy. Multilingual learners' meta-linguistic awareness (how language works), and contrastive awareness across different language systems bolster overall literacy proficiency. For students who come to school as English learners, the simultaneous development of both English and their home language is associated with stronger performance in English than students who are educated monolingually (College Board, 2017).

In one study, the effects of Spanish immersion on children's English vocabulary were studied. Matched on grade, sex, and verbal scores on a fourth-grade Cognitive Abilities Test (CAT), a sample of fifth- and sixth-grade immersion students and a comparable number of English monolinguals were asked to complete a Peabody Picture Vocabulary Test (PPVT)—a measure of a student's receptive vocabulary. The results of the CAT and PPVT revealed comparable verbal ability between the two groups, but on the PPVT, the experimental group (immersion students) outperformed the control group (monolingual students) because of their knowledge of cognates (words that sound alike and have similar meaning between two languages). Cognates allow students to make connections between words in the students' home language and their second language, thus reinforcing and honoring content that students already know and connecting a second language to that. It is a more efficient process than beginning with no content or language at all. On SECT, immersion students significantly outperformed students in the control group. Findings support the idea that Spanish immersion has English-language benefits and that positive transfer (cross-linguistic influence) occurs from Spanish as a foreign language to English receptive vocabulary (Cunningham & Graham, 2000).

MULTILINGUAL LEARNERS

These studies and others (e.g., Thomas, Collier, & Abbott, 1993) demonstrate the academic and achievement possibilities for multilingual learners in multilingual programs. Our multilingual learners can and will rise to the level of our expectations, especially when their linguistic and cultural histories are honored and built upon. Next, we will explore the cognitive benefits of multilingualism.

Cognitive Benefits of Multilingualism

Multilingual proficiency strengthens how the brain functions, and bilingualism is associated with more cognitive flexibility and better problem-solving abilities. Psychologists Ellen Bialystok and Michelle Martin-Rhee and researcher Albert Costa (2008) have concluded that the primary difference between monolinguals and bilinguals is "a heightened ability to monitor the environment." During one study, bilingual and monolingual students were asked to sort red squares and blue squares in a computer program. First, the children were asked to put the blue circles in a digital bucket marked with a blue square and red squares in a digital bucket marked with a red circle. The sorting by color was relatively easy for both groups of children. Next, the children were asked to sort the squares and circles by shape, which meant putting the red squares in the bucket marked with a blue square and vice versa. The bilingual children outperformed their monolingual counterparts in the speed that it took to complete the task, demonstrating that bilingualism improves the brain's executive function, or the control center, which handles the processes we use for planning, problem solving, and critical thinking. Such processes assist with staying focused, switching attention from one thing to another, and holding onto information (Bialystok & Martin-Rhee, 2008). The ability to problem solve and think critically are also higher-order skills that have been identified as important to success in 21st-century society and workplaces by educators, business leaders, academics, and governmental agencies (www.p21.org). Such cognitive benefits of multilingualism allow multilingual learners to reach their highest potential in higher education and the workplace.

Cultural Benefits of Multilingualism

Research also shows us that people who are able to speak, read, and write in two or more languages are able to participate in multiple cultural and language worlds. Since culture and language are intertwined, learning a new language makes one more receptive to new cultures and open to broader perspectives. These qualities promote biculturalism and can better prepare students for a global society and economy. An example of negotiating multiple languages

> Put this sentence on a poster in every school! High expectations and valuing students' linguistic and cultural assets are essential mindsets that make or break educators' impact. Multilingual schools help educators collectively and systemically build on multilingual learners' assets by design!
> —**Tonya**

and cultures is *language brokering.* The term *language broker* refers to children who interpret for their immigrant parents. A research study investigated the relationship between language brokering and academic performance, biculturalism, academic self-efficacy, and social self-efficacy. The study found that the many adult-like experiences of children who broker on a regular basis led to accelerated cognitive and socioemotional development in contrast with the development of children of immigrant families who rarely or never language broker. The researchers established a positive correlation between language brokering and biculturalism; in turn, both of these variables were found to be positively related to academic performance. In addition, the strongest predictor of academic performance was academic self-efficacy (Buriel, Perez, De Ment, Chavez, & Moran, 1998).

The academic, cognitive, and cultural benefits to multilingualism are endless. For decades, the evidence has been clear that multilingual learners benefit from quality bilingual programs that validate and build upon their primary language as an asset for learning English. For too long, we have stripped multilingual learners of this valuable asset, as if they were blank slates, without any language and cultural capital or foundations of their own. Instead, we must now use sound research on effective bilingual programs and pedagogy, to ensure that inequities are eliminated and *all* children are prepared for a global world and economy.

THE VISION

By valuing and advancing multilingualism as a principle of social justice, communities, and schools can join forces to ensure that multilingual learners have equitable opportunities to pool their talents and resources. School leaders and teachers must be sensitive to the linguistic and cultural connections of students with their homes and communities. More important, these stakeholders can readily continue to nurture this relationship while respecting the students' multilingual language development. The question at hand is how might this goal be accomplished when there is still a strong anti-bilingual sentiment that has a grip on educational policy and practice in many a district? The upcoming section offers a vision for promoting and sustaining multilingualism in schools.

The Multilingual Advantage

The irrefutable evidence of the assets of knowing and using more than one language should justify our schools' commitment to multilingualism over monolingualism. Multilingual persons possess more resources that further their learning that monolingual English speakers simply do not and cannot have. Multilingualism is an *advantage,* not a liability. In addition to the many assets mentioned earlier in the chapter, multilingual learners' competencies in using multiple languages help shape their thinking and form relationships with others (Cook, 2016).

Our vision is based on the premise that multilingualism should be the mission of every school, irrespective of its student population, but it is a necessity for schools that educate multilingual learners who have a familial history of varied linguistic and cultural influences that are integral to their development. As an educational community, we need to reconceptualize how to approach multilingualism as integral to schooling and recognize the multifaceted reality of linguistic practices for multilingual learners as part of teaching and learning. Multilingual voices should permeate the halls, the lunchrooms, and classrooms all day long, every day. Just think about it: Having access and opportunities to use multiple languages within a school environment enables students of the same language group to

- Interact with each other within and across languages in social and academic contexts inside and outside the classroom.

- Interpret information from multimodalities, such as text and video, from an expanded number of sources.

- Use each other as linguistic and cultural resources to increase their knowledge base.

- Learn deeply by integrating their conceptual knowledge that has been pooled from their multiple languages and cultural experiences.

- Apply concepts from a variety of contexts or perspectives through a multilingual/multicultural lens to new learning.

- Synthesize information that draws from their full linguistic repertoire, inclusive of the sum of their languages and cultures.

- Understand multilingual/multicultural nuances, such as gestures, idiomatic expressions, and ways of being.

A WHOLE-SCHOOL COMMITMENT TO LINGUISTIC AND CULTURAL SUSTAINABILITY

Linguistic and cultural sustainability is a term that is applied to pedagogy as well as the classroom and school environments (Paris, 2012). The notion of sustainability goes beyond the idea of cultural relevance or responsiveness by not merely accepting linguistic and cultural differences but by *insisting upon* the preservation and maintenance of the multiple languages and cultures of minoritized students. Linguistic and cultural sustainability ideally is a school-wide (or better yet, district-wide) commitment to appreciating, celebrating, and infusing multilingual learners' identities into the fabric of teaching and learning (Miramontes, Nadeau, & Commins, 2011).

One of the first steps in honoring and perpetuating multilingualism and multiculturalism, the essence of linguistic and cultural sustainability, is to engage the entire school community—from family members to students, ancillary staff to the principal—in crafting a mutually agreed-upon language policy that is reflective of its mission, vision, and values. That is exactly what La Asociación Escuelas Lincoln, an international K–12 school in Buenos Aires, Argentina, did in the development of its core values with multiple references to its multilingual/multicultural demographic, including

- Inspire globally minded citizens.

- Find strength in bilingualism and cultural diversity.

- Celebrate and welcome differing world views (see https://www.lincoln .edu.ar).

In addition, the school has adopted a set of belief statements and evidence-based practices as part of its language philosophy that exemplifies its values and highlights the strength of multilingualism. These language principles include: (1) affirmation—ownership and validation of multilingual learners' home language as essential for family communication, cultural identity, meaning-making, and thinking; (2) transfer as the basis for learning between languages; and (3) enrichment—respect for students' languages and cultures, while viewing their linguistic and intercultural journey as enriching the community.

VALUING FAMILIES' "FUNDS OF KNOWLEDGE" AND STUDENTS' "FUNDS OF IDENTITY"

The lived and relevant experiences of the students should be framed as resources that serve as the backbone for teaching and learning. This pedagogy that relies on the linguistic and cultural capital of students, their families, and households exemplifies the seminal theoretical work of Moll and González (1994). Their research underscores students' "funds of knowledge" that have been accumulated from historical and cultural practices rooted in community life which forms the basis for sound instructional practice (González, Moll, & Amanti, 2013).

As an extension of this concept, "funds of identity" is a personalization of a household's or community's "funds of knowledge" that helps define a person (Esteban-Guitart & Moll, 2014, p. 31). In other words, identity is shaped by personalizing meaning making from one's community and family resources. Viewed as a sociocultural construct, "funds of identity" implies linguistic and cultural ownership by individual students within the context of family and community life. For multilingual learners, we consider "funds of identity" an expression of their individual multilingual multicultural beings.

In both "funds of knowledge" and "funds of identity" students must be able to see themselves and act from their own perspectives. By being able to rely on their individual experiential bases as a springboard for learning, students will more likely gain confidence in themselves, become more motivated to learn, and move towards being self-regulated autonomous learners. Valuing student engagement and investment in learning ultimately yields social, emotional, and academic benefits (Christenson, Reschly, & Wylie, 2012). In addition, students' identities lead to agency, where they can advocate and act on their own behalf. As a result, students seek meaning in their world and act with determination and persistence to reach desired goals for themselves and others (Gottlieb & Castro, 2017; Vander Ark, 2015). Several examples of student goal setting can be found in Chapter 7, "From Assessment *of* Learning to Assessment *for* and *as* Learning," of this book.

DESIGNING A CHALLENGING MULTILINGUAL CURRICULUM

It is advantageous for multilingual learners to be members of high-challenge, high-support classrooms where language and academic literacy are taught in context and where curriculum is amplified, not simplified, as teachers provide information in multimodal ways. In these classrooms, there is ample scaffolding so that students are supported until they can work independently (Gibbons, 2009). Chapter 3, "From Watering Down to Challenging," explores when it is appropriate to introduce (and to remove) scaffolds. In addition, teachers target and highlight academic language use within content-area instruction as multilingual learners perform hands-on, engaging activities (Gottlieb & Ernst-Slavit, 2014; Zwiers, 2008).

While all these features of curriculum planning and implementation for multilingual learners are sound, they fail to address multiple language use in teaching and learning. Just as the integration of content and language is becoming the mainstay of classroom instruction for multilingual learners, we also must come to accept student interaction in multiple languages to communicate ideas and concepts, negotiate understandings, clarify misunderstandings, or to deepen their learning (Gottlieb, 2016). One way to be inclusive of multilingual learners' multiple language use is to recognize translanguaging as a schoolwide policy, practice, and pedagogy (Garcia, Ibarra Johnson, & Seltzer, 2017).

As discussed earlier and reiterated here, our national policy context is one in which student literacy in languages other than English has been discouraged and undervalued (Hornberger & Link, 2012). As a result, multilingual learners' communicative repertoires that encompass translanguaging practices have not been acknowledged as authentic and valid pathways to their academic language development. Translanguaging, an individual's strategic use of multiple languages in oral and written communication, is a natural phenomenon for multilinguals as they traverse their full linguistic repertoires. By identifying translanguaging expectations and targets for learning, the status of both languages is elevated and multilingual learners' multiple ways of knowing are acknowledged (Hilliard & Gottlieb, 2018).

> What a powerful point to layer upon all initiatives of academic conversations for multilingual learners. The point of classroom conversations isn't just to build academic English but is also to engage students as thinkers, collaborators, and learners who use their linguistic and cultural assets to make meaning and express themselves authentically. Value translanguaging as part of this process!
>
> —Tonya

As an example, a translinguistic expectation for a unit on families might be: Multilingual learners will analyze the use of languages in family discussions and their different audiences (e.g., grandparents, young children, siblings). To meet this expectation, multilingual learners will play the role of ethnographers; first they will identify words and expressions in their home language that describes their families (e.g., *mi hijito*). The students will then examine and relate the discourse used with family members in English. As a final activity, multilingual learners will relate their family's bilingual patterns of language use to a peer of the same language group and reflect on the use of language with different members of their families.

OFFERING DEEP PROFESSIONAL LEARNING OPPORTUNITIES

Professional learning centered around educating multilingual learners, where teachers, school leaders, and administrators work together on an ongoing basis to enhance teaching and learning, can yield tremendous benefits to the greater educational community. A prime example of an effective program is one that integrates the arts into the language and cultural fabric of school, such as the one funded by the USDE Professional Development for Arts Educators Grant for K–12 educators. Several school districts in Illinois received this grant and participated in a focused, deep, and layered examination of the arts to enhance curriculum design. The following description of a three-module professional learning institute illustrates how the arts can transcend linguistic and cultural boundaries to become infused throughout school.

> Arts are an ideal medium for educators to explore the intersectionality of language, culture, and content and is a panorama for understanding social justice issues that relate to curricular choices and instructional implementation. In the first module, teachers and district leaders were introduced to a multilingual curricular framework before engaging in the second module, a rich series of field experiences with artists and cultural experts in Oaxaca, Mexico. The third module focused on making district curriculum more culturally and linguistically appropriate. Data from post-institute surveys and evaluations confirmed the positive impact of this multidimensional approach to professional learning where participants see the value of sustaining and amplifying the home languages and cultures of their multilingual learners to use as learning tools to access complex content. (Hilliard & Gottlieb, 2018)

Professional learning within school and beyond should offer teachers opportunities to grow personally and professionally while serving as an apprenticeship for experimenting with new ideas. For example, teachers may delve into action research to investigate questions revolving around multilingual learners' use of languages in different contexts—at home, in the community, and at school. Through professional learning communities, teachers and other staff can then analyze the data from their research to better understand the complexity of language learning and the variability of language use.

It is the responsibility of administrators and school leaders to create and instill a vision of excellence for its student population. As an extension, ideally, educational programs should be inclusive of community participation and support. These actions lead to the ultimate vision for schools to be linguistic and cultural sustainable, representing and reflecting the students' multilingual/multicultural lives and experiences.

THE CALL FOR ACTION

California: A Case Study in English Only to Multilingualism

California offers us an example that other states can learn from, as it is the nation's most populous state, with the highest percentage of multilingual learners of any other state. California is also home to a significant percentage of Long-Term English learners (LTELs)—with 59% of all multilingual learners at the secondary levels being identified as LTELs (Olsen, 2012). California's history with bilingual education has not always been a positive one, as few multilingual learners were instructed in dual language bilingual settings over the past 20 years. Despite 1.4 million students enrolling as multilingual learners, the number of these students receiving bilingual education dropped precipitously from 30% in 1998 to less than 5% in 2013 due to Proposition 227. Although two decades ago the state adopted this antibilingual education policy and was heading in the direction of a monolingual English-only state, citizens overwhelmingly passed Proposition 58 in Fall 2016. Under Proposition 58, multilingual learners (and proficient English speakers) in California once again are being honored for their languages, and have an opportunity to become bilingual *and* biliterate. California's current comprehensive, large-scale, and well-funded implementation of Proposition 58 is about righting a historical wrong.

In this way, at this point in history, we are well poised to ensure language equity on behalf of multilingual learners. Key leverage points and systems in California—including the California-English Language Development Standards, English Language Development/English Language Arts Framework, the English Language Proficiency Assessments for California (ELPAC), the EL Roadmap, and Proposition 58—make this a pivotal time for multilingual learners to make measurable academic progress, in the manner that they have always deserved. This section will focus on systemic efforts that California has taken to transform itself from an English-only state into a multilingual leader.

Systems for Change: Global 2030 and the English Learner Roadmap

Thanks to systemic efforts and visionary leadership, California now boasts over 300 two-way dual immersion programs, with more added each year. In 2018, Tom Torlakson, California State Superintendent of Education, launched his Global 2030 California initiative. Global 2030 seeks to double the number of world language classes taught in California schools, more than double the number of bilingual teachers authorized each year, and more than triple the number of graduating high school students who receive a state seal of biliteracy on their diplomas. Perhaps most importantly, it seeks to quadruple the number of dual language immersion programs to 1,600 by 2030 (Torlakson, 2018). Global 2030 is an ambitious goal that is only possible due to other recent multilingual learner policies in California that have paved the way, including the English learner Roadmap.

The California English learner Roadmap State Board of Education Policy: Educational Programs and Services for English learners was passed by the State Board of Education on July 12, 2017. In essence, this new policy eliminates the rigid English only policy that Proposition 227 supported. The EL Roadmap is intended to provide guidance to local educational agencies (LEAs) in order to welcome, understand, and educate the diverse population of students, with a special focus on multilingual learners attending California public schools (CDE, 2017). The vision and mission of the EL Roadmap, according to the California Department of Education website, are as follows, and further provide direction for educational systems regarding *how* to create equitable educational environments for multilingual learners.

EL ROADMAP VISION

Multilingual learners fully and meaningfully access and participate in a 21st-century education from early childhood through Grade 12 that results in their attaining high levels of English proficiency, mastery of grade-level standards, and opportunities to develop proficiency in multiple languages.

EL ROADMAP MISSION

California schools affirm, welcome, and respond to a diverse range of multilingual learner strengths, needs, and identities. California schools prepare graduates with the linguistic, academic, and social skills, and competencies they require for college, career, and civic participation in a global, diverse, and multilingual world, thus ensuring a thriving future for California (CDE, 2017).

The four principles that undergird this new policy include

- **Principle 1: Assets-Oriented and Needs-Responsive Schools**—Pre-schools and schools are responsive to different **multilingual strengths, needs, and identities** and support the socio-emotional health and development of multilingual learners. Programs value and build upon the **cultural and linguistic** assets students bring to their education in safe and affirming school climates. Educators value and build strong family, community, and school partnerships.

- **Principle 2: Intellectual Quality of Instruction and Meaningful Access**—Multilingual learners engage in intellectually rich, developmentally appropriate learning experiences that foster high levels of **English proficiency**. These experiences integrate language development, literacy, and content learning as well as provide access for comprehension and participation through **native language instruction** and scaffolding. Multilingual learners have meaningful access to a full standards-based and relevant curriculum and the opportunity to develop proficiency in English and **other languages**.

- **Principle 3: System Conditions that Support Effectiveness**—Each level of the school system (state, county, district, school, pre-school) has leaders and educators who are knowledgeable of and responsive to the **strengths and needs of multilingual learners** and their communities and who utilize valid assessment and other data systems that inform instruction and continuous improvement. Each level of the school system provides resources and tiered support to ensure strong programs and build the capacity of teachers and staff to leverage the **strengths and meet the needs of multilingual learners**.

- **Principle 4: Alignment and Articulation Within and Across Systems**—Multilingual learners experience a coherent, articulated, and aligned set of practices and pathways across grade levels and educational segments, beginning with a strong foundation in early childhood and appropriate identification of strengths and needs, and continuing through to reclassification, graduation, and higher education. These pathways foster the skills, **language(s)**, literacy, and knowledge students need for college- and career-readiness and participation in a **global, diverse, multilingual, 21st-century world.** (CDE, 2017)

Together, these four principles can lead to educational and linguistic equity for multilingual learners in California. Californians Together and other advocacy groups across the state have been training educators and administrators, as well as trainers of trainers, so that the EL Roadmap becomes deeply engrained in districts and schools across California. The next section will discuss the impact of new educational policies at the classroom level, for both teachers and multilingual learners.

Multilingual Learner Proficiency Assessments and California English Language Development Standards

At the teacher level, the California-English Language Development (ELD) standards provide direction regarding the rigorous language expectations that our multilingual learners need to succeed in both language and across content areas. The California ELD standards align with the ELA standards, as well as the English Language Development/English Language Arts Framework, whereas historically the two sets of standards did not closely support each other. Teachers no longer need to learn a whole new set of standards for multilingual learners that do not connect with their teaching throughout the school day. There is also no longer a disconnect between what is expected of proficient English speakers and multilingual learners. Instead, the two sets of standards—ELD and ELA—work in tandem with each other. During Integrated ELD, content-area standards are at the forefront, but the ELD standards are used to provide a *language scaffold* for that content. The focus, then, of Designated ELD (protected time during the school day—typically 30 minutes—for English language study) should be language with the ELD standards at the forefront, and instruction *connected to content*. That is, teachers are now free to do what we have known was best all along: connect language to content, so that language instruction is not disconnected from what happens throughout the rest of the school day.

Similarly, the English learner Proficiency Assessments for California (ELPAC) are aligned with the ELD standards, and assess listening, speaking, reading, and writing. Instead of assessing language out of context, this rigorous language assessment is also contextualized and embedded in content. For

FIGURE 8.1 **Integrated and Designated ELD: Working in Tandem**

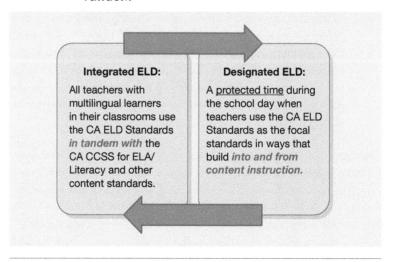

Source: Adapted from 2014 English Language Arts/English Language Development Framework, https://www.cde.ca.gov/ci/rl/cf/.

example, multilingual learners are no longer expected to listen to and retell a story about chocolate chip cookies, but instead must actively listen to an academic presentation and paraphrase key content. This suggests that we must know and teach to the ELD standards deeply, in order for multilingual learners to be successful. These two instructional and assessment shifts, when understood and implemented, are the key levers to language equity for multilingual learners in California. Students who demonstrate proficiency with the CA-ELD standards and the ELPAC can have entryway out of Multilingual Learner programs and into grade-level expectations. Multilingual learners in bilingual programs can continue on their pathway to biliteracy and can be acknowledged for that asset at graduation, which will be described further in the next section.

Seal of Biliteracy

An additional incentive for bilingualism is the state Seal of Biliteracy. In 2012, California became the first state in the nation to award a state Seal of Biliteracy to graduating seniors with demonstrated proficiency in two or more languages. This groundbreaking step was an acknowledgement of the economic and social value of multilingualism, the realities of a global century, and of the high level of academic achievement associated with attaining literacy in multiple languages. Ten thousand Seals were awarded in the first year for proficiency in 29 languages, including American Sign Language. One year later, in June of 2013, the number had more than doubled with 197 school districts, 19 charter schools, and six county offices of education providing 21,655 awards to graduating seniors. Across the nation, other states were inspired to follow California's lead. In 2013, New York, Texas, New Mexico and Illinois adopted state Seals of Biliteracy. In 2014, Washington state followed suit, and three additional states have pending legislation, including Florida, Massachusetts, and Maryland (Californians Together, 2017).

Findings from a survey regarding students' perceptions of the Seal of Biliteracy conducted by researchers Kristin Davin and Amy Heineke (2018) have promising results. Specifically, they surveyed 215 high school seniors in three suburban high school districts in Illinois, nine focus groups with a total of 47 seniors, 23 of whom were pursuing the Seal of Biliteracy. The results suggested that these students valued bilingualism. According to a summary of the results in New America,

> Both English-dominant students and linguistically diverse students shared their interest in being able to communicate and interact with more people. Linguistically diverse students who spoke languages such as Arabic, Korean, Portuguese, Russian, Spanish, and Vietnamese expressed their desire to connect with their own heritage. Overall, students valued being bilingual more (i.e., oral language abilities in a language other than English) than their perspectives on the benefits of being biliterate (i.e., reading and writing abilities in a language other than English). Yet, in two focus groups, linguistically diverse students were interested in learning how to read and write in their home languages. (Colon, 2018)

Such results from student voices point to the possibilities of spreading multilingualism across the country. The next generation of students yearns for connection with each other, across cultures and languages. They see the value, and we must provide programs and opportunities for multilingualism to flourish.

Strengthening Bilingual Teacher Pipelines

Although several bilingual systems and initiatives have flourished in California over the past few years, recent efforts have focused on strengthening the bilingual teacher pipeline, in order to insure that there are enough bilingual teachers to meet the demands of Global 2030. This current shortage is in large part a consequence of years of suppressing bilingual education under Proposition 227. A report by Californians Together (2017) suggests that, "while most districts (58%) have plans to expand bilingual education opportunities in the future, an overwhelming majority (86%) reported facing a shortage of bilingual teachers as a hurdle to realizing those plans. Half of these districts say they expect a major shortage, and overall districts anticipate the shortage will primarily impact early childhood and elementary school levels."

What is important to emphasize in this context is that good intentions and brilliant policies alone are insufficient as drivers of large-scale change. Unless such programs are adequately funded and resourced, change is unlikely to happen. As such, in 2017 the California Department of Education (CDE) announced a Request for Applications (RFA) to fund projects that provide professional learning opportunities to teams of eligible teachers, principals, and paraprofessionals for the purpose of increasing the number of teachers who obtain a bilingual authorization as a result of participation in the program and the number of teachers with a bilingual authorization who return to teaching in a bilingual or multilingual setting. The Bilingual Teacher Professional Development Program (BTPDP) was established to ensure that California can meet its demand for bilingual teachers. The CDE, in consultation with the Commission on Teacher Credentialing (CTC), established eight awards, based upon merit, for $625,000 per award, to at least five of the 11 regions designated by the California County Superintendents Educational Services Association.

Ensuring an adequate supply of qualified bilingual teachers must begin with developing excellent teacher preparation programs. In fall 2018, the Commission on Teacher Credentialing announced the availability of competitive grant funding for eligible Local Education Agencies (LEA) to apply for $25 million in funding to create bilingual teacher residency programs. A school district, county office of education, charter school, or regional occupational center was eligible to apply for funding of up to a maximum of $50,000 per grant to support a collaborative partnership between the eligible LEA and Institute of Higher Education that offers a Commission-approved

This is so inspiring! In addition to the many benefits for multilingual learners, educational pathways towards a Seal of Biliteracy also raise the bar for how English-dominant students learn a new language. It's a common experience for English-dominant students, like me, to take a second language in high school and graduate without fluency or literacy in that language. Since biliteracy programs benefit all kids, be sure to design and refine your programs with an equity lens so they don't widen opportunity gaps, but truly serve multilingual learners.

—Tonya

teacher preparation program. This funding is intended to develop the partnerships' capacity to develop and operate a teacher residency program for bilingual education residents.

Foundations in California have also followed suit in funding bilingual teacher pipeline initiatives. One notable example, the Sobrato Family Foundation, a Northern California real estate foundation, awarded the California Association for Bilingual Education (CABE) with a grant to increase the supply of bilingual teachers and education leaders who are focused on multilingual learners. As such, CABE developed the Bilingual Educator Strategic Training (BEST) Program.

The CABE BEST Teacher Cohort outcomes are as follows:

- Develop expertise around dual immersion (DI) pedagogy with a special emphasis on linguistic transfer and academic Spanish.

- Understand the academic language needs of students in dual immersion programs via DLI shadowing.

- Develop expertise around the Guiding Principles for Dual Language.

- Understand the similarities between the ELD and SLD standards, as well as the role of designated ELD in DI programs.

MULTILINGUAL LEARNERS

Next steps for the BEST program include launching two more teacher cohorts across California, as well as a BEST Administrator Cohort, in order to ensure that administrators can support the growth of bilingual programs in California. Many other such initiatives—either by foundations or education agencies—must be established in order to build, strengthen, and retain bilingual teachers.

The systemic initiatives outlined in this section prove to have promising results for multilingual learners and multilingualism in California. Although the state is still in the early stages of expanding and implementing professional learning programs for bilingual educators, the future of multilingualism in California is bright. This is an exciting time to be a bilingual teacher, as despite our political climate, educational policies are valuing, validating, and supporting multilingual programs that have the potential to close achievement gaps on behalf of multilingual learners.

Summary and Conclusions

The United States is a tremendously rich multilingual/multicultural nation, yet paradoxically, it seems to retain a monolingual, anglocentric identity that tends to be perpetuated in school and beyond. In the name of being a civilized and cultured society, we as a nation must discard this monolingual language ideology in favor of a multilingual one that is reflective of our collective heritage (Garcia & Torres-Guevara, 2010). The irony of maintaining this linguistic stranglehold on English as the language of power is that in this era of globalization, it is multilingualism, not monolingualism, that is not only a necessity but also the norm around the world.

As educators of multilingual learners, we must remove our nation's shackles of xenophobia and isolationism that tend to perpetuate monolingual views and obscure our vision of a multilingual/multicultural mosaic. Instead we must advocate for social justice—the right of our students, their families, and communities to own their languages, cultures, and identities. We can only nudge schools and communities into accepting and transmitting multilingualism, however, their commitment to linguistic and cultural sustainability should be a starting point in positively influencing and gaining acceptance of the true makeup of our society.

Multilingualism is the mainstay of North American life (it always has been), and all indicators point to continued growth of a multilingual school-age demographic in the future. As educators of multilingual learners, we must come to accept and respect the linguistic pluralism of our schools and our nation. In doing so, we should weave communities' "funds of knowledge" and expertise into an integrated curriculum of content and language to shape students' "funds of identity" that is reflective of their individual linguistic and cultural experience and tradition. The rich heritage of our students should be infused into lessons in every classroom to create linguistically and culturally sustainable schools. At the same time, we also must realize that the power of English will not be lost and that our students will be able to use their full linguistic repertoire to reach new academic heights.

We are beginning to see the joining of forces and the sharing of goals within and across language education communities. Our California case study is one example of an entire state mobilizing around a multilingual imperative. We've witnessed the coming together of the fields of language education through the lens of multilingualism-including dual language, immersion, bilingual education, and "foreign language" or world languages in theory (as in the seminal article by The Douglas Fir Group, 2016) as well as in practice (as in Utah's dual language immersion program). The Seal of Biliteracy has become a reality in school districts and states; it is currently awarded to students, whether previously exposed to multiple languages or not, who have attained proficiency in two or more languages, usually at the close of high school, according to specified criteria (see https://sealofbiliteracy.org). We have seen how California Together and other grass-roots advocacy organizations around the country have banded together in a campaign to support and grow multilingualism in K–12 settings while empowering students and teachers.

We have also witnessed how states, school districts, schools, and organizations are initiating multiple pathways to multilingualism whether through acceptance of student interaction in natural settings, participation of growing numbers in multilingual programs, or recognition of bilingual excellence by meeting local language criteria. At the same time, teachers are becoming more aware and accepting of the benefits of having multilingual/multicultural students bring their diverse perspectives and worldviews into classrooms and school life. Through extended coursework, professional learning opportunities, conferences, and digital networks, teachers and school leaders are becoming more attuned to the wealth and richness of their surrounding multilingual community resources that help enlighten stakeholders and enrich their schools.

As educators, we must ensure that students in this digital age have the communicative skills to engage in and contribute to an ever-expanding global network. To do so, we must invite students' participation in deep learning through rich, challenging, and stimulating curriculum that integrates content and language while highlighting academic language use in meaningful contexts (Gottlieb & Ernst-Slavit, 2014). We must have linguistically and culturally sustainable classrooms and schools where multilingual learners have opportunities to learn in multiple languages. Through gradual release of responsibility, we must lead students to become autonomous, independent, and self-regulated thinkers and learners.

High schools should become laboratories for students to explore entering the field of multilingual education within their own communities. Internships, mentoring programs, and tutorials, both internal and external to school, should apprentice students to possible options for the future. In addition, students should have a venue for sharing cross-cultural and cross-linguistic resources, including digital connections, international exchanges, and global projects that can make a genuine positive impact.

Teacher preparation programs must become responsive to the changing demographic of our schools and our nation's youth who are entering the work force as paraprofessionals and beginning teachers. We need to revisit the notion that a single course on multilingual learners will suffice and infuse multilingual/multicultural perspectives throughout undergraduate and graduate programs. Practicums inclusive of multilingual learners should be offered throughout community colleges and universities and should become the mainstay of coursework in education.

The goal of education should be to strive to achieve excellence through equity for every student (Blankstein & Noguera, 2015). In the future, we envision equity for multilingual children and youth being achieved through languages and cultures that connect school to home and community. Thus, we improve the likelihood of our multilingual learners to feel a sense of efficacy and be equipped with resources to combat social injustice.

We envision a time when all teachers prepared to understand the complexities of language development so that they can seamlessly interweave content and language in their classrooms and defend the right of multilingual

> This is so true especially to ensure English-dominant white educators like me (about 80% of teachers) build the cultural competencies, assets-based, anti-racist practice, and pedagogical skills to effectively teach in linguistically diverse schools. When the shift to multilingualism Margo and Ivannia call for in this chapter becomes the norm, future teachers will begin developing these competencies though their own K–12 multilingual learning!
> —Tonya

learners to communicate in the language of their choice during learning. In the future, we foresee the education community respecting monolingualism while embracing multilingualism as a means of learning, a way of life, and a cherished value of our society.

References

Barac, R., & Bialystok, E. (2011). Cognitive development of bilingual children. *Language Teaching, 44*(1), 36–54.

Bialystok, E. (2009). Bilingualism: The good, the bad, and the indifferent. *Bilingualism: Language and Cognition, 12*(1), 3–11.

Bilingual Education Act (BEA) (81 Stat. 816), Title VII of the Elementary and Secondary Education Amendments of 1967 (Pub.L. 90–247, January 2, 1968).

Blankstein, A. M., & Noguera, P. (Eds.). (2015). *ExcELence through equity: Five principles of courageous leadership to guide achievement for every student.* Alexandria, VA: ASCD.

Buriel, R., Perez, W., De Ment, T. L., Chavez, D. V., & Moran, V. R. (1998). The relationship of language brokering to academic performance, biculturalism, and self-efficacy among Latino adolescents. *Hispanic Journal of Behavioral Sciences, 20*(3), 283–297. From PsycINFO database.

Californians Together. (2017). *Multiple pathways to biliteracy.* Long Beach, CA: Californians Together.

Castañeda v. Pickard, 648 F.2d 989 (5th Cir. 1981).

Christenson, S. L., Reschly, A. L., & Wylie, C. (2012). (Eds.). *Handbook of research on student engagement.* New York, NY: Springer.

College Board (2017). Class of 2017 SAT Results. College Board.

Cook, V. J. (2016). Premises of multi-competence. In V.J. Cook & Li Wei (Eds.). *The Cambridge Handbook of Linguistic Multi-Competence.* New York, NY: Cambridge University Press.

Cunningham, T. H., & Graham, C. R. (2000). Increasing native English vocabulary recognition through Spanish immersion: Cognate transfer from foreign to first language. *Journal of Educational Psychology, 92*(1), 37–49. From PsycINFO database.

EL Roadmap (2017). Sacramento, CA: California Department of Education.

Esteban-Guitart, M., & Moll, L. C. (2014). Funds of identity: A new concept based on the Funds of Knowledge approach. *Culture & Psychology, 20*(1), 31–48.

Garcia, O., Ibarra Johnson, S., & Seltzer, K. (2017). *The translanguaging classroom: Leveraging student bilingualism for learning.* Philadelphia, PA: Caslon.

Garcia, O., & Torres-Guevara, R. (2010). Monoglossic ideologies and language policies in the education of U.S. Latinas/os. In E. G. Murillo, S. A. Villena, R. T. Galván, R. S. Muñoz, C. Martínez, & M. Machada-Casas (Eds.), *Handbook of Latinos in education: Theory, research, and practice* (pp. 182–193). New York, NY: Routledge.

Genesee, F. (2016). *At-risk learners and bilingualism: Is it a good idea?* Retrieved from http://www.colorincolorado.org/article/risk-learners-and-bilingualism-it-good-idea

Gibbons, P. (2009). *English learns academic literacy and thinking: Learning in the challenge zone.* Portsmouth, NH: Heinemann.

Goldenberg, C., & Coleman, R. (2010). *Promoting academic achievement among English learners: A guide to the research.* Thousand Oaks, CA: Corwin.

González, N., Moll, L. C., & Amanti, C. (2013). *Funds of knowledge: Theorizing practices in households, communities, and classrooms*. London, UK: Routledge.

Gottlieb, M. (2016). *Assessing English language learners: Bridges to equity* (2nd Ed.). Thousand Oaks, CA: Corwin.

Gottlieb, M., & Castro, M. (2017). *Language power: Key uses for accessing content*. Thousand Oaks, CA: Corwin.

Gottlieb, M., & Ernst-Slavit, G. (2014). *Academic language in diverse classrooms: Promoting content and language learning, Definitions and contexts*. Thousand Oaks, CA: Corwin.

Heineke, Davin, & Bedford (2018). The Seal of Biliteracy: Considering Equity and Access for English learners education policy analysis archives, [S.l.], v. 26, p. 99, aug. 2018. ISSN 1068-2341. Available at: <https://epaa.asu.edu/ojs/article/view/3825>.

Hilliard, J., & Gottlieb, M. (2018). *Language, Culture, Literacy, Art and Virtual Education Bilingual Curriculum Development Institute (La Clave) de Oaxaca, Module 1*. Chicago, IL: Paridad.

Hornberger, N. H., & Link, H. (2012). Translanguaging and transnational literacies in multilingual classrooms: A biliteracy lens. *International Journal of Bilingual Education and Bilingualism, 15*(3), 261–278.

Kieffer & Thompson (2018). Hidden Progress of Multilingual Students on NAEP. *Educational Researcher*. https://doi.org/10.3102/0013189X18777740

Lau v. Nichols, 414 U.S. 5637 (1974).

Martin-Rhee, M., & Bialystok, E. (2008). The development of two types of inhibitory control in monolingual and bilingual children. *Bilingualism: Language and Cognition, 11*(1), 81–93. doi:10.1017/S1366728907003227

Menken, K. (2008). *English learners left behind: Standardized testing as language policy*. Tonawanda, NY: Multilingual Matters.

Miramontes, O. B., Nadeau, A., & Commins, N. L. (2011). *Restructuring schools for linguistic diversity: Linking decision making to effective programs* (2nd Ed.). New York, NY: Teachers College.

Moll, L., & González, N. (1994). Lessons from research with language minority students. *Journal of Reading Behavior, 26*(4), 23–41.

Olsen, L. (2010). *Reparable Harm: Fulfilling the unkept promise of educational opportunity for California's Long Term English Learners*. Long Beach, CA: Californians Together.

Olsen, S., & Brown, L. (1992, Spring). The relation between high school study of foreign languages and ACT English and mathematics performance. *ADFL Bulletin, 23*(3), 47–50. From ERIC database.

Ovando, C. (2003, Spring). Bilingual education in the United States: Historical development and current issues. *The Bilingual Research Journal, 27*(1), 1–24.

Panetta, L. (2018, August 6). Americans are losing out because so few speak a second language. *The San Francisco Chronicle*. Retrieved from https://www.sfchronicle.com/opinion/openforum/article/Americans-are-losing-out-because-so-few-speak-a-13135901.php?utm_campaign=twitter-premium&utm_source=CMS%20Sharing%20Button&utm_medium=social

Paris, D. (2012). Culturally sustaining pedagogy: A needed change in stance, terminology, and practice. *Educational Researcher, 41*(3), 93–97.

Rodríguez, D., Carrasquillo, A., & Lee, K. S. (2014). *The bilingual advantage: Promoting academic development, biliteracy, and native language in the classroom*. New York, NY: Teachers College Press.

The Douglas Fir Group. (2016). A transdisciplinary framework for SLA in a multilingual world. *The Modern Language Journal, 100*(S1), 19–47.

Thomas, W., Collier, V., & Abbott, M. (1993). Academic achievement through Japanese, Spanish or French: The first two years of partial immersion. *Modern Language Journal, 77*(2), 170–179. From PsycINFO database.

Torlakson, T. (2018, August 20). This is why California needs to expand bilingual education. *The Sacramento Bee*. Retrieved from https://www.sacbee.com/opinion/op-ed/soapbox/article216851715.html

Umansky, I., Valentino, R., & Reardon, S. F. (2015). The promise of bilingual and dual immersion education (*CEPA Working Paper No.15-11*). Retrieved from Stanford Center for Education Policy Analysis: http://cepa.stanford.edu/wp15-11

Vander Ark, T. (2015, December 21). 10 tips for developing student agency. *Education Week*. Retrieved from http://blogs.edweek.org/edweek/on_innovation/2015/12/10_tips_for_developing_student_agency.html

Westly, E. (2011, July/August). The bilingual advantage: Learning a second language can give kids' brains a boost. *Scientific American, 22*, 38–41. Retrieved from http://strawberrychildcarec.ipower.com/pdf/The-Bilingual-Advantage-Scientific-American-August-2011.pdf

Zwiers, J. (2008). *Building academic language: Essential practices for content classrooms, grades 5-12*. San Francisco, CA: Jossey-Bass.

chapter nine

From Nobody Cares to Everyone/Every Community Cares

DEBBIE ZACARIAN
AND MARIA G. DOVE

PREMISE

As educators, our individual perspective, despite our most sincere commitment and dedication to bring out the best in our students, has not led to closing the opportunity gap between English learners and their American English-fluent peers. Supporting educators as well as teacher educators to build and sustain programming developed from open and flexible partnerships with students and families, as well as the school and the local community can better assist us in closing these gaps and helping students to flourish in school and their lives.

VIGNETTE

Javier is a fourth-grade student who spent his first six years of life in a rural village in Guatemala. His family fled their village home overnight after it was overtaken by a group of armed criminals, who were assaulting and extorting their neighbors and friends. When Javier finally arrived in the United States with his mother and younger sister, he was confused, anxious, and afraid. He was enrolled in school for the first time in a second-grade class; he had had no formal schooling in Guatemala. The screening process for new entrants identified Javier as an English learner (EL) at the beginning stage, and subsequently, he was placed in an English language development program that supplemented the instruction that he received in his regular class to support his acquisition of English language and literacy skills.

Javier's overall progress during his first year in school was identified as slow, at best. Initially, he had some minor behavior problems—being uncooperative with his teacher and other students, having occasional emotional outbursts, and refusing to abide by certain class rules. At other times, he appeared to be quite sullen, indifferent, and detached. After a few short months, his behavioral issues began to subside, and he had gained enough English to make himself understood, but his literacy and math skills were far below his peers, which, at first, was understandable for an EL newcomer.

By the time he reached fourth grade, Javier was able to understand spoken English well and use his oral language skills to spontaneously respond appropriately and fluidly in routine situations as well as discuss concrete academic topics in school. In spite of these gains in developing his English language skills, Javier continued to struggle academically as well as socially and emotionally. He was significantly behind his peers in reading and mathematics, and his behavior problems began to resurface. His teacher became increasingly concerned. As a result, she thought she would request that Javier be further evaluated through the committee on special education (also commonly referred as the child study team). After an initial discussion with the principal and school psychologist, Javier's lack of English proficiency was cited as the most likely cause affecting his academic progress and behavior. They recommended delaying any further evaluation of Javier in order to give him more time. As a consequence of this decision, Javier's issues were not investigated or systematically mitigated any further, and his mother was never consulted about any of these matters. Indeed, his mother rarely attended any events at his school, as almost all of the communication with them came in a routine form in a language that she did not understand. By the end of fourth grade, Javier continued to struggle in school.

THE URGENCY

In the shadows of our classrooms hiding in plain sight, there are English learners, such as Javier, who have secrets they never tell, troubles they never share, or voices that are never heard. While we often think of such children and their families as merely having language barriers that can be remedied with translators, we inevitably miss the important and significant distinctions among this diverse group. Many of these children and their families have not had prior schooling and literacy experiences, and/or their experiences are quite distinct from what typically occurs in American schools while others have had interrupted and limited educational experiences. Although these families bring with them their own rich traditions, as well as personal, social, and cultural assets and experiences, many of them are unfamiliar with

American public schooling and the cultural ways of being and acting in the United States.

Furthermore, some of these families live in extreme poverty and are unfamiliar with or fearful of the services offered to those in similar conditions. Additionally, there are also a significant number who have experienced or are experiencing some form of significant trauma that is causing them significant physical or emotional stress—such as serious illnesses, the death of a loved one, abuse, neglect, food instability, homelessness, the chronic stress of being undocumented or being a citizen child of an undocumented parent who may or may not have been deported, as well as those that have experienced war, civil unrest, extreme natural disasters, and so on.

When children who are English learners have or have had one or more of these various experiences and do not perform academically as expected, the pervasive effects of their experiences are often not called into question. Instead, traditional steps are generally taken to remediate students' learning through the development of their basic knowledge and skills either within the same assigned classes as American English-fluent peers or in segregated specialized classes to narrow the gap. If improvement does not develop within a specified timeframe, special education committees often investigate students' learning and cognitive abilities to further explore the reasons for these deficits in achievement. What exacerbates these complexities even further is, unfortunately, conventional methods of academic evaluation that often do not reveal the underlying strengths and assets of such students and their potential for student achievement. Further, all too often, parents/guardians are distanced from being true partners with us on behalf of their child's learning and membership in the classroom and school communities.

On the flip side, most educators are not familiar with their English learners' and families' prior experiences and the majority has never been trained to work with students and families whose life experiences are different from their own. It is much too common a practice for school leaders and faculty to dismiss the academic struggles of ELs and blame their lack of academic progress on their absence of English language proficiency. Further, ELs are viewed as a homogeneous group of learners with a single shortcoming (that of needing to learn English) instead of being individual learners with richly complex strengths and assets as well as needs. Partnering with families, particularly with those who speak a language other than English, can also seem daunting for some school leaders, teachers, and staff, especially those with little personal and professional experience or formal training working with culturally and linguistically diverse people. It takes special skills and additional effort to open the lines of communication with these families to capitalize on their diverse personal, social, cultural, and world backgrounds and the unique knowledge and perspectives they bring to our school community.

In this chapter, we attempt to break down the wall of impassivity and unresponsiveness to children and families from diverse experiences by moving

Debbie and Maria succinctly describe what is happening in so many schools! I hope the schools and policy makers begin conversations that lead to swift action.

—**Margarita**

away from *nobody cares* to *every community cares*. We show how it is much more possible to close the gaps that we are experiencing when we work in partnership with students, their families, our school and local communities, as well as faculty from institutions of higher education to support this type of partnership effort in preparing pre and inservice teachers to meet the ever-changing needs of English learners.

THE EVIDENCE

In 1988, educational scholar, Lisa Delpit called for educators to value the differing perspectives and experiences of students, families, and family communities. She argued that to do this, we have to be willing to acknowledge the power imbalance that occurs when we work with marginalized student and family populations. In addition, she called for us to embrace the strengths of the languages, literacies, cultures, and experiences of students while at the same time supporting them to be successful in school. She aptly argued that taking this stance required that educators honor and value the strengths and assets that all students and families possess and bring with them as they become involved in our schools. Her words are as relevant today as they were over a quarter of a century ago. While English learners had historically been educated in urban districts, they are now enrolled in rural, suburban, and urban districts across our nation (U.S. Department of Education, 2015). Further, it is almost impossible to ignore the persistent gaps that occurred during the decades before she spoke and have continued right up to the present time. For example, 32% of eighth-grade English learners scored at the basic level or above in reading versus 78% of English-fluent students (National Assessment of Educational Progress (2017). Further, far fewer English learners graduate from high school than do almost every other group (National Center for Education Statistics, 2017).

These realities have led many scholars to research and rethink how to address these poor outcomes. One area that is critical is how educators can raise the amount of meaningful, purposeful, and relational communication with students and their families so that we can make school a more inclusive positive, productive, and successful experience for everyone. To do that, it is important to rethink the practice of partnering with English learners and their parents/guardians and families so that we may be more in tune with the vast strengths and assets that they possess and support schools to be more of a match for their skills and interests than they have been.

A First Step in Transforming Practice

A first step in engaging in this type of thinking is to have a deeper understanding of the rapid and dramatic demographic changes that are occurring in our student and family populations. For example, suburban schools that had recently been all white are seeing rapid growth and dynamic changes in students and families from culturally, economically, linguistically, and racially diverse student and family populations (Edwards, Domke, and White, 2017). Additionally, while schools in high poverty and/or urban areas employ a higher percentage of diverse teachers, the overwhelming percentage of the nation's school principals and teachers are white (U.S. Department of Education, 2016). Moreover, and startlingly, over half of the nation's students live in poverty (Southern Education Foundation, 2015), and an overwhelmingly epic number of English learners live in extreme poverty. According to a 2013 Grantmakers for Education report, 60% of English learners' families had incomes that were 185% below poverty level. What constitutes a family is also evolving in our contemporary diverse society. It now includes children being raised by two parents, a single parent, foster parent, grandparent, blended parent, and/or with extra-familial supports (Zacarian & Silverstone, 2015) as well as students being reared in institutional settings, such as the more recent apprehended undocumented children who were taken from their parents to live in tents on our southern border and throughout our country like seeds in the wind. It is also critical to consider that English learners are one of the most rapidly growing groups across the nation (National Center for Education Statistics, 2018). In addition, it is almost impossible to ignore the epic number of students experiencing trauma, violence, and chronic stress. According to the Data Resource Center for Child and Adolescent Health (2011/2012), over half of the nation's students have had one or more significantly adverse childhood experiences including physical, sexual, or verbal abuse; physical or emotional neglect; a parent who is addicted to alcohol or drugs; witnessing a mother who is abused; a family member in jail; the loss of a parent to death, abandonment, or divorce; and/or mental illness of family member. While many English learners' families have experienced these adversities, millions have had adverse experiences that are distinct from these. For example, many are refugees who have come to the United States from African, South Asian, Asian, and Latin American nations fleeing crises in their homelands (U.S. Department of State, 2015). In addition, millions are undocumented or are citizen-children of at least one parent who is undocumented and live in chronic fear of being deported (Menjivar and Cervantes, 2016).

While the need for working closely with these increasingly diverse populations is an urgent need so that we may become familiar with one another and work together on behalf of students' success, many educators have found themselves mistakenly questioning whether culturally, economically, linguistically, and racially diverse families actually value education and really care about their child's educational successes and failures (Noguera, 2001). Further, while we know the value of parent involvement and engagement, we often find ourselves doing this work in the same ways and by doing the same things that we have been doing for decades. Perhaps this is occurring because the vast majority of us are white (U.S. Department of Education, 2016) or white and middle class (Hollins and Guzman, 2005). Further, we received our post-secondary education in institutions of higher education that are overwhelmingly and predominantly dominated by full-time faculty who also are white (National Center for Education Statistics, May 2018). Another challenge is many of us who teach people of color in poor urban and rural areas were "fast-tracked" into teaching in these communities without the level of adequate training and preparation that we and, more importantly, our students and their families sorely need us to possess (Zeichner, 2012).

A Second Step in Transforming Practice

These disparate realities require that we rethink how to meet the academic and social-emotional needs of English learners, and how we can truly partner together and more closely with their families on behalf of their child's success in school and beyond. To do this, it's also helpful to look back at history to examine whether schools have kept pace with the rapid changes that are occurring to our nation's population. Prior to the 1954 landmark U.S. Supreme Court *Brown v. the Board of Education* decision, which sought to end the inequities that were occurring nationwide, a universal public education was mostly intended for white Americans (Flores and Halsall, 2017). Since 1954, there have been a variety of actions and initiatives that point to the importance of working more closely with students and families and to become more familiar with these practices—all intended to lead to better outcomes. These include the Civil Rights Movement of the 1960s, the charter school movement in the 1990s, the No Child Left Behind Act of 2002, the Race to the Top Initiative of 2009, the Common Core Standards of 2010, and the Every Child Succeeds Act of 2015. Each of these has been intended to remedy the persistent and pervasive gaps that have been occurring amongst underrepresented populations (Swanson, 2011). In addition, while family involvement has long been known as a critical element in a child's education, most educators learn how to work with families as they are actually doing it or "on the job" as opposed to engaging in formal or even informal professional development about it (Henderson, Mapp, Johnson, & Davies, 2007).

THE VISION

Educators frequently witness students who are struggling in schools—they cannot read or write on grade level; they have trouble recalling basic math facts; they have problems paying attention or exhibit troublesome behaviors in school. Yet, many school administrators, faculty, and staff have yet to discover the root cause of what is impacting an alarming number of students whose experiences are distinct from their educators and, as important, how to best support this diverse population of students. A way of approaching these issues is to adopt a strengths-based teaching and school-community partnership framework in which all students and families feel and experience a sense of belonging, acknowledgment, value, and competence (Zacarian, Alvarez-Ortiz, & Haynes, 2017; Zacarian & Silverstone, 2015).

Although there is little doubt how much time educators spend developing their skills and strategies to effect student outcomes positively (Grant & Ray, 2016), much less time seems to be devoted to pursuing efforts to engage diverse families and empower parents in some school districts. Yet, family engagement is a crucial part of advancing school reform efforts (Cavanagh, 2012; Mapp & Kuttner, 2013). First and foremost, there needs to be a positive mindset among all members of the school community regarding family engagement. School leaders and teachers, who foster and maintain positive family engagement, have been determined to be most effective with bringing about successful student outcomes. According to Henderson and Mapp (2002), studies suggest that students with engaged parents, regardless of their cultural background or socioeconomic status, generally do the following:

- Earn higher grades.
- Enroll in higher-level programs.
- Are most often promoted or pass their classes.
- Have regular school attendance.
- Exhibit positive social skills and school behaviors.
- Graduate and continue their education.

Yet, barriers to engaging students' families, and in particular, those families who are from diverse backgrounds and/or speak a language other than English, presents unique challenges to schools. According to Grant and Ray (2016), "Despite research to the contrary, unfortunately, some teachers think that families are not valuable resources in educating students, and hence, they do not promote family engagement" (p. 10). Other sources of barriers to school-family engagement are from families who may have their own time constraints, lack English skills, or hold cultural traditions that distinctly separate their roles as parents from the roles of educators, as well as the school community, who may create policies and practices that make families feel unwelcomed and family engagement a low priority (Grant & Ray, 2016).

THE CALL FOR ACTION

When people in general are asked how they accomplish what others seemingly cannot, invariably they respond by talking about priorities—what you focus on, you accomplish. In the same way, our call to action is to have school communities making school-family-community partnerships a critical concern. Having these partnerships as a most valued goal requires efforts from the various factions involved in these partnerships.

TRAINING EDUCATORS

First and foremost, change needs to begin in the way we prepare teachers and administrators for working in the field. Some institutions of higher education (IHEs) offer separate coursework about culturally and linguistically diverse students, but the majority of IHEs do not incorporate such studies into their general coursework for developing educators. In all preparation programs, pre-service educators must be provided not only with formal training to work with diverse students who are culturally, linguistically, racially, and economically different from their own experiences (Darling-Hammond & Rothman, 2015), but also with the ability to recognize and develop the necessary strategies for working with children and their families from diverse backgrounds and, more importantly, building sustained partnerships with them on behalf of their child's membership in their school and classroom communities and their academic development.

Pre-service teachers are given little if any guidance to work with their students' families, and when parents or guardians speak a language other than English, it can cause even greater anxiety and avoidance on their part. Walker & Dotger (2012) note that "communicating with families is a central facet of the teaching profession, yet few teacher education institutions help candidates develop their knowledge, skills, and dispositions for family school partnership" (p. 71). Unfortunately, most student-teaching experiences are not organized to include pre-service teachers' engagement with students' families on a regular basis.

Student teachers, when placed in the field, may also experience the negativity that some inservice teachers have toward certain parents and parental groups. Spending time in the teachers' lounge or lunchroom can expose teacher candidates to the unfavorable discussions teachers sometimes have about particular students and their families. At times, ill-conceived notions about students' ethnic and racial backgrounds and misconceptions about students' cultural heritages are bandied about with certain teachers proclaiming their general bias about how particular family groups do not care about their children's education. These first encounters about relationships with students' families can be disheartening to budding teachers. They may also intensify the preconceived notions of inexperienced teachers when they encounter families unlike their own. Moon and Neville (2017) advise that "ridding pre-service teachers of negative assumptions about students' families is a critical step in ensuring improvement of communication between home and school" (p. 5).

One of the key challenges for teacher education programs is ensuring that they embrace family engagement practices with our ever-increasing diverse populations of English learners' families. Doing this requires that teacher educators adopt the ideals of family engagement by

- Having an expectation of a positive outcome.
- Unconditionally accepting families.

- Building a community of trust in which all members are interdependent on the other on behalf of students' social-emotional and academic development. (Zacarian & Silverstone, 2020)

To do this, teacher educators must use an assets-based approach with pre- and inservice educators in which educators' engagement with families of English learners is always, consistently, and routinely intended to provide families with a feeling that they are welcome, valued, honored, and competent. Teacher education programs need to offer pre-service teachers better opportunities to learn about, see models of, and practice building positive and productive relationships with families as well as community organizations that assist family groups to develop the skills and strategies for welcoming parents to participate in their children's education. Further, teacher educator programs need to support pre- and inservice educators in engaging activities that move beyond traditional parent-teacher conferences and "open house" events (as these are full of implied rules and meanings that are generally understood by native speakers of American English) to build the kinds of partnerships that are needed with families of English learners. To further these goals, schools of education must support teacher candidates to do the following:

- Understand the importance of and have opportunities to practice consistent, positive communication with students' families to fulfill their student-teaching requirements.

- Build strategies for corresponding with families who speak little or no English such as using school and community resources as well as technology to translate information.

- Role play or participate in mock parent-teacher conferences and other forms of parent-teacher communication that may require difficult conversations.

- Avoid stereotyping, making assumptions, or drawing conclusions about families based on their ethnic or racial background, cultural heritage, religious beliefs, and so forth.

- Develop realistic expectations for fostering family-school relationships.

- Create classroom and school-based events that are intended for building meaningful relationships with families, showcasing students' learning, drawing from the rich resources of families, and creating a home-school culture of learning. (Zacarian & Silverstone, 2015)

COLLABORATIVE DISTRICT-BASED PRACTICES

In order to better serve the needs of English learners, building collaborative district-based and/or school-based communities of practice, where the formation of teaching partnerships and teams yield continuous learning about ELs, should be the norm. Yet, effective collaboration can only occur when there is a systemic understanding of the need for such practices as well as the time, structures, protocols, and specific goals in place for it to occur. School leaders must consider how to ensure that faculty and staff have the understanding, training, and opportunities for sharing their expertise, investigating solutions, planning instruction, and creating a culture that fosters all members of a school to become a part of a community of learners (Dove & Honigsfeld, 2018; Honigsfeld & Dove, 2019). These collaborative practices are particularly crucial in diverse communities:

> When complex learning environments are as diverse as they tend to be in classrooms across the United States, curricular and instructional decisions must be made carefully and intentionally. . . . In the best interest of the students, educators must collaborate and develop innovative strategies to design classroom instruction. (Honigsfeld & Dove, 2019, p. 2)

Moreover, collaborative practices can create opportunities for teachers to explore concerns that go beyond instructional considerations to create safe learning environments and truly support the complex issues that some culturally and linguistically diverse families face such as homelessness, food insecurity, undocumented immigration status, family member deportation, and so on.

Collaboration is key in order to be able to support English learners through an assets-based approach. Drawing on students' cultural, linguistic, and social knowledge, interests, strengths, and talents, assets-based teaching can uncover English learners' true potential by tapping into these assets. Collaborative partnerships can support teachers to surrender their ideas of deficit-based models of instruction in which ELs are viewed as limited due to their absence of English-language skills. This shift to strength-based teaching can be instituted through the negotiation and development of instructional supports and strategies that build on students' strengths as well as make them more successful academically.

Having a diverse mix of collaborative partners allows for a richer exploration of knowledge and ideas that can enhance and foster reciprocal learning opportunities to uncover cultural understandings and consider multiple perspectives. Various types of school and community partnerships can create opportunities to develop more culturally inclusive school curricula that reflect the values, attitudes, and beliefs of both minority as well as mainstream cultures. These are the most beneficial when the partners work from a strengths-based disposition in which all members, students, families, school communities, and community-based partners see and operate from the assets and strengths that each possesses.

Debbie and Maria help us to see that it is not just the one bilingual or ESOL teacher in the school who is responsible for engaging parents. It takes the preparation of all the teachers in the school!
—Margarita

PARENTS AS PARTNERS

Experts in family engagement, Henderson and colleagues (2007) use the term *partnerships* to define the special qualities that can occur when students, educators, parents, and community members work closely together. To do this, we must work relentlessly to build a strong sense of value, trust, confidence, and competence in working with each another on behalf of students' social-emotional and academic development. School communities first need to consider how to foster such relationships. This consideration should begin by working from the premise that *all* families have strengths and assets that can and do support students. The type of strengths-based perspective that we are referring to occurs when we take time to meet with families for the purpose of building relationships with them and honoring, valuing, and acknowledging the special resources and strengths that they possess so we may develop strong, lasting, and mutually fulfilling partnerships (Saint-Jacques, Turcotte, & Pouliot, 2009). What is particularly helpful to this end is showing our curiosity and interest in getting to know the families of our English learners on a personal level.

If we consider our typical enrollment process, however, more often than not, parents/guardians travel either to a centralized location or to their child's local neighborhood school to complete a set of standardized documents (such as the school's emergency contact form as well as a student's medical and prior school history form). Once these are completed successfully, children are generally enrolled without their educators really knowing much about their and their families' interests, talents, hopes, and dreams. Further, within the span of a few weeks or months after the enrollment process, parents and guardians are generally invited to attend an *Open House* or *Curriculum Night* at their child's school where parents and guardians usually sit passively while their child's teacher shares what students are learning (Zacarian & Silverstone, 2015). Parent-teacher conferences generally replicate the same type of passive participation among families and rarely result in engendering the type of reciprocal relationships that we are seeking as we attempt to build real partnerships with families (Lawrence-Lightfoot, 2003; Zacarian & Silverstone, 2015).

It's helpful to think of every meeting that we have with families as partnership meetings that occur for the purpose of a positive outcome, unconditionally valuing and welcoming family involvement, and for building a community of trust with and among families. To do this, according to family expert Joyce Epstein (2011), we must care for families in the same way we care for their children.

Using this idea as a springboard for parent partnerships, here are some ideas and tools for building partnerships families of English learners. It is helpful to be guided by three overarching questions when working with families:

1. How can I keep parents/guardians continuously informed of what their child is doing well?

2. How can I express this even in the smallest of ways to celebrate the successes of their child?

3. How can I support families to celebrate the assets, strengths, and resources that they bring to their child's learning? (Zacarian, Alvarez-Ortiz, & Haynes, 2017)

In the beginning of our chapter, we presented a short vignette of a student, Javier. In it, we described the limited contact that the school had with his mother. Let's change the vignette to show how educators can respond to the three guiding questions to better ensure the type of parent partnerships that we are describing.

When Javier was enrolled in a fourth-grade class, his teacher, Mrs. Nelson, eagerly met with his mother during the first week of school. Mrs. Nelson first sent a note home, ensuring that it was also written in Spanish. The letter stated that she was eager to have Javier in her class and looking forward to meeting with her and any other family member that she would like included. The letter also provided a possible date, time, and place for them to meet and asked if she could come. It also asked that Javier's mother provide an alternative if the date, time, and place didn't work. Javier, his younger sister, Anna, and mother came to school a few days later. They came with a family friend. With the support of a translator, Mrs. Nelson welcomed everyone. With the support of a whole-school practice regarding the engagement of parents of English learners whose home language survey indicated that they were most comfortable communicating in their home language, she set aside double the time that she normally allotted for parent meetings conducted in English only. This practice better ensured that their two-way communication was translated meaningfully and that she could ask questions that supported a partnership purpose. These included the following questions (adapted from Zacarian, Alvarez-Ortiz, & Haynes, 2017):

1. What are Javier's special interests?

2. What are some things that you particularly enjoy about Javier?

3. What particular talents and skills does Javier possess?

4. What are some things that you enjoy doing as a family?

5. We want our classroom and school to be a welcoming place for you and your children. What would make coming to our school or my classroom more enjoyable?

6. I welcome working in partnership with you. Is there any particular way that you would like to help me to make Javier's school experience a great one?

7. What special talents or interests would you like to share with the students in Javier's class or with their families?

8. What are your hopes and dreams for Javier's education?

9. What questions do you wish I had asked and would like to be sure are included?

Mrs. Nelson listened attentively throughout the meeting. She found out that Javier loved to play soccer and that he treasured his sister and often doted over her. She also found out that one of his favorite activities was listening to stories about his family. Javier's mother also shared some of the tragedies that they had experienced in their homeland and why they had fled. She shared that Javier often had nightmares and that they were all having a hard time coping with what they had experienced. When asked about her hopes and dreams for Javier, his mother stated that she wanted Javier to be happy and to make friends in his new school.

Armed with this information, Mrs. Nelson told them about the town's soccer team and that she would be happy to reach out to her school's liaison to help Javier join the soccer program. She explained that she knew that many of the children in her class participated and that she was sure that the liaison would be happy to help Javier be included. Mrs. Nelson also took time to share with Javier how special it was that he had a little sister and that she knew her teacher also would be welcoming her to the second grade.

Later the next week, the soccer coach did, indeed, reach out to Javier's family and, with help from a family from Mexico who speaks Spanish, encouraged him to join the town soccer team, which he did. Within the first month, he was an active and well-liked member of the team. Mrs. Nelson also had the support of a bilingual translator who came to her class during mathematics, science, and social studies to translate what was occurring. And, while the translator was assigned to work with Javier and other English learners in her class, she had a desk that sat adjacent to Mrs. Nelson's, and all of the students in this fourth-grade class saw her as a member of their classroom community. In addition, Javier received instruction in English language development during his entire language arts block where he joined peers who were also English learners.

During the first few days of school, when Javier began crying at recess, Mrs. Nelson and the translator met with Javier and his school's counselor. Javier shared that he was afraid to go outside because he feared that someone would be killed. Empathetically and with support of his mother and the school's counselor and translator, Javier slowly learned to feel more comfortable on the playground.

In addition, when Mrs. Nelson and Javier's ESOL teacher communicated with his mother to discuss Javier's progress (and they did this frequently), they always had the support of a translator who provided a flow of communication among them that would otherwise have been impossible. Further, whenever they communicated, Mrs. Nelson positively spoke about the successes that

Javier had experienced in school and shared what she observed by drawing from the many strengths that she had noticed. Here are some examples:

"It is great to see Javier come to school on time. He demonstrates such responsibility! Thank you for helping him to get ready for school and come to school on time! Thank you for being such a great partner with me!"

"I appreciate how much time Javier is taking to participate in class. Today, for example, he volunteered an answer in our mathematics class. He is so enthusiastic about learning!"

Throughout the year, Mrs. Nelson conveyed the importance of her partnership with Javier's mother. For example, when she found out that Javier's mother was a seamstress, she solicited her support in creating sock puppets for a play that the students were enacting about their social studies unit, and his mother readily agreed. In addition, Mrs. Nelson consistently and routinely conveyed four key messages to Javier's mother about the importance of their partnership. Drawing from Zacarian & Silverstone (2015) and Zacarian, Alvarez-Ortiz, & Haynes (2017), this included:

- The importance of their getting to know each other
- How she valued Javier's mother's participation and contributions
- How the classroom community was a place where they could work together on behalf of Javier and the students in his class
- How she was comfortable with her questions and engagement

In addition to understanding the value of frequent personal contacts with families, it is helpful to bring families together to demonstrate our interest partnering with them in support of their children. Classroom-based events that are targeted for this purpose are a wonderful means for supporting student engagement and academic growth. Four types of classroom-based events include the following (Zacarian & Silverstone, 2015, 2017; and Zacarian, Alvarez-Ortiz, & Haynes, 2017):

1. Gathering families together for a social purpose. Events such as a pot luck meal, an art, a music, or a dance event can do a lot to share mutual interests with families and to create positive momentum for working and socializing together.

2. Curriculum-centered events where students engage in showcasing their learning provide students with an opportunity to share their learning and parents and guardians with an opportunity to celebrate their child's successes. Events such as poster presentations, plays, science explanations, and whatever we might creatively cocreate with students can provide invaluable opportunities for students to create, practice, and then share a short presentation with their families.

3. <u>Drawing on the rich resources and assets of families</u>. All families have great skills, talents, and interests. Tapping into these can greatly support families' participation in partnering with us and, most importantly, enhance a student's engagement in learning and mastering academic content. For example, Javier's mother greatly contributed to her son and his classmates' "sock puppet" play about early settlers in the United States, by supporting their understanding of the reason that the settlers came to the New World.

4. <u>Fostering a shared culture of learning between home and school.</u> One of the key findings of family expert scholar and researcher Joyce Epstein (2011) is that parents and guardians want to support their child's learning, regardless of their educational backgrounds or experiences. Student and families interacting about a child's learning is a way for families to share in their child's learning. It is helpful to think of activities that children can do at home with their parents/guardians or others such as reading to them, sharing their assignments with them, or soliciting a parents/guardians' support in or contribution to an assignment. An example is Mrs. Nelson's social studies class. She asked students to go home and interview a family member or friend about their immigration experience. Family curriculum events are also helpful times to share what children are learning. For example, Mrs. Nelson invited families to learn how to play some of the math games that students were engaging in school.

Throughout the school year, Mrs. Nelson engaged families in a range of activities. At first, Javier's mother came reluctantly. Soon after that, when she became familiar with other Latino families, she participated regularly. During the school year, Javier made a great amount of progress. Though still catching up to meet grade-level expectations, there was no doubt that he was well on his way to be an active learner and participant in his classroom and school.

COMMUNITY SUPPORT

Just as family partners are great supporters of students' social-emotional and academic growth, the same is true of community partners. They, too, can be invaluable to the success of students. To create successful community partnerships, it is essential to identify, build, and sustain partners who operate from the same strength-based approach that we use to ensure that students and families feel the four essentials. It is also important to recognize that every school is uniquely positioned to understand the needs and desires of its students and to identify individual, agency, and institutional partners from their local community. An example is the Kansas City Public Schools. It partnered with the Truman Medical Center Behavioral Health to address a need that it had—to implement a model of Trauma Sensitive Schools (Zacarian, Alvarez-Ortiz, & Haynes, 2017). The training was intended to develop and

> Perhaps, as a staff collaborative activity, teachers can collect or construct other key sentence frames that they have taught their students in the past.
> —Margarita

enhance students' coping skills. An empowering strategy that some of its elementary-school students learned, for example, was how to recognize stressors that might result in a negative response and how to change that to a positive and empowering one. One, for instance, is the sentence prompt: *When I feel a negative emotion I can take this action.* Had Javier attended this training, he might have responded:

"When I feel angry at someone, I can use words instead of my fists to explain how I feel."

It's important to for individual schools to take time to map out the type of student-community partnerships that are needed for their particular students. Figure 9.1 is intended for this purpose.

At Javier's school, for example, many students had been identified as living with adverse childhood experiences. They partnered with a nearby university that has an advanced degree program in social work. The school liaison worked closely with the director of the program to discuss the ways that it could address the challenges that the school had identified and be of benefit to the university. At Javier's school, graduate students work with individual and small groups of students under the close supervision of the director of their studies. One of the graduate students, for example, is a native of Guatemala and has been working with Javier. The school liaison also contacted the town's soccer program director, who helped facilitate Javier joining one of the fourth-grade teams.

FIGURE 9.1 **Steps for Mapping Out School-Community Partners**

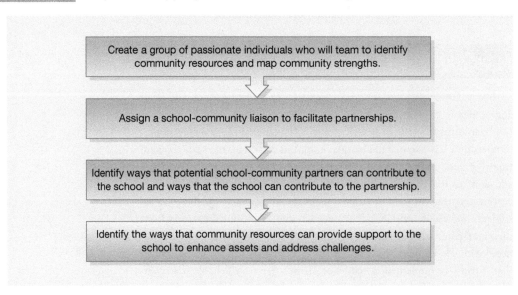

Source: Zacarian, Alvarez-Ortiz, & Haynes (2017, p. 182).

Summary and Conclusions

In this chapter, we presented the urgency for supporting teacher educators and K–12 educators to build and sustain programming by creating open and flexible partnerships with students, families, schools, and local community partners. We discussed how such partnerships can better support us in helping students to flourish in school and their lives. We also discussed the importance of supporting students and families to feel safe, a sense of belonging, acknowledgment, and competence. We showed how we can do this by using a strengths-based partnership approach.

In many ways, understanding and fostering the strengths of culturally and linguistically diverse children and families is crucial to their success. While we understand that many teacher educators and K–12 educators have experiences that are quite distinct from the dynamically diverse and ever-growing, ever-changing population of English learners, it does not mean that we cannot work closely together with students, families, and community partners. Moving in this direction is not just critical to do; it is urgent to do now if we are ever going to close the opportunity gaps that our nation's students have been experiencing. Moving to a place where *everyone and every community cares* about our students shows great promise for us all, today and in the future.

References

2017 Reading Grades 4 and 8 Assessment Report Cards: Summary Data Tables for National and State Average Scores and Achievement Level Results. Retrieved from: https://www.nationsreportcard.gov/reading_2017/files/2017_Results_Appendix_Reading_State.pdf

Cavanagh, S. (2012, April 4). Parental engagement proves no easy goal. *Education Week, 31*(27), 16–17.

Darling-Hammond, L., & Rothman, R. (2015). *Teaching in a flat world: Learning from high performing systems.* New York: Teachers College Press.

Data Resource Center for Child and Adolescent Health. (2011/2012). National Survey of Children's Health. Retrieved from http://www.childhealthdata.org/docs/drc/aces-data-brief_version-1-0.pdf

Delpit, L. D. (1988, August). The silenced dialogue: Power and pedagogy in educating other people's children. *Harvard Educational Review 5*(3), 280.

Dove, M. G., & Honigsfeld, A. (2018). *Co-teaching for English learners: A guide to collaborative planning, instruction, assessment, and reflection.* Thousand Oaks, CA: Corwin.

Edwards, P. A., Domke, L., & White, K. (2017). Closing the parent gap in changing school districts. In S. B. Wepner & D. W. Gomez (Eds.), *Challenges facing suburban schools: Promising responses to changing student populations* (pp. 109–123). Lanham, MD: Rowman & Littlefield.

Epstein, J. (2011). *School, family, and community partnerships: Preparing educators and improving schools* (2nd ed.). Philadelphia, PA: Westview Press.

Flores, R. L. & Halsall, J. (2017). The rising gap between rich and poor: A look at the persistence of educational disparities in the United States and why we should worry, Cogent Social Sciences, 3:1, DOI: 10.1080/23311886.2017.13

González, N., Moll, L. C., and Amanti, C. (Eds). (2005). *Funds of knowledge: Theorizing practices in households, communities, and classrooms.* Mahwah, NH: Lawrence Erlbaum Associates, Inc.

Grant, K. B. and Ray, J. A. (2016). Home, School and Community Collaboration: Culturally Responsive Family Engagement (3rd Edition). Thousand Oaks: Sage.

Henderson, A., & Mapp, K. (2002). A new wave of evidence: The impact of school, family, and community connections on student achievement. Retrieved from www.sedl.org/connections/resources/evidence.pdf

Henderson, A., Mapp, K. Johnson, V., & Davies, D. (2007). *Beyond the bake sale: The essential guide to family-school partnerships*. New York, NY: New Press.

Hollins, E., & Guzman, M. T. (2005). Research on preparing teachers for diverse populations. In M. Cochran & K. M. Zeichner (Eds.), *Studying teacher education: The report of the AERA panel on research and teacher education* (pp. 477–548). Mahwah, NJ: Lawrence Erlbaum.

Honigsfeld, A., & Dove, M. G. (2019). *Collaboration for English Learners: A foundational guide to integrated practices* (2nd ed). Thousand Oaks, CA: Corwin.

Lawrence-Lightfoot, S. (2003). *The essential conversation: What parents and teachers can learn from each other.* New York: Random House.

Mapp, K., & Kuttner, P. (2013). *Partners in education: A dual capacity-building framework for family-school partnerships*. Austin, TX: SEDL. Retrieved from http://www.sedl.org/pubs/framework/

Menjívar, C., & Cervantes, A. G. (2016, November). The effects of parental undocumented status on families and children. *CYF News.* Retrieved from https://www.apa.org/pi/families/resources/newsletter/index

Moon, A., & Neville, A. L. (2017, March 2–4). *Are pre-service teachers prepared for family-teacher relationships*, to be presented at the American Association of Colleges for Teacher Education (AACTE) 69th Annual Meeting in Tampa, FL.

National Center for Education Statistics (2016–17). Retrieved from: https://nces.ed.gov/ccd/tables/ACGR_RE_and_characteristics_2016-17.asp

National Center for Education Statistics. (2018, May). *Characteristics of postsecondary faculty. The condition of education.* Retrieved December 21, 2018, from https://nces.ed.gov/programs/coe/indicator_csc.asp

Noguera, P. A. (2001). Transforming urban schools through investment in the social capital of parents. In S. Saegert, J. P. Thompson, & M. R. Warren (Eds.), *Social capital and poor communities* (pp. 189–212). New York, NY: Russell Sage Foundation.

Saleebey, D. (2000). Power in the people: Strengths and hope. *Advances in Social Work, 1*(2), 127–136.

Saint-Jacques, M. C., Turcotte, D., & Pouliot, E. (2009). Adopting a strengths perspective in social work practice with families in difficulty: From theory to practice. *Families in Society, 9*(4), 454–461. doi:10.1606/1044-3894.3926

Southern Education Foundation. (2015). *A new majority: Low income students now a majority in the nation's public schools.* Retrieved from https://files.eric.ed.gov/fulltext/ED555829.pdf

Swanson, C. (2011). *Nation turns a corner. Diplomas count 2011: Beyond high school: before baccalaureate.* Retrieved from http://www.edweek.org/ew/toc/2011/06/09/index.html

U.S. Department of Education. (2015). *Digest of education statistics, 2014.* (NCES 2016-006). Retrieved from https://nces.ed.gov/programs/digest/2015menu_tables.asp

U.S. Department of Education. (2016). *The state of racial diversity in the educator workforce.* Retrieved November 27, 2018, from https://www2.ed.gov/rschstat/eval/highered/racial-diversity/state-racial-diversity-workforce.pdf

U.S. Department of State, Diplomacy in Action. (2015). *Cumulative Summary of Refugee Admissions.* Retrieved from: https://2009-2017.state.gov/j/prm/releases/statistics/251288.htm

Valencia, R. R. (2010). *Dismantling contemporary deficit thinking: Education thought and practice.* New York, NY: Routledge.

Walker, J. M., & Dotger, B. H. (2012). Because wisdom can't be told: Using comparison of simulated parent-teacher conferences to assess teacher candidates' readiness for family school partnership. *Journal of Teacher Education, 63*(1), 62–75.

Zacarian, D., Alvarez-Ortiz, L., & Haynes, J. (2017). *Teaching to strengths: Supporting students living with trauma, violence and chronic stress.* Alexandria, VA: ASCD.

Zacarian, D., & Silverstone, M. A. (2015). *In it together: How student, family, and community partnerships advance engagement and achievement in diverse classrooms.* Thousand Oaks, CA: Corwin.

Zacarian, D., & Silverstone, M. A. (2017, September). Building partnerships through classroom-based events. *Educational Leadership: In Sync With Families, 75*(1), 12–18.

Zacarian, D., & Silverstone, M. A. (2020). *Raising student voices together: A collaborative approach for empowered learning and teaching in diverse classrooms.* Alexandria, VA: ASCD.

Zeichner, K. (2012). *Two visions of teaching and teacher education for the twenty-first century.* Dartmouth, MA: University of Massachusetts, Dartmouth, Centre for Policy Analysis.

INDEX

A SAGE Publishing Company

CORWIN HAS ONE MISSION: to enhance education through intentional professional learning.

We build long-term relationships with our authors, educators, clients, and associations who partner with us to develop and continuously improve the best evidence-based practices that establish and support lifelong learning.